A Reluctant Servant

A Reluctant Servant

—⟋⟍—

Dennis V. Neely

ISBN: 1508643288
ISBN 13: 9781508643289

Dedicated to the more than fifty-eight thousand men and women
who made the ultimate sacrifice.

My sincere
acknowledgment and gratitude
for the overwhelming support that
I have received from my spouse, Carole,
and
my daughter, Shannon Leigh, who
have helped me beyond thanks.
Thank you, Carole and Shannon.

I also thank those who were kind enough to read and comment
on my preview releases.
Your encouragement spurred me onward.

Contents

A Starting Point

—〰—

As I sit at my PC and wonder why I have spent the last several months writing of things in my past in which most will have no interest, I cannot help but compare my present emotions with those I held in the late sixties and early seventies. Back then, I did not participate in the drama of the antiwar movement or over the legalization of recreational drugs or the tolerance or intolerance of diverse social behavior. I lived day by day, synchronous with all of those movements and directions. I never felt the need to represent or object to any one of them. As long as they didn't influence my life and my living of it, I couldn't care less.

My story relates to my naïve and extremely innocent views of that time compared to those of an older and more experienced, if not a wiser, man. I reflect mainly on the "meaty" parts of my life and the effects that they had on the finished product. Some of my tales I tell with a smile and a warm spot in my heart, while others are terrible and nearly unspeakable, evoking a tear or the need of immediate relief with two fingers of JD on the rocks, which, unfortunately, I gave up nearly twenty years past.

A good part of my story is based on my personal experiences while some parts are from recollections given to me by my family, comrades, and patients who took part in my life's events. In that some of the material is second or third-hand and weathered by forty-five years of good living, there may exist some embellishments or errors of fact. I have changed most of the dates and nearly all of the names so that no one will be required to relive any part of their history if they do not care to do so. However, while reading this, all of those who have had similar experiences might wish to reflect on their own memories and benefit from the healing.

I do not have difficulty remembering the ambitious, naïve, innocent faces of so many of the cherries (new guys) and how they changed to mature hardened, focused, and determined ones after their first few weeks "in country." Many of them, may God bless, are not still alive—some are dead, and some are just not living. A great number, 58,209 (as of 2015, this includes those missing in action [MIA], assumed dead, and died in captivity),[i] paid the ultimate price and were not able to share their historical contributions with those back in the world, while another nearly 153,303 were wounded and 1,627 remain MIA.[ii]. Many who survived their wounds were not able to relate their stories without reprisal and hatred. To all of them, I dedicate my stories.

I also make my position clear on those we fought and the treatment of them in my stories. It is clear to me that regardless of the particular side one fought on, humans are products of the environment that shaped them, the economies that ruled them, and the leadership that directed them. They should not be faulted for any of that. The loyalties to their country and their causes were strong, and they should not be condemned. Their families grieved the injured and dead just as our folks "back in the world" grieved our losses. My use of slang such as "gook," "dink," "slope," and a handful of other terms are meant to associate your reading with the authenticity of the period. The validity of the story would suffer, as would its importance, if the dialect of the time were not honored.

Me, Ron, and the Worms

—⟋⟍—

RON (AGE ELEVEN) AND I (age eight) loved to fish. We fished together frequently until separated by our adult lives in 1967. Our early ventures took us many times to Mong's Pond in the middle of the little town of Seneca, Pennsylvania. It was just an old cow-pasture pond that held more organisms than imaginable, and it infected our skin on a routine basis.

Ron and I were never good "wait-and-see" fishermen. If things didn't happen on the end of the line within a few minutes, we moved to a new spot, changed hooks, or changed bait if we had the choice. Sometimes we just quit and went swimming or did something else that amused us. My uncle worked for the dairy farm that owned this pond, and they retailed milk, cream, cheese, and, most important, ice cream. There was a new flavor every day, and it was the policy of Dick Mong to give any kid a cone who wanted it—at no charge. So, a lot of kids, fisherpersons or not, traveled through the ice-cream shop in the back of Mong's Dairy Store to claim their free soft cone of the day. They were never shabby in size and you could have as many as you wanted, one at a time, as long as you were not wasteful. Great man, Dick Mong!

We did, however, spend a lot of time pondering on how to be better fishermen, as this was truly a calling for both of us. We were certain of it. We would frequently spend a good part of a summer afternoon making concoctions that might entice the finny little bastards more readily to the hook. We made yarn baits, tin-can baits, wooden baits, and plastic baits. It just seemed like our fish were different from those we had seen on the outdoor and travel cinemas at the local theaters, as they would never consider anything other than insects or red meat. We even painted minnows with Merthiolate to make them orange and more attractive. Goldfish were illegal as bait in Pennsylvania, so we figured artificially colored orange-silver fish would work great. And they did.

One particular day, Ron and I were digging up garden worms to add to the supply of a couple of dozen night crawlers we had caught the night before. It seemed like we were both struck with the same genius idea at precisely the same time. We worked on the details of our new plan while running to my house, bait worms in hand. The idea was for sure an earth-shaking method that would change fishing forever! We had reckoned that neither of us, or anyone we knew, for that matter, ate meat raw. Why would a big, old trout be drawn to raw meat except for stupidity? Were we just knocking off the smallish, dumb trout and not even realizing that the big, smart ones still remained because, up till now, we had been stupid?

It so happened that this was pie day. My mom had the oven cranked up to 350, and two cherry pies sat on its lower rack. With the top rack totally free, it was obvious what we should do. We found an old, tin pie plate and spread the crawlers evenly around the bottom, chucking them into the oven as quickly as possible so as not to lose a single one. We watched for a short while, not really sure what to expect. As they squirmed, Ron swears to this day that "they squealed like little pigs."

When they slowed their squirming, Ron opened the oven, and with some tongs that Mom used to lift corn on the cob out of hot water, he relocated worms that had slithered over the tin to the lower rack, over the pie, and onto the lower shelf, leaving a faint bit of artwork on one of them. We were sure it wouldn't show once baked. Noticing that Mom had about twenty minutes left on the oven timer, we felt we could make much better use of our time by playing catch for a bit, our second love in life.

Time really does fly when you're having fun, but that fun ended abruptly when, shortly after the timer went off, my mom was on the back porch, waving the hickory stick. She was yelling some words that I think were telling me to get my ass into the house right away and that Ron was to go home to face his mom, Alma.

The rest is history. I spied the two pies in the garbage can with my crispy night crawlers, coal black and immobile, right on top. My mom was spilling out words that I had been taught each Sunday not to even think about, let alone say, and she assured me that my fate would be further judged when Dad got home from work. Two switches across the back of my bare legs made me wince, but I refused to demonstrate the pain by crying. I was to wait on the porch until Dad returned home from work at 3:00 p.m. He normally would quickly prepare for his second job that started at four o'clock—only an hour to wash up, eat dinner, have cherry pie, and leave for work again. But now, he had no cherry pie, and he had to deal with me. This could be pretty bad.

Dad was very tired on his return home. He just slumped onto the glider on the porch and asked Mom if she would bring him some iced tea. He drank the tea and said he'd just have a piece of the cherry pie that Mom had promised, rest awhile, and then head to work in Oil City. Well, this opened up the can of worms, and I was soon in tears in front of my dad with him telling me that I was old enough to be responsible and that I needed to use my head before pulling off all these stunts. He told me that I should be doing much more around the place other than getting into trouble on a daily basis. He had this truly disgusted look on his brow like he'd given up on me amounting to anything. It made me very sad. I felt worthless, and after I received a minor slap across the ass, I was already laying down the plan for what I would do the next day to please him and make him happy with his son.

Even though his discipline was severe and contact emotions like hugs and an occasional peck on the head were not his style, I loved and admired him and always hoped he at least loved me. But, most of all, I wanted him to be proud of me, and that seemed like it might never happen.

My Uncle Dan

—ᴍᴍ—

MY UNCLE DAN, MOM'S BROTHER and youngest of the Slater clan, spent a lot of time at our place. Dan did not do well around other men, whether they were relatives, bosses, policemen, or any authority figure, and there was almost always some sort of trouble certain to occur.

On the other hand, my uncle Dan, who was only five years older than I, the result of a late twinkle in my Grandpa Slater's eye, loved being around females. I do believe that he loved every woman he met. He was sexually active very early, I believe eleven or twelve. He hooked up with some neighborhood gals and visited them from time to time as he pleased.

Testosterone is powerful magic, and my uncle Dan certainly suffered no shortage of it from a very young age. His conversations would almost always become sexual, either with a story or an educational adventure, and he was always the star. He fantasized all the time and would say, "Hey, how would you like to take a crack at that one?" He spoke loud enough that I am certain others could hear, and I was generally humiliated enough to melt into my shoes. I would wander off away from him for a while until my mind was going somewhere else, and all would be OK until the next time he embarrassed me. In spite of my frequent humiliation, my time with him was always an exciting adventure. He made me aware of lots of things at an early age. Though I didn't understand a lot of the new feelings that emerged, it was exciting, and his talk about girls was not uninvited.

Dan was terrible in school and would do most anything to keep from going there. I recall the time when my grandmother Slater, a sweet, generous, loving woman, was my caregiver while my dad worked three jobs and my mom worked two just to scrape by financially. Out of necessity, I would be taken to Grandma's house early in the morning, around 6:00 a.m., and left there while Mom went on to work. I was made to go up to the boys' second-floor bedroom and take my place in a double bed between my uncle Dan and my uncle Bud.

My uncle Bud was a large man, actually obese as a sixteen-year-old, and he occupied the majority of the mattress space. Dan was not large but was very aggressive in seeking out his share of the bed. Both would be in that deep sleep that neither an act of God nor a turkey dinner with all of the fixings could come close to awakening them. Their snoring, bubbling, and whistling were incredible. I often wondered how they made such sounds and wondered if I might do the same when I was fast asleep. The air was thick with the gasses produced from the fat-rich diet that both of them so enjoyed. Everything in that house was cooked in pork fat, and the heavy, lingering smell was predominant throughout. I'm sure it was very obvious to visitors and infrequent guests. At times, I would play a private game to see which one farted the most but made a large error one morning by telling them who was the winner. They roughed me up quite a lot. So I played the game for my own satisfaction from then on.

After sleep time was over, my grandmother would climb the creaky stairs, open the door to the boys' room, and tell them that breakfast was ready and they needed to get up and get dressed for school. Bud was always prompt and was first out, with me a close second. I think Bud dreamed of breakfast the entire night. He always took the first huge helping of fried potatoes, at least three rashers of thick country bacon, three eggs, and four slices of toast—and that was usually only his first serving. Potatoes were cheap, eggs were home raised, and my grandpa usually made deals with the local farmers for a half hog or so by trading carpenter or brickwork. Of course, Grandma made the bread, and sixty years later, I remember it being the best I ever tasted.

Most times, Dan would not yet be at the table after Bud's second round, and Grandma would once again hobble up the creaky stairs and into the boys' room, only to find Dan missing. He would usually climb out of the second-floor bedroom window and sit Indian style on the roof, most often in a T-shirt and his boxer shorts. There was no amount of conversation that would bring him back inside, regardless of the weather or the season. He would sit there until that yellow-and-black bus pulled away with Bud and a few other kids in the neighborhood who used the Slater house as the bus stop. Dan would then climb back into the room and go back to sleep until his mind became infected with an adventure. Then, off he would go, past his mother's parting reprimands and promises of great punishment from his father when he returned from work. This was no concern to Dan, as he was a champion at withstanding physical punishment. He hated verbal punishment and criticism, and unless my grandparents were dishing it out, he would not take it without retaliation. He would not take it from his brothers, friends, me, or his teachers. He had several expulsions from school because of his aggressive reactions toward his teachers. I guess that is why he avoided school so frequently—to save the teachers.

On those rare days that, for some reason, Grandma's words sank in enough to bring him off the roof, Dan would walk the five long miles to school, arriving late but at least gaining a present-but-tardy status. Then, after a period or two, usually following shop or art class, which he liked very much, he would leave. He would shit his pants just enough for him to go to the school nurse, complain of diarrhea and shitty, smelly pants, and insist on going home.

Dan did this number so frequently that, after a while, no one batted an eye at his antics. If the school nurse happened to see him limping down the hall to her office, she would just motion him to go ahead and leave. The fatty-food diet and the close quarters in the classrooms probably made him incompatible with other humans, and sending him home was the best of all solutions. Dan, however, would rarely go home. He most often came to our house. He would go to our cellar (a dirt-floor bomb shelter at best), take off his soiled underwear, wrap them up in a newspaper—which my dad stored there to start coal fires in the winter—put his blue jeans back on, sans briefs, and make himself at home until my mom arrived home from work with me in tow.

After a time, his behavior brought a small committee of sorts to my grandma Slater's house near the end of Dan's eighth school year. The group consisted of the principal, assistant principal, the school nurse, and Dan's bus driver. They insisted strongly that Dan be removed from school, as it was obviously not going to lead to anything positive. There were problems that most likely would occur again and again involving the teachers and confrontations with other students. My grandmother, in the absence of her husband, agreed and reluctantly signed some papers to take Dan out of school. These things were never decided by the women in those days, even though they were much more inclined to be best at it. They spent most all of their time with the kids, relatives, and neighbors. The man worked twelve to fourteen hours a day and had minimal contact with his family. He seemed more like a visitor than an active family member. Many of the men of this period knew little about their kids until they retired, and often, that was too late.

Dan's tumultuous life eventually resulted in three wives and five kids who knew him only while their mothers were married to him. My uncle's episodes of mild success were ruined by alcohol and came to crashing failures. They caused my grandmother tremendous guilt. Fortunately, she preceded him in death, never knowing that he would pass very young from alcoholic heart failure. I will forever remember him as a notable masculine figure in my life. I will blame my faults on the sin that he taught me and thank him for all the skills that he shared with me. Yes, I have very fond memories of my uncle Dan.

The Cornfield Chapter

—m—

I RECALL VIVIDLY THAT THE only defense against the wrath of my mother and my father for my misbehavior and my bad deeds, which they assured me no other kid had ever done before, was to do something really, really nice before they found out the full details of my "crime."

One such occasion was a result of our "war games," one of the most popular activities of the group of twenty or so kids in our small neighborhood. Considering the number of combatants involved, the game we called "army" involved quite a lot of planning. Several of us movers and shakers would get together to decide on the day and the place we would play. The place could be any one of a number of favorites—Kerr's woods, Mong's pond, Egypt Road, or, most frequently, Morrison's farm.

The farm was a great place, with all of the super elements a kid of eight to fourteen needed for the imaginative excitement of army games. There were the hay lofts with tons of bales two stories high that we many times molded into intricate tunnels, rooms with booby traps, and secret passageways that led to surprise open areas on the level below. The silo was a large space where we would take prisoners. It was rich with a lot of organic corn silage that, after just a short while, required the prisoner to be dragged out into fresher air because he was acting really crazy or becoming hysterical. The alcohol content of the air must have been phenomenal.

There were the fields that held crops during certain seasons that could be super hiding places for a squad of army guys. The cabbage and carrots not so much, but the wheat field and the supreme court of battle, the cornfield, always saw action. Of course, the whole property was laced with fences and named landmarks that we laid out for both sides while establishing the rules of engagement. Finally, embedded in all of this exciting real estate were the black-and-white heifers and their one rather cross overlord who took great pleasure in chasing one, two, or a small group of us around the property. Nearly all of us found ourselves up a tree at one time or another.

One particular tree about four inches in diameter held battle marks for nearly a decade from that bull's rage and determination to uproot it with us humans as the favored fruit at the top. Fortunately, he never caught any of us, although Ron, being tall and lanky, did have some close calls when he snagged his flannel shirt while trying to dive through the barbed-wire fence in the fifty-foot race from the base of the tree to safety.

After we had decided on "D-Day" and the "theater of operations," we had to call up the troops. We would make a list on lined, yellow school paper and split it up into groups. Two assigned captains would be responsible for notifying the others on the details of the game. They all lived within about three square miles, and since there were very few other activities in this small town, most of the guys showed up on a regular basis.

If there was a conflict with a baseball game or such, we would have a confab, and all of us would end up maybe playing baseball. The group was close knit and most often congenial. We all got along wonderfully. There were very few serious altercations and no competition between one side of the town and the other. There were no exclusive clubs or gangs. We just all played together and never imagined a situation in which any person would intentionally injure another. Naïve? Possibly. But it was in the best way.

Even though our hearts were pure and friendships were etched in concrete, it is not to say that we didn't cause some hell in the neighborhood or even with each other. With that many kids involved, the casualty

index (wounded in action, or WIA) was considerable and into triple dig-
its, but we all took it as a matter of fact and continued our games un-
fazed. I am happy to say, we had zero missing in action (MIA) and zero
killed in action (KIA) throughout our childhood adventures. Most of
the guys would never tell their parents, however, as they might have to
divulge too many secrets about our play and ruin everything.

One of these casualties occurred one Saturday afternoon with the
war games at Morrison's. There were three guys from the red team and
two guys on the white, including me, who were taken prisoner. We were
all sitting at the edge of the pond in the middle of the farm, next to the
cornfield. Those who had BB guns would screw out the barrel and, after
cocking the lever, drop a lighted firecracker down the barrel and shoot.
It made a half-ass realistic effect, and it dissuaded almost everyone from
using BBs in their rifles for the games.

We had heard about the big BB gun war held about one kid generation before us that resulted in, yes, an eye being shot out (never verified),
several other superficial injuries, and considerable property damage. In
that case, the cops were called, and all the BB guns in the neighborhood
were confiscated. There were some legal activities as well, so the story
went. We were not interested in a repeat of that story, so we figured out
our own safe ways to have fun by shooting firecrackers out of our rifles.

Back to the battle. The red team was waiting for more of their group
to arrive and take us prisoners to the silo but got bored and started toss-
ing firecrackers up in the air over our heads. Most of them exploded a
few feet above us, but one had a faulty, slow fuse that didn't go off. It was
lying right beside my left thigh, unexploded but kind of smoking a bit.
I quickly picked up the cracker and side-armed it toward our captors.

Tom, one of the veteran war-game kids, had a lot of realistic gear that
he had bought with hard-earned lawn-mowing money, and among that
gear was a dandy pair of combat boots. They were the kind that laced
up to the ankle, had a flap that went around the lower leg just above it,
and buckled with two buckles. Black beauties, for sure, and expensive
for our time and financial situations. Tom never buckled the tops of his

boots. They kind of hung open at the top and flopped around when he walked, making his swagger even more exaggerated. What happened next changed that habit for good.

The damned firecracker landed perfectly in the top of Tom's left boot. I saw it, he saw it, and the entire red team saw it at the same time. We all looked at each other in frozen anticipation. To our amazement and horror, within a second, that damned thing exploded. It had apparently slid down past the leather flap inside, sliding all the way down his foot. When it exploded, it was snug between the leather and the sock. All of us had our eyes fixed on Tom's foot and the expression on his face as a gaping hole opened up on the side of his boot. (Firecrackers were real firecrackers in our day, not the duds that are sold now.) We were aghast, and I felt certain that I had maimed him for life.

Tom's face was screwed up and contorted just as though he had ripped a loud fart in the middle of English class, bringing all eyes to him in shock, horror, and amazement. At first, he was actually fearful of removing the boot and finding a major wound that would take a lot of explanation to his mom and dad as well as a trip to the hospital. Even with all of these anticipated evil probabilities on his mind, he soon came to his senses and was doing double-time removing the boot. As he worked on the laces, he seemed to be holding back on breaking into tears, with his lips clenched tightly and his eyes nearly squinted shut. The boot seemed to take forever to unlace, but finally, off it came, and a large black spot showed on his white sock.

He jerked off the sock, and to his and our utter amazement, all that presented was a reddened area on the skin about the size of a quarter. He played with it and flexed it and finally arose, walking on it while hobbling on one boot. He said it didn't hurt at all, but we all knew that it did as he limped and hopped around. He picked up his boot, and I could tell that this is where Tom felt the true pain. The boots were a favorite possession, and now he had one with a big hole in it.

His voice was now exaggerated and strong to make up for the near-tearful moment. As Tom put his sock and boot back on his foot, he looked at me and sputtered, "You're gonna spend a good helluva long time in the goddamned silo today." Thank God, the cows moved in, followed by the bull, who was never happy, and we called the game by running helter-skelter to escape the resident bully.

The next day, no remorse, no bad feelings. We were friends, and Tom knew that I would never try to hurt him intentionally. He probably won't ever forget that particular moment when I ruined his army boot and, more important, nearly made him cry in front of his friends. Hopefully, it's not a totally bad memory.

Our next war game was about a week later on a Saturday, and the weather in Pennsylvania was beautiful with the early October change. The trees were a beautiful panorama of color on our rolling hills and mountains, and it made fall my favorite season of all. We gathered once again at my place, which was just adjacent to Morrison's Farm. We had only a group of thirteen, and the guys were really anal if one team had to do with one less man. Dumb logic starts at a young age, and after all, what did we know? We were young kids, with Ron and Jimmy being the eldest of our usual group.

Ron and I lived across the street from each other and were constant companions. We fished a lot together, played baseball whenever a free moment permitted, and last, played a lot of army games. We all had our favorite sport or activity, but once again, everyone was also willing to cooperate and participate with the "game of the day" and actually had fun in doing it. Seems different now.

Our house was never locked, and Uncle Dan was frequently sitting on the back porch or in the living room when my mom arrived home from work with me in tow from Grandma's. Some days, however, he would show up on a Saturday and would be a part of our group in the army game. Such was the case on this particular day: the fourteenth player would be Dan. Being five years older than me, he would always act as though he was reluctantly going along with us young kids, but you could tell by his face that he enjoyed it as much as we did.

The battlefield chosen was once again Morrison's pasture, as there were so many neat things going on there during October. The leaves were turning, and our Indian summer was just perfect, with low humidity and comfortable temperatures allowing a long fall day of vigorous warring. This was also the time just before the corn harvest when the stalks were bone dry and rattled in the breeze and the bright-yellow cobs burst out of their sheaths. They became the "hand grenades" that we used in Morrison's cornfield.

The cows, and therefore the bull, stayed a lot closer to the barn, as the grazing was much less interesting out in the field at that time of year. They mostly munched on hay and some grain concoction the Morrison brothers used in their feed bins. We tried it a few times and found it to be sweet but very chewy and not nearly as good as the hallucinogenic stalks of silage we chewed in the silo at times. Ron and I once really got into the silage stuff, and we caused a real panic upon returning home. Neither of us could stand in one place without swaying or falling down. We planted a real seed of doubt in our parents' minds about the other parents' supervision, as they thought we had raided their liquor cabinet. Actually, neither family kept liquor in the house. Ron I had checked that out carefully a long while back. Oh, well, our parents were starting to get too chummy anyway. The chummier they got, the more they talked of their kids, and the fewer secrets Ron and I were able to keep.

The game we played that day was not necessarily the interesting part of the story but rather the run-up to the end of the game, which was hugely memorable and exciting. It ultimately resulted in the worst punishment of my life.

The seven-"man" teams had avoided each other's domination for most of the day, and at about four in the afternoon, two of each team were prisoners in the silo, leaving five for each team at large. There was a large horse-chestnut tree near the edge of the cornfield and a small creek that had a marsh like edge running beside it. From time to time, it attracted a duck or two, and at this time of year, it had quite a lot of cattails that had dried and fluffed out, releasing their seeds to drift in the air. It was near that horse-chestnut tree, having crossed the muddy, sludge-filled marsh and creek, that we sighted the five members of the red team: Jimmy, Jack, Phillip, Rick, and last, my uncle Dan.

Upon seeing us, Jimmy and Dan (Jimmy was also older than the others) immediately led the reds into the safety of the huge cornfield before we were able to react. It would be a tough end to the game with the corn nearly six feet high and the wind rustling the shocks, blocking out any noise. The abundance of the yellow grenades was worrisome to us also. Most of us at one time had taken one of the cobs loaded with dried corn to the upper torso or head, and believe me, they really packed a wallop. They were a wicked weapon, and now the red team had control of a whole lot of them.

Ron had filled his small canteen bag with about ten or twelve of the hulled horse chestnuts, which had very sharp, stinging barbs all around the shell. I had thrown one at Ron several days before, hitting him in the neck, and after yelping for a minute or two, he said it stung like hell and seemed to get worse and worse. I took a quick look and sure enough, one of the barbs was sticking in the skin on the back of his neck. I was able to remove it, but it left a very large, red area about the size of a golf ball and Ron said it hurt like crazy for several hours thereafter. Ron was sure the arsenal in his canteen holder would be a big contribution to his victory over the red team if we could find them and roust them out into the open.

We had no sooner started to make a plan when a barrage of yellow grenades came flying out of the corn, scattering the white team to the base of the chestnut tree for protection. They apparently were stockpiling corncobs at various spots in the field and were cluster-bombing us as fast as they could hurl. Only one of us was really hit. Bob took a full cob in the face, and after moving his lower jaw at about twenty different angles and directions decided he was OK, but he was super pissed. A couple of the white-team guys had loaded up their canteens with some gasoline, and after the first round of grenade attacks, they took off for the marshy area and returned with armfuls of fluffy cattails. I knew immediately what was going to happen and was sucked into the plan before any common sense was engaged.

Bob and Ron poured some gas into a paper cup that one of them had in his pack and began dunking the dry, fluffy cattails. They trimmed the stems so that just the fluffy part and a couple of inches of the stem fit into the end of the BB gun barrel. After the gun was cocked, Ron lit the projectile up with a Zippo. Bob held the BB gun like a mortar and shot off the first round. To our amazement, it flew about five feet into the corn. Even though we were duly impressed with the spectacle, we immediately realized that we needed much more distance.

We set up an assembly line of sorts, soaking cattails and laying them out on the ground with Bob and Ron lighting them up and us side-arming them manually into the corn. We continued this exercise until about a dozen flaming cattails were hurled into enemy territory. With no more corncobs coming out of the field at us, nothing seemed to be happening. We sat down to ponder if more cattails were needed or whether we should develop a new plan. After a short while, we decided we would split up and go through the tall cornstalks in the ready position, row by row, hoping to come upon our enemy.   We made it just a short distance into the corn when I heard the unmistakable voice of my uncle Dan. "Jesus Christ, what the fuck is wrong with you guys? Are you fucking crazy?" With that, the five of them busted out of the field. We thought we had them as we trained our BB guns on them. They were totally off guard and seemed to give up. Dan shouted, "You set the fucking corn on fire, you dumb-asses!"

He'd barely got those words from his mouth when we saw the plumes of gray smoke coming from several different areas of the corn. Soon we saw little whiffs of flame shooting up in various places, and before long, big sections of the corn were wildly ablaze—in places, flames were up to six feet high. About five out of the ten guys beat it for home, and the remaining five of us—Dan, Ron, Bob, Jimmy, and me—were left standing there looking at each other with our mouths agape.

My uncle Dan more or less took command and told us to wet our shirts in the creek and try to beat some of the flames down. He told Bob to head home and get someone to call the fire department. The four of us headed into the corn but were soon beaten back by the smoke and fear of the flames that were already shooting several feet above the corn shocks. All the time, Dan was chanting, "We are all fucking going to go to jail over this one. You watch, we're fucked."

We waited and waited, backing up further and further from the heat and smoke when Dan discovered the gasoline in the cup and canteens. He yelled at Jimmy, "Get rid of this shit!" Unthinking, Jimmy started to pour it out on the ground until Dan called him a stupid shit and told him to carry it down to the creek and dump it there. After Jimmy came back from the creek, he apologized to Dan for being stupid. My uncle Dan just looked at him like he was a fucking freak or something. "Is that all you're worried about? We are going to go to fucking jail, and you're worried about being a stupid, fucking dumb-ass?" Jimmy lowered his head, and Dan conceded, "Well, I know you didn't set the field on fire, because you were with me. Denny, your ass is going to jail though, you can bet on that!"

We waited for nearly an hour with no fire department, no Bob, just the last bit of corn burning and smoke as thick as I had ever seen. Suddenly, Dan jumped up and started running toward the opposite end of the field closest to the barn, the cows, and the hay. The dried scrub grass was now on fire, and with the wind blowing in that direction, it could be trouble. Dan ran on to the silo and released the four guys and told them to beat it home and call the fire department, as Bob had apparently gone AWOL. They stumbled through the field, half-drunk from the silage vapors, and we finally watched them climb the fence to the main road about half a mile away. Dan told us to wet our shirts down again in the water trough at the barn and start fighting the fire. I thought this was kind of neat and strangely felt that it might get me off the hook a little if the parents knew I had saved the barn and the cows and the hay.

With soot on arms and face, smelling of smoke and my uncle Dan's recently purchased school shirt now with huge burn holes throughout, we gave up and headed home. We found Bob sitting on the bank of the main road, still sobbing, his eyes red from crying and irritated from smoke. He told us he was afraid to tell his mom to call the fire department, so he had left the house and settled on the bank to watch. The fire department never came while we were there. The police department, two cars' worth, did come, however, and they took us one by one inside the cruiser and asked us all kinds of questions. It turns out that the gasoline issue and the firecracker issue and the cattail issue never came up from any one of us.

When it was my turn to talk, the cops were convinced that one of the older boys had been careless with a cigarette, and it was assumed to be the unfortunate cause of the fire and all of the destruction. Apparently, one of the cops asked if anyone smoked, and after two of us assured them that the older guys both did, the cops drew their own conclusion. Finally, the fire department showed up, and about a half-dozen men with spray packs on their backs piled out of the trucks, headed for the field that was now just a smoking patch of black earth with a little tuft of flame shooting up here and there.

Shortly, a small crowd formed alongside of the road, leaning out of their car windows or standing and chatting with each other. As all of this official stuff continued, our fear of reprisal welled up more and more. I was actually nauseous with the fear that we had created the largest crime ever in this little community's history by burning down Morrison's cornfield.

We played the cigarette bit until midevening, and the phone at my house began ringing constantly. By the tone of my mom's voice, I could tell things were going from bad to worse even though Mom did not yet know the whole story, only that Dan and I were involved. It was about 8:00 p.m., and it was still light around the back porch, as Dad had installed a mercury yard light there. I went out and sat on the porch and thought of what I might do to make this situation better.

Dad had mentioned that the wood porch looked pretty rough and would need painting soon. *That's it—the perfect job! Maybe he will be proud of me and we can let this cornfield thing go as just bad luck.* My dad had a bunch of partially used gallons of paint in various colors in the garage, and without hesitation, I picked out a bright, barn red to liven up the appearance of the back porch.

My dad was a fanatic about keeping the outside of the house in immaculate shape and during the previous summer had constructed a beautiful concrete sidewalk leading from the porch and extending to our driveway about twenty feet away. The sidewalk was bermed and even had all of our initials in the concrete off to the side by the porch. My dad was really proud of that sidewalk.

The paint was very thick and difficult to put on, especially between the open slats on the porch. I knew that it would never last at this rate and I would never finish before Dad got home around 11:00 p.m. There was a hose outlet at the base of the porch steps with a small section of hose attached. My plan was to thin the paint down so that I would have enough for the job, and it would go on much easier as well.

Holding the hose in one hand and bending to reach the faucet with the other, I turned on the water, and it shot out of the hose nozzle like a jet, hitting the paint can and tipping it over onto the cement. My heart stopped beating, and I stood staring at the mess. I tried to spray the paint off the sidewalk, but, unknown to me, it was oil based. So it repelled the water, and most ran down half the length of the walk. I sprayed tons of water on the concrete with little effect. I got my mom's scrub bucket with some Fels-Naptha soap and tried to scrub it off, but all I created was red foam that emphasized the mess even more.

What I did achieve was to gain my mom's attention. She came out on the porch but stopped dead in her tracks. She gasped and assured me that I was so near being a dead kid. She now had received the truth from several of my friends' parents. My goose was cooked! She turned before I could warn her and walked back into the kitchen, tracking red paint onto about six feet of the linoleum floor. I heard her shriek, but I didn't go in.

I gathered up the buckets and brushes and after putting them away, sought out my only dear friend in the world right at the moment: Elmer, a little English sheepdog that I learned was a female long after I had named her. I sat on the bare ground, telling her that I probably wouldn't see her again and that she should run away at first chance and try to find another kid who might love her as much as I. She licked my face and lay her head in my lap. I knew she felt my pain, if not the cause of it.

Dad, Me, and My '38 Chevy

—〰—

MY FIRST VEHICLE WAS A '38 Chevy coupe that my dad and I saved from my grandfather Neely's pasture. The car was virtually a bubble of rust and had sat for the better part of fifteen years. It actually had grass and small trees growing up through various openings in the vehicle. My grandfather kept it only for the memories. He was granted considerable amusement, however, over the thought of my resurrecting the old Chevy to its original purpose after it nearly had returned to the earth from old age.

After chopping the car out of the holding vines and small trees, Dad inspected the whole engine and drive train and said that it really should start if we did the right things and did them properly. The tires had dry rot, and all four wheels were sitting on the rims. Dad had me get measurements from the tires and write them down on a small note pad. We then started taking notes on the engine, the drive train, the suspension, and the exhaust system.

After spending half the day in the pasture with that car, we retreated to the farmhouse, where Grandma Neely had lemon-drop cookies and fresh, cold milk for the two of us. We chatted for nearly an hour while enjoying the snack, and finally, my dad asked my grandfather what he would need for the car. My grandfather thought intently for several minutes, making obscure verbal references that we could not hear while dipping the last lemon-drop cookie into his cup of milk. Finally, laughing loudly, he blurted out, "Thirty-five dollars, as it sits."

We immediately said "Deal," and Dad and I headed to the city and the Western Auto Store for some tires and parts.

The following weekend found my dad and me in my Granddad Neely's pasture field once again. This time, we were loaded down with tools and the smaller of the needed parts to fix the old '38 Chevy. I was just sixteen, and although I was on the short side, my dad had me in very good shape, mostly through child labor. I was his helper on jobs that occupied his evenings and most every weekend.

Carrying concrete blocks for two professional bricklayers while also ensuring they had fresh cement for laying the blocks without interruption kept me nearly breathless for hours at a time. It wasn't all that bad until they had laid seven or eight courses of blocks, at which point I had to lug two ten-inch blocks up a doubled-up two-by-ten, walk across a narrow scaffold, and stack the blocks just behind them in the direction they were going. The job was a ballbuster but created some terrific muscle groups that helped me prevail in most of the thoughtless attacks upon me because of my short stature.

Another major job that was a real killer was laying new roofs on houses or utility buildings. It required hefting quarter squares of shingles up a ladder, up and across a usually steep roof, opening the bundle with tin snips, and placing the shingles within easy reach of the shingle layer, all in horrid heat. It was an awful job, and at the end of the day, it left you black from the asphalt of the shingles. Little, gritty granules stuck to your skin while you lost torrents of precious, salty sweat running in filthy, black streams into your undershorts. Once again, however, the delts, biceps, and the pecs all benefited.

So, I was quite prepared to hustle the four tires we had mounted on the rims that Dad had removed during a weekday visit to the farm while I was in school. The damn things were heavy at two at a time, and I will remember to this day the second trip in which I thought it might be easier to carry one while bouncing the other gingerly beside me. As I dropped down over the embankment into the lower pasture, the tire and rim alongside of me quickly took the lead, and I realized I would not catch up with it anytime soon. The damn tire seemed alive as it bounced and danced in the air in huge, beautiful arcs, right past Dad and the car and on down the hill toward the barn. Unfortunately, it piled up right on the entrance door to my granddad's chicken coop. The door exploded as if hit by a grenade. The door being shattered and demolished, the fucking chickens scattered to the winds. My grandpa was watching all of this from the porch swing, and I can imagine him now, laughing in his grave at his dumb, fucking grandson over the chicken stunt. He did not laugh long that day, however, as he informed me that the reason the chickens were penned was that they were not safe outside the coop. Something had been picking off one or two a night until it seemed he would lose the whole flock until he saved them with the coop. Building a new door to the coop and catching two dozen chickens and a mad rooster took me most of the afternoon, and my dad had to work without his helper. He never complained.

By early evening, the Chevy had four wheels and tires installed, and the drive shaft was broken loose from all of the rust. Dad lubricated all of the required parts on the underside of the suspension and axles. He had dumped some fluid through the engine where one would put oil and let it run straight out of the oil pan into a bucket. Miraculously, no water had accumulated in the engine, and hopefully not in the gas tank, either. We thought about removing the tank and tipping it to remove any water or rust, but the bolts holding it in place were so frozen that the first two were twisted round without breaking loose even after heavy doses of penetrating oil. We decided to leave it, and Dad dumped something in the tank and rocked the car back and forth. I could hear the gas sloshing around in the tank.

Dad had purchased material and cut all new gaskets for the oil pan and the cylinder heads. He also made new gaskets for the exhaust manifold. He disassembled the entire carburetor and cleaned it with a brush and pipe cleaners until he was satisfied that it held no foreign debris. He sloshed it around in a small bucket of gasoline and suggested that I rub some gasoline on the layers of chicken scratches on my arms and face before they became infected. I looked at him as though he were an idiot trying to trick me into a stinging on my arms. I did it, however, and yes, it hurt like hell, but I never had even a hint of infection from the filthy chicken-claw scratches.

A new battery, a new solenoid, a cleaning for the new battery's starter cables, and a check of the belts, and we were ready for the grand test. We were certain there had to be crap collected in the gas tank and we would eventually have to take it off and deal with it properly, but on the fourth or fifth crank after pouring a little gas into the throat of the carb, the old Chevy coughed. On the sixth or seventh crank, it exploded into a blue, smoky song in six-part harmony. We, of course, had no muffler for it, so it was fairly unsettling to run, but we had to keep it running to make sure that all the fuel going to the carb was clean. The continued loud symphony scared the living shit out of the cows to the extent that none of them would milk that night, and my grandpa was somewhat pissed about that.

We put the old Chevy in gear, and sure enough, we were driving toward the house up through the old pasture field. The transmission was pretty rough and needed some work. It wouldn't go into reverse, so I had to keep in mind the wide turn radius I would need for a 180 until we got it home and fixed the problem. It turned out we used every available junkyard tranny for the '38 Chevy in the tri-county area in the first six months of driving it. The engine was just too powerful for the transmission, as we drove much differently than intended some twenty years after its manufacture. Dad and I ended up replacing the transmission with a later-year tranny that fit up without too much trouble, and it lasted for the remainder of the time I had the car.

The fenders were easily one-eighth inch thick, with one-thirty-second of that being rust. The main body itself was not too bad except around the lower door panel. My dad had a good friend who owed him some money, and he worked out a deal on the bodywork and a custom metallic paint job in lieu of payment. In the meantime, a good friend of mine had a father in the auto-repair business who had two right-side '38

Chevy fenders complete and unpainted and still in the paper in the attic of his garage. I paid fifteen bucks for one of them, and the paint guy did it up nice and replaced the right, dented original one. The old Chevy really looked quite nice by now—at least on the outside.

The interior was a disaster and had become a Red Carpet Inn for the field mice and a nesting place for some kind of small bird. The headliner was hanging down from the roof like a huge cobweb, and it stunk to high heaven from rodent urine and God knows what else. The seat covering was ripped badly in many places, and the mice had helped themselves to the stuffing to decorate their penthouse nests. The interior door panels were in pretty good shape, as was the paint on the dashboard. No radio and no rubber pads on the clutch or the brake pedal survived. My mind was going like crazy, fantasizing ways of making this a real nice boat.

To make a long story short and much less boring, I removed literally all that was removable from the interior of that car. Unfortunately, the floor material covered some small, escape-hatch holes through the floorboards that I'm sure the mice used to avoid the owls and hawks, making them look very clever for sure. I learned how to use the welder for the first (and hopefully the last) time. All that was not metal was ditched.

I replaced the headliner with some nice, black cotton material that my mom measured and cut for me. I found a black seat cover out of a junked 1950 Plymouth that was rolled and pleated and fit into my color scheme perfectly. I also salvaged the front bumper from that same Plymouth, which was about six inches wide and chromed. The bumper on the Chevy was spring steel that once hit something so hard that Dad and I, after multiple attempts with crowbars and chains, were unable to straighten, so it was replaced. Ultimately, we had the car painted a metallic candy-apple red, and the interior was mostly black. It really was a beauty and served me well through high school and my first two years of college. I ultimately sold it for $450.00 to the guy who did the paint job.

My purpose in boring you with this story is not to brag about my car or the extraordinary transformation my dad and I made of a pile of rusting junk. It's an example of how determined I was to make the very best of a situation, regardless of how difficult or unlikely I was to succeed. This trait was partly hereditary but mostly a gift from Mom and Dad. I was never permitted to leave a task completed to less than near perfect, and my own criteria for that became even more demanding than theirs in later life.

School Daze

—✺—

HAVING GRADUATED FROM A VERY small high school in rural Pennsylvania, I set out on my journey to a college education with a rather smug and self-confident attitude. After all, I was one of the top ten graduates out of a total of a hundred or so classmates! Hints of reality began to set in, though, upon receipt of iffy letters from some colleges to which I had applied, while others rejected me outright. I was accepted by some of my less desired schools, which I felt were as likely for me to attend as a guy going into the nursing profession in those days. Well—wrong on both counts. My ultimate choice among the three welcoming institutions of higher learning was a small, Methodist college in Western Pennsylvania with a very good track record in premeds.

I will not mention the school by name. I think they are still looking for me and some others regarding some damage caused during a scavenger hunt for our initiation into the fraternal order *Alpha Alpha* Delta. The special items that were on my team's list had been on the lists for every prior year of the scavenger hunt. Unknown to us, however, the "big five" had never been collected in the Delts' history. The brothers really didn't expect us to collect them either. They were on the list to justify handing out more punishment during our hazing. We worked very hard at our assigned task, and we had a great team. We did collect every item on the list, which was historical, immoral, and ultimately fatal to the fraternity.

The first item was ten gallons of piss. We assigned two guys to this task. They first went to a grocery and bought ten one-gallon jugs of a fruit-aide drink. They drank one of them and dumped the rest in the sewer drain so we'd have the ten empty bottles. Our guys actually had a great plan: they knocked on every door of the three dorms and the seven frat houses on campus, politely asking everyone if they would kindly contribute by pissing in the jug. Even a few ladies participated along the way.

The second item we had to get was a pound of cigarette ashes. This sounds quite easy, but it's not. A pound of cigarette ash is a hellacious amount. We assigned two pledges to this task, and they followed the guys on the piss-collection rounds, asking if they could have the contents of all the ashtrays. They then traveled downtown and visited the bars and party stores and a Friday-night dance place. Honestly, we never really did get a whole pound of *cigarette* ash. We topped off our shoebox containers with burned magazine and newspaper ashes we skimmed from a barrel that we found beside a house downtown. We just pulverized them until they looked very similar to the cigarette ashes and went with that. We counted on the brothers to be so drunk when we returned hours later that they wouldn't be able to tell the difference.

Our third and fourth items came from the same source. We were to collect a black 46D bra. There was a restriction on this one, however. It had to come from the female physical-education instructor on campus. She was quite young and quite voluptuous but had been a part of this hunt for a few years already. The biggest problem we had was getting her address. Once we had it, we were a bit hesitant to knock on her door. However, upon hearing our introduction as Delt pledges, to our surprise, she responded, "Oh, I know what you want!" She left us at the door and soon returned with the bra that met the exact specifications. She toyed with us a little with some jokes I really don't remember, but it certainly put me and the other two guys at ease.

This task had been completed so easily that I decided to ask if she could help us with the fourth item, which was "a female breast impression in whipping cream." We had had the piss collectors purchase a can of whipping cream for us so we would be prepared upon finding a willing subject. She looked at us kind of strangely at first and then gave us a sexy grin and took the whipped-cream can from my shaking hand and left us at the door once again.

She returned after a short while, now wearing a robe instead of the baggy T-shirt she had had on before. In her hand was a copy of *LOOK* magazine with a whole pile of cream on top and a perfect breast imprint right in the middle. What a gorgeous nipple! I couldn't believe this was happening. If it hadn't been for the timed element of the scavenger hunt, I might well have offered to help her take care of the excess whipping cream under the robe. We thanked her and excused ourselves as I sent one guy back to the frat house with the two items, as the whipped-cream imprint wouldn't last long, and it was way too precious to lose.

I and the remaining Delt pledge set out to obtain the last item on the list. The guys who had collected the cigarette ashes had told us about the Friday-night dance and said there were a lot of really shady characters there. Well, my new friend and I figured that there must be, out of all of those shady characters, at least one prostitute or her pimp, so we hustled to the dance, paid our admission, and started asking shady-looking guys about "a date." It wasn't long until a female about twenty years old approached me and ask me to dance. She fulfilled all of the criteria with her makeup, dress, and brash approach.

She started grinding on me like a crazed cow and right up front said, "I hear you are looking for a date."

"Yes, I am, but maybe not the way you are thinking. I need to return a working girl to our frat house up on college hill and have her just admit that she sells her tail for a living, and that's it, if you want it that way." Just as I was about to give her more details, her pimp showed up and roughly pulled me to one side. He started his little pricing spiel, and I interrupted him to explain what I needed. I think he thought at first that one in the hand was better than several in the bush, and he wanted me to pay right now for the little dance and a follow-up performance in the boys' room. When I said no, he pulled a long, skinny knife out of his jacket pocket, and I immediately started to rethink his proposition.

I told him that he needed to lose the fucking knife before anything got discussed, and when he finally slid it back into his pocket, I offered to pay twenty dollars up front just to get her in the door with about twenty-four frat brothers. I could see the dollar signs clicking in his head, and he soon thought it was a great idea. I insisted that only the girl enter the house and not him. He was hesitant at that. He said, "Well, she isn't fuckin' goin' in there alone. I'll send another girl in there with her."

Not to make the deal look so perfect, I said, "Well, I don't know about that. If that is a condition, I'm not going to pay an extra twenty."

He said, "Nah, just for the one."

The deal was struck, and my friend, who was literally shaking in his fucking shoes during this whole scenario, joined me and the two whores as we walked up to the big Delt house on the hill.

When we made our entrance into the basement party room of the Delts, it was like a New Year's celebration. All the other stuff from my team had been turned in, and the whore was all that was left—and we brought two. The brothers were yelling and clapping, whistling and chanting, and we felt like we were coming home from the war! They put on some really hot songs, and the whores fit right into the picture by doing some dances on the pool table and eventually getting totally naked. The guys at first just put dollars in their bras and panties, but as the booze flowed and the clothes were all gone, tens and twenties started showing up. Each of the darlings would disappear for the very short period of time that such things take when you are stoned out of your fucking mind and you are a young, sex-crazed college student. Of course, the pledges were not permitted to join in. They insisted we be tormented with drinking and memory games until well past 2:00 a.m., at which time most of the brothers were finally passed out.

So, that is the history of the first and last totally fulfilled scavenger hunt in *Alpha Alpha* Delta history. Even though I felt very good about it at the time, bad shit was to follow. One of the female guests of one of the brothers had an uncle who was on the college alumni board, and word soon permeated ears that couldn't handle this type of entertainment.

Word had it that our zealous efforts to become Delts put the fraternity's charter in default and restricted its social activities to near convent level. This was a devastating sentence given that the Delts had the reputation of being the wildest and most party-loving fraternity in the region.

The smug and conceited school, fearing for its prestige among other institutions, did not keep secret its disapproval and its attempts to get rid of the Delts. Having failed on previous attempts to rid its campus of these heathens, the college jumped on the scavenger-hunt incident like flies on shit. Every minor infraction that followed resulted in a downward spiral for the fraternity until its charter was withdrawn at the end of the following year.

By that time, I had transferred to another university and was taking classes at one of their satellite locations not far from my home. I commuted each day, but my financial resources ultimately became nonexistent. I had spent every dime I had saved since age fourteen and had exhausted all scholarships, loans, and the humble donations provided by my parents. I did take on a part-time job at the hospital's emergency room, where the staff told me that I was fucking insane for wanting to work in medicine. "Your life is never your own. You're always taking care of or worrying about someone else as well as your own family. You can make just as much as a plumber." Sounded sanely correct to me, but I had no alternate course. The job did help me pay for my second year even though I loathed missing some of the fun times of evening life.

My lifelong dream had been to be a doctor. All of my planning, saving, and dreaming had been directed toward that goal. However, I found myself in a dilemma. I had two years of college and needed two more, followed by four years of medical school and at least a one-year internship—yet I had not a single penny to pay for it. I had to work very hard to make the As and Bs required for acceptance into med school during my first two years of college. Working enough hours to support myself financially while going to school felt monumental, and my savings were at near-poverty level. Something big had to happen, and quickly.

I was broke at the end of my second year, when I heard a rumor about an army-enlistment program that paid for your final two years toward a bachelor's degree with a payback of serving twice the number of school years in active military service. Additionally, board, lodging, books— and, most important, salary—were paid for during one's entire time in college. Being a poor boy from a poor family in rural Pennsylvania, my life experiences had been pretty much limited to a hundred-square-mile area around my home in Seneca, a small community about forty miles northeast of Pittsburgh.

The longest trip I had ever taken was to Ocean City, New Jersey, for a summer vacation with the family. I had never flown in a commercial aircraft and considered it to be for the wealthy only. Now, here came the army, offering a paid ride for attaining a bachelor's degree and spending a little time with them after graduation in return. The only drawback was that the degree had to be in nursing. *Nursing!* I had never seen or heard of a male nurse, and the obvious connotations immediately filled my mind.

Having been reared, no pun intended, through the fifties and sixties, a man being a nurse was almost inconceivable to me. Men in traditionally female professions were considered to be effeminate, if not outright "queer," "homo," or whatever term you might choose. These words are not socially acceptable now in the twenty-first century, but they were used in "the day" regarding a subject that few knew anything about, and I was one of them.

As a kid, I knew of only one person who was "queer." His name was Oddly Green, and he was a hairdresser. He had pink hair, drove a pink, Mary Kay–ish Cadillac and hit on every young boy he passed. We were all terrified of him in my neighborhood. Every boy's father knew of Oddly and scooted him out of the area on sight. I was very comfortable with my gender and never felt really threatened, but I likewise knew nothing about homosexuals or of Oddly actually being one. So I left it at "queer" and knew there were some feminine traits there and figured it probably was the cause for his odd behavior toward boys.

My father, himself poor all of his life, was a hard worker and some-what of a jack-of-all trades. He taught me most everything, whether I wanted to be taught or not, and I cherish his influence on my life some twenty years after his passing. His son, the nurse? No fucking way! At the time, I thought maybe I should just run it by him. It would be fodder for a good laugh, if nothing else.

With Mom and Dad perched on the sofa in our living room on a Friday night following a wonderful shrimp dinner at a favorite little res-taurant and bar, I proceeded with my uncomfortable announcement. My mom cried, and my dad just looked right through me in that way that I never knew whether I was about to get my ass kicked or hear some profound input concerning my life and how it should progress. To my amazement, Dad turned to Mom and said, "What are you crying for? I think he has come up with a perfect solution for finishing college and getting his degree, don't you?"

Mom nodded halfheartedly and sobbed, "I had just hoped he would be a doctor. And what about the war? He will most certainly have to go. I don't know if I could stand that." Dad pulled Mom close to him in the kind of consoling hug that I rarely witnessed. Dad was never one to dis-play a lot of love or emotion openly. It was always there and you knew it, but he just never appeared comfortable in displaying this "weakness."

Sitting in shock at the prospect of my folks actually seeing my plan as feasible and now almost locking me into it through their approval, I left the room. A lot of thinking to do. Only three weeks to make a decision and go through all of the paperwork if I chose this direction.

August of 1965 found me exploring the huge, bare square foot-age of a second-floor apartment on Maryland Avenue in a suburb of Philadelphia. It would be my home for the next two years while I attend-ed the University's School of Nursing. The place was huge, with three bedrooms, a large kitchen, dining room, and living room. It was larger than the whole first floor of our home in Seneca. Suffering from years of neglect, the woodwork and wall coverings were in terrible disrepair. The floors were creaky and void of color except for faded, varying grains of neglected wood. The place had a kind of musty, stagnant odor that would have to change. No problem. Mom was here, and I could read her mind while she made mental notes for the task ahead. Although she didn't like the place at all, she had already given up any hope of changing my mind to rent it versus living on campus in a dorm room.

Philadelphia was a huge, overwhelming place compared to my little community of Seneca, and I was awed by the activity and the expanse of it all. My apartment would be about six miles from the main campus, requiring a reliable means of transport to and from class. Catching the bus required a short walk of only four blocks, and it ran right through the campus and my clinical class areas.

Having left Mom to her plans, Dad and I took a trial run to check out the transportation system. We were gone for hours as we checked out most of the restaurants and bars on the way, a true necessity for someone who would be spending the next two years there. The area proved to be quaint, with a mixture of college students, aspiring artists and writers, and a smattering of older folks still wishing to be young. A future favorite hangout would be a jazz-and-blues bar, a smallish place downtown with a beatnik-like atmosphere. For the life of me, I can't remember its name.

Upon returning to the apartment, I couldn't believe my eyes or my nose. The place not only looked clean and livable but actually pleasant, and it smelled quite nice. Mom once again had performed her magic on the toxic-waste dump. The place was magnificent.

As I watched Mom and Dad leave, a feeling of excitement mixed with sadness overtook me. I was about to embark on a tremendously exciting adventure for the first time without my parents' influence, but a feeling of fear and of loss nearly overwhelmed me. I realized that my relationship with my parents would change forever, and for the first time in my life, I would be truly alone—the kind of alone that means there would be only one decision on issues from now on. My answers had to be the right ones, as there would be no one else to help me with the consequences. God, I missed my mom and my dad!

Philadelphia today is a more upscale, modern metropolis surviving the downfall caused by Asian interests in our steel industry and our willingness to hand it over to them. My memories of the city, unfortunately, are of the stalled-out slums and empty, decrepit factory buildings left to rust before high tech replaced the steel yards and factories. My few visits back to the city during my early adulthood amazed me. How could a place that was so dead so few years ago be so alive and vibrant now? My mind would flood with memories of my earlier experiences in the city, wonderful and terrible in equal number. Philly had been the setting of one of the greatest and most demanding times of my life: attaining a degree in a predominantly female profession. I was only the second male ever in the school's history to matriculate into the program for a degree in nursing.

The apartment, after two weeks of additional touch-up and furnishing from the secondhand store, now had some real character. I took on a roommate, thinking it would really help bring down the costs. Jerry agreed to split everything fifty-fifty. He was a navy veteran and had some kind of compensation from the government, but he never would talk much about any details. He also made frequent visits to the VA Clinic where he got all of his health care. After a couple of months, I did learn that he had some type of intestinal problem that caused considerable gastrointestinal (GI) bleeding from time to time, especially following one of his heavy drinking sprees laid atop his usual fifth-every-two-days habit. He was good with his share of the rent and utilities, so I was fairly tolerant of his at times obnoxious behavior, especially when my friends visited. He was very intelligent on most any topic and extremely creative in fixing up some of the beat-up furniture we acquired. He reminded me, in a lot of ways, of my uncle Dan.

Jerry spent nearly eight months in the apartment up until one day in the early spring, when I came home to find the door wide open and no one around. Upon checking the place out for missing items, I found a note tacked to the inside of the door from my upstairs neighbor informing me that an ambulance had been there earlier and Jerry was taken to the hospital. I checked Jerry's room in hopes of finding the number of his mom, who I knew lived somewhere in Philadelphia. Instead, I was stopped in my tracks by a huge, dried puddle of blood on the wood floor of his room. It appeared as though he had vomited the blood and became weak, as items were tipped over on the nightstand and elsewhere on that side of the room.

I started canvassing the hospitals in the immediate area, and after many calls and a bunch of runaround bullshit, tracked him down to a suburban hospital not too far from our apartment. I rushed over right away but found myself waiting for nearly three hours before someone important decided to allow a nonrelative into his room.

I was blown away when I saw Jerry, who had been very much alive and active just the day before at age twenty-seven, now connected to IVs, a Foley catheter (a tube in the penis for draining urine), nasogastric tube, and, most terrible of all, a respirator. From what little info I could gather from his nurse, who made me take an oath of silence on the source, the EMTs had surmised that he apparently made it to the phone just in time enough to call 911 before passing out. The ambulance folks, with the police in tow, had forced the door and found him unconscious on his bedroom floor. He apparently smelled strongly of alcohol when rescue arrived and had been unresponsive since his transport to the hospital. The hospital had thus far not been able to contact next of kin. I stayed with Jerry that night until he died at eight thirty the next morning.

A Saturday afternoon in March found me among a group of total strangers along a peaceful little stream near Haverford. Jerry's memorial was very moving, and I learned more about him from his mother and his uncle than I had in the entire eight months we had lived under the same roof. Jerry had been a reader and was very quiet except when under the influence, and then his verbal torrents on every subject under the sun were somewhat unbelievable and always loud. I believe now that many of his tales were more than likely true and wish that I had had the fore-sight to take advantage of his loquacious gifts and historical knowledge. Instead, I had written off most of what he'd said as bullshit. We do learn valuable lessons throughout our whole lives. There is never a time when we know it all or have a total grasp on "how things are" regardless of our intelligence or life experiences.

Jerry's mom explained to me how he had entered the navy and that his deceased father and his uncle were both navy men. She knew little other than superficial stuff about Jerry's military life, like where he had been stationed and a postcard now and then while he had been on R and R, and, of course, his visits home to see her when on leave.

From what I gathered, and this is very sketchy, Jerry had spent near-ly a year on a navy ship in the South China Sea somewhere off the coast of Vietnam. He said little about his time there in his letters home. His mother did discover, however, that he had some physical problems that the navy was taking care of, and he had told her not to worry. It turned out to be Crohn's disease, a progressive ailment of the bowel that causes a lot of digestive problems as well as bleeding. The disease is also not tolerant of alcohol. I'm not sure when Johnny Walker be-came Jerry's friend, but they were inseparable in the best and in the worst of times.

Jerry's mom hadn't spoken to him or heard from him in nearly a month when, one evening in February of 1965, she answered a knock on the door. He had been discharged from the military and assured her that it had not been dishonorably. In fact, he would be receiving care for his GI system from the navy until things were resolved. He also said the navy would be sending him small monthly compensation check. That is about the extent of the information that I was able to garner on my roomy of eight months, except that his uncle had thought a lot of him and seemed destroyed over his passing.

After Jerry's ashes were sprinkled into the little creek that he and his father used to fish many years ago, the twelve or thirteen people there mingled. Some laughed, some cried, and others were silent with bland emotion. I thought, *Jerry was in the midst of these people and had some kind of relationship with each of them, and the best we can do is chuckle, cry, or do nothing?* I became somewhat outgoing with these strangers and started sharing stories of some of our antics—some good, some not so good—and it seemed to break the ice. Soon, people were in small groups, talking, laughing, and sharing their past memories of Jerry—something Jerry would have wanted.

Following the memorial, Jerry's mom invited me to her home to join them for supper. I cringed silently. I didn't want to go, but I immediately said yes. I loved this woman, as her kindness was sincere and her concern was real, and she appreciated me as Jerry's friend. It was just like my mom would respond under similar circumstances.

She made me sit in the parlor while she prepared dinner. Jerry's pictures were all over the place: him fishing, playing ball, partying. She seemed to live on the parts of his life when he had been willing to share. There were many things he did not share, however, that would impact her life in a very different way down the road.

Jerry's uncle shared several stories with me about Jerry as an adolescent that were quite usual for most boys of his age. Later, in his mid-twenties, he fell hard for a girl just before he was to depart for Southeast Asia. They had planned together to meet on an R and R and become engaged, but the uncle had heard from a friend of Jerry's that when the time came, the girl never left the States and Jerry spent the R and R on his own. I thought, *This is turning out to be the typical boy-girl in love, boy goes to war, girl meets new guy and Dear Johns the boyfriend, runs off with new guy. Fuck Jerry.*

Jerry's mom cooked us a delightful meal of pierogi, a light soup, coffee, bread, and plum pierogi for desert. The meal was delicious. I had never tasted Slavic food before. I ate my fill and sat with Jerry's uncle, planning the move of Jerry's stuff from the apartment. He said he had room on his second floor and could furnish a whole room there and still have space left. I explained that Jerry's stuff wasn't exactly from the Ritz, and he chuckled. "Hell, mine isn't either." So the remainder of Saturday evening and all of Sunday were spent making trips in his small pickup truck back and forth from my apartment to his house. On about the fourth trip of the ten-mile jaunt, I suggested that we drop this last load, which was kind of a no-matter, shitty load anyway, at the Salvation Army, and maybe he would be blessed for sharing a little part of Jerry with the homeless.

The Salvation Army Center was closed, it being Sunday, but there was a sheltered area in the back where it appeared things could be dropped off. We unloaded the several remaining pieces of furniture. As we were off-loading a small writing desk, Jerry's uncle lost his grip, and the piece fell to the ground on one end with me holding the other. It did not damage the desk except for a small scuff on one of the legs, but three of the small drawers fell out onto the concrete. As we picked them up and replaced them into their slots, I noticed a small key taped to the bottom of a drawer. I removed it and gave it to Jerry's uncle, and I thought no more about it. We finished up the work, and Jerry's uncle took me home. We parted with no expectation of seeing each other again.

When I left Jerry's uncle's company in March, I assumed that only a few superficial memories of my roommate would remain. I was very surprised that, one day in early May, a knock at the door came just about the time I was finishing my schoolwork. I was amazed to find Jerry's uncle there. He gave me a very warm greeting and apologized for not letting me know ahead of his visit, but he didn't have my phone number and thought he would just stop in. I suggested we go across the street to my favorite food-and-beverage hangout.

The bar was owned by two Greek brothers, Gus and Nick, who had been very cordial and warm to me from day one. The first time I went, they learned that I lived next door, was in the military, and was paid just once a month, so they offered to let me have a tab I could settle each payday. I actually did a lot of studying there over a beer and the best burger ever. The brothers put out a good bar menu, and I ate there at least four times a week.

Jerry's uncle seemed very anxious to tell me something, so after our beer was ordered, he proceeded to tell me more of Jerry's history. He had pursued the origin of the key that we had found and discovered it was to a safe-deposit box in some bank near Jerry's family's home. After getting permission from Jerry's mother and the bank manager, he opened the box and found some very interesting information that only added to the mysteries of Jerry's existence in his last couple of years.

The box had contained a few old stock certificates from US Steel, about a thousand in cash, and some old letters he had received from his girlfriend while he served in the navy. There were also two medals, one for heroism and one for getting wounded in action. The certification for the heroism medal described a firefight between Jerry's unit and the Vietcong in which over half the members on his craft were killed and the remainder wounded. He was commended for taking over an automatic-weapon post that had been operated by one of his dead comrades and, even after being seriously wounded, fought from the disabled craft until fire support and air support came to the rescue. He was credited with repelling a sizeable enemy force from boarding the craft and killing or capturing his remaining crew members.

Jerry had never mentioned anything about his experiences in Vietnam or the abdominal scarring that I had assumed was all from his Crohn's disease. I respect Jerry for his sacrifices and his humility and only wish that I and his family might have known some of these details so that a military proceeding could have honored his actions after his death.

Jerry had been a lot of company over the first several months at the apartment on Maryland Ave. After he was gone, I spent a lot of time on campus with my schoolmates—more than fifty women—at the student union and at a couple of bars that didn't check ID very closely. I was twenty-one, but the majority of the ladies that I hung out with were not. At first, my associations were only random meets at "the union," but after a while, I began casually dating several of my classmates. It was quite comfortable, as the classwork was difficult, and the most any of us expected in a date was fun and not any additional serious baggage.

Several of my friendships lasted years after graduation. I felt it very important to remain low profile for at least the first year, and I found shortly after my first day of classes that it was going to be a very tough trip. I would be graduating from a very prestigious school run by a bunch of very opinionated and prejudiced instructors who seemed intent on keeping the profession exclusive of men—by any means.

On August 22, 1965, day one of my classes at the School of Nursing, I walked into the educational facility used by the combined medical services and was overwhelmed. The facility was very modern. There were four floors surrounding a huge, lobby-like common area with a high ceiling at the top. Each level was served by a set of wide stairways that gave access to a multitude of classrooms, labs, and even a morgue that was used by doctors, dentists, and, finally, nurses.

Needless to say, nurses, as the third in line at the morgue, found the cadavers were pretty rugged and many times had strange anomalies, such as hearts on the right side and males with uteri, and so forth. All of these antics were perpetrated by our co-participants while they became the medical superstars of the future.

I was feeling pretty comfortable up to this point. The classroom schedule didn't look too difficult, and my experience as an orderly the previous summer would really help on the clinical side. We were herded into a huge classroom with our instructors sitting before us and went around the room with the usual introductory stuff: name, hometown, and why we would want to be nurses. My answer was not very well received. "Well, I really didn't want to be a nurse, but I didn't think I had the brains or the money for med school. I had already invested two years in the sciences, so I figured nursing might be the next best thing, considering." I heard the collective sighs of the instructors, all four of them nearly in cadence, along with the giggles from the other freshman nursing students who knew that I had committed the greatest of sins and that I would live a hell on earth here at the School of Nursing for the next two years. They were right.

The following day, when I reported to microbiology class, the instructor, Dr. Carner, handed me one of the pink memo slips that were so popular in the day, instructing me to go directly to the dean of nursing's office. I thought immediately that some terrible accident or worse had happened at home, and I nearly ran to the dean's office on the second floor. I introduced myself to the receptionist and was asked to have a seat. I sat and remained there for nearly an hour.

The receptionist received calls and shyly looked at me over the top of her glasses while talking very softly to whom I guessed to be the dean just on the other side of the door. Finally, I was told that I could see the dean, and I knocked softly. As I entered, I was nearly floored to see all four of my clinical instructors and the dean sitting in Supreme Court style along a deeply shined, walnut-paneled wall clustered with countless old portraits of past nursing notoriety at the university. I stood speechless and was gruffly asked to sit down because the discussion today might take some time.

The dean presented the case. "I was informed that you stated in front of all of the instructors and your classmates that you really didn't want to be a nurse, but in lieu of your ability to be a doctor decided to give us a chance anyway. I will inform you, Mr. Neely, before you begin, that the university is and has been one of the most prestigious educational facilities in the East, with the School of Nursing helping to lead the way. We are not enchanted with a student taking up a space of enrollment who is not truly honored to be here. Are you honored to be here, Mr. Neely?"

"Of course I am. I was not able to pursue my original desire to become a doctor because of financial and educational problems, but I am now more than happy to be able to have an alternative choice." The pack of hounds bristled and looked at each other like I had disrobed in front of them or called them a clutch of whores or something. I had simply been taught to say what I mean and mean what I say, so to reverse the actual thoughts in my head—right, wrong, displeasing, or otherwise—was foreign to my behavior and my upbringing, and I stated that in so many words.

Ms. Stark, a leather-faced matron of the anti-male movement, pushed out her chest in a threatening posture and in a voice as deep as mine, said, "Do you realize that because of your decision, it is a fact that if you do not make it through this program with your degree, the military will send you to medics' school and you will be sent to Vietnam and combat in the field instead of a military hospital?"

"No, I really never thought of that. I never really thought of failing the program."

"Do you think the program is so easy that there is no chance of you failing?"

"No, I never considered failing because of the program not being challenging. I have worked in hospitals as an orderly and was quite good at it and feel that I would make a good nurse as well."

"You know there is a huge ocean between the skills and responsibilities of a nurse compared to an orderly, don't you?"

"Of course I do, but the knowledge and skills should come with education and experience, and I think that I can achieve that."

"What did your father do for a living?"

"He still works. He is a machinist at a tool-and-die company."

"Has anyone in your family *ever* gone beyond high school in their education?"

"No. I am the first."

"Has anyone told you how difficult this program can be, even for female students?"

"Is it more difficult for male students?"

"Maybe not. Men certainly suggest that they are much stronger. Is that how you feel?"

At this point, I really felt like I was being interrogated by a group of lawyers or judges and regardless of what I said, it was not going to turn out well for me, so I decided to be a lot more assertive. "Yeah, I guess men are a lot stronger in many ways. Certainly, I can see where physical strength might be an asset to a nurse, along with education and common sense, of course."

"Oh, you think that common sense and physical strength will make you a good nurse."

"Not in itself, but it would be of great benefit."

I studied the faces of the instructors as Ms. Stark poured questions at me. It appeared that all were enjoying the show except for the youngest, Ms. Key, the psychiatric instructor. She was in her late twenties and was exceptionally good-looking. She had long, black hair, a narrow face, and a tall, gorgeous figure with smallish, firm breasts, rounded hips, and long, slender legs. I noticed today and the previous day, during our intros, that she favored skirts that were very short. I wondered what the other biddies actually thought of her, as she looked very much out of place alongside them.

As the other three glared at me for most of the interrogation, Ms. Key actually cracked a pleasant smile in my direction on several occasions. My God, how could I be thinking about how gorgeous one of my instructors appeared when the other three were burning me at the stake? It appeared that the others wanted to punish me some more, but suddenly, the dean looked at her watch and stated, "This meeting is over. And, Mr. Neely, make sure you get the notes from someone on the micro class you just missed."

I was stunned, as there wasn't any closure on the fucking meeting. It seemed like they just wanted to get together and beat on me a bit and then go about their business, appearing as though nothing had ever happened! I was now aware that this was going to be a tough road.

For the rest of the first week, there were more tours of the many places where we would be working and studying for next two years. We met a thousand people, it seemed, and were expected to remember the names of most. Our clinical rotations would be held at one of the specialty hospitals, most within walking distance of each other.

There were also several academic courses that most of us had to complete while wading through the nursing curriculum, and most of those classes were held at the main school campus. Many of the liberal-arts students had classes there as well, and it was good to meet folks for a change of pace who weren't being indoctrinated into the science professions. The classes there were a cakewalk compared to what was in store for me at the nursing campus. I would soon be the prime target of three out of four of the nursing instructors, and it would take all of the energy and perseverance that I could muster to survive.

I was excited to attend my first microbiology class. I strolled into the room with anticipation and found a seat. As others filtered in, I had to change seats several times, as apparently there was some random order of seat assignments, a tactic utilized back in grade school. After moving four times, I just took a lean against the wall by the door until it appeared everyone else was in their proper positions, and I sat down in one of the three remaining seats.

"I see we have the honor of Mr. Neely being in our classroom today," bellowed Ms. Carner. "However, you are sitting in our 'guest seat,' Mr. Neely. Would you kindly move to the seat by the door?" She continued, "I would like to emphasize that micro is an extremely difficult class, and attendance to all of the units in my class are very advisable to pass this subject in the manner needed for the nursing curriculum. Missing a class will make it very, very difficult for anyone to succeed here, and missing two will make it impossible. Does everyone understand that?"

I thought, *Yes, you are truly a bitch, just as I have heard from the second-year students, and you have just divulged the trap you plan to use to run me out of this curriculum, out of Philadelphia, and off to a field-medic job waiting in*

Vietnam. I swore to myself, *I will not fail in this class.* The obvious prejudice had given me a conviction for victory. At the end of the period, a dozen of my fellow students gathered around me in support, calling Ms. Carner names that I would not use and some that I had not heard. They assured me if that I chose to take exception in the dean's office, I would have their support. For the short time we spent together in class, they were very supportive and kind, and these same women would play a huge part in my attaining a degree at the university.

The following twelve weeks involved a lot of classroom study and nursing-skills practice, and it was not difficult for me to get the grades I needed. In my clinical work that came later, however, it was apparent to me that my performance would always be under more precise scrutiny than that of the others. It was so severe and obvious that my classmates actually made an issue of it, unknown to me, with a group visit to the dean of nursing. I was not aware of that fact until the last two months of my matriculation, and it turned out to be a lifesaver. That is an understatement.

—⚒—

By the fourth month, it was time to start our clinical rotations. Our class was broken up into roughly five groups, with each group starting in a particular specialty and advancing to the next by rotation. There were no provisions for repeating any of the clinical rotations if one were missed or failed. Under extreme circumstances, the dean could offer a second chance to complete the curriculum and graduate, but this had never actually happened in the school's history.

My first rotation was in surgical pediatrics, well known to be the most difficult. I found myself in the company of Ms. Stark and the brightest and most advanced classmates, who viewed the selection as an honor. I viewed it a bit differently, as I was the only one in the group who, despite good grade performance on tests, was awarded a passing B for the first classroom quarter. I guess I was fortunate to get that.

Pediatrics was difficult because it not only included medical and surgical patients, but everything was in miniature. The anatomy was much smaller, the medicine doses were much smaller, the math was much more difficult, and the emotional stress of dealing with a nonadult was huge. Additionally, the parents of the children needed a lot of attention, and at times, they were the most difficult to manage.

Each student was given one patient to start clinicals with, and being the last to receive my assignment, which is the way it would be for nearly two years, I accompanied each of the nine other students to the rooms in which their patients were located. This was a surgical postop unit, and so far, all of the assigned patients had been two or three days postoperative and in a pretty much stable, controlled stage of treatment. Finally, I was led to my room and introduced to the child's mother at the door. She had a horrid, frantic look on her face as I was taken to her son's bedside.

Anthony M. had been transferred to the surgical floor this morning after two days in ICU. His surgery had been a correction of Tetralogy of Fallot, a genetic heart problem that involves four different defects, each relying on the presence of the others for compensation to permit the patient to survive through birth and early childhood. I distinctly remember Anthony in his blue diaper and cotton T-shirt that also served to keep his wires (pacemaker wires that led to the ventricles of the heart in case things went wrong) out of sight and out of his hands. Under his shirt, he had a narrow dressing extending from his sternal notch down to his abdomen. He was under an oxygen tent and was standing up, clinging to the side rail, wailing and sobbing, with blue lips and bloodshot, reddened eyes. He had an intravenous that entered into his left femoral vein.

I was speechless for nearly fifteen seconds, and finally, upon recovering from the shock and the flood of ideas zooming through my brain, I dove in with what little experience I had gained thus far. While dropping the side rail, I spoke with the mom, telling her things would turn out OK and for her not to be overly concerned about disturbing all of the wires and tubes. Anthony certainly needed the human contact, and after a short while, with the attention from me and his mom, he was asleep in mom's arms in the rocker beside the crib, working on the pacifier that he refused to give up under any circumstances.

I spent the next four hours with Anthony and his mother, and at the finish of my day, I was physically and mentally drained. Every time I had to leave the room to get a med or a supply item, Ms. Stark would pull me aside and pommel me with questions about Anthony's anomaly. For those missed, I was told to write them down and that I would be queried on them the next day prior to my revisiting the room, as she did not want anyone taking care of patients who didn't know what they were doing. I hated her from that day forward, supporting my same feeling about her from weeks before.

As I said good-bye to Anthony for the day, his mom approached me and took my hand and thanked me as sincerely as I have ever been thanked. I learned that day the true bond between a mother and her child and the importance of all of the love in between.

I returned to my apartment about 7:00 p.m. after stopping at the library and doing all the scut work Ms. Stark had laid on me. I was starved but simply sprawled across the bed and didn't awaken until around 9:30 p.m. I was famished and thirsty. I threw on a pair of jeans and a T and went to the Greek bar for a burger and beer. We were sworn to an oath not to discuss patients by name outside the school, but after a few beers, Gus, the bartender, was a good ear for the events of my day. He could not believe how cold this bitch was, and what the fuck she was even doing in a "people job" as important as that? I had to agree with him as I finished my fourth sixteen-ounce Miller and dozed off, leaning up against the wood back rest of the booth.

I guess Gus tried to wake me a couple of times to no avail, so he just let me stretch out in the booth, covered me with a blanket, and provided a pillow for my head. I remained there until awakened by the smell of bacon and eggs. It was 7:00 a.m., and Gus was making breakfast. He had made his wife breakfast before she left home and was jokingly complaining about all the fucking worthless people he had become responsible for. I liked Gus, and we did favors for each other whenever we could.

We both loved beautiful women, and Gus knew this gal on the North Side that would give you anything you wanted for ten bucks. When my best friend, Fred, visited, we had several beers and after a while became bored. Gus suggested we go see his girlfriend. Fred and I obliged and took off for the North Side, a place where white boys usually do not venture.

After two or three close calls asking for directions, we finally found the address. It was a well-kept three-story house with a bunch of adolescents' toys on the porch. Fred knocked on the door, and a young girl around ten answered it. Fred looked over his shoulder at me with half a frown. I shook my head to assure him Gus wouldn't do that to me. Soon, the girl's mother came to the door, and we stood there staring at each other until finally, the mother told the little girl she needed her to go to the store for some milk and butter.

The daughter left without hesitation, and the mother looked at us and said, "Gus said you were pretty young. How old are you?" Fred and I were legal, me at twenty-one and Fred just shy at twenty and three-quarters. "Well, who's first?" Fred was on his way up the stairs before we were able to discuss the matter. They both were back down within fifteen minutes.

I followed her up the stairs and turned to put the ten on her dresser, and when I turned around, she had her dress pulled up over her waist and was lying on her back with legs spread-eagled. She showcased a bushy, black-haired pussy that under most circumstances would turn me off and make me fearful of critters climbing up hair shafts to greet me as I plunged into the forest. I commented that it didn't seem like a very romantic position. She said, "You're here to get your rocks off for ten bucks. What do you want?"

"I want to see your breasts." I didn't even get my knee on the bed, and the shirt and bra were on the floor.

I undressed and lay bedside her and kissed her once on the cheek and was headed for the lips when she pulled away and said, "We aren't going to take this seriously, are we?"

I said, "No, I don't take my hand too seriously either," and I just dove in, climaxing almost before I crossed over the pubic hair. It had been a long time. I dressed and started down the stairs. Fred was there at the bottom, actively urging me to hurry and leave before she came down. He ushered me out the door just as her daughter returned home, and off to Shadyside we headed, helter-skelter, in Fred's car.

"What the hell was with you, Fred? We should have waited and said good-bye and thanks, at least. Gus will be pissed with our rudeness."

"No, we shouldn't have."

"Why?" I asked.

"Because I ate the pork chops that were cooked on the stove that she and her daughter were having for dinner."

"Holy shit, we need to make it up. Give me five bucks." He fought, but I got the five, and we circled around the block. I bailed out in front of the house with my five and his five and kind of just barged into the house to find her, her daughter, and a large guy with gold front teeth and a shit-eating grin on his face. "My friend and I thought you should have this. Thank you. Bye." I never returned.

I prepared with endless hours of study on Tetralogy of Fallot and knew every variation and complication and treatment—everything! I felt very much in control as I entered the pediatric postop unit on the next day of my rotation. I made my way through the nurse's station, as report had not yet begun from the off going shift, and peeked into Anthony's room. For the first time, he looked truly comfortable in his sleep.

As I was watching, Ms. Stark came from behind and asked me to join her in the conference room. I followed her, and soon the remainder of my classmates showed up as well. "I have your assignments," Ms. Stark declared. It turned out that everyone else kept the same patients they had had on the previous Friday—except me. "Mr. Neely will have two patients today: a female with spina bifida and a three-year-old male postop splenectomy due to trauma from a car-pedestrian accident. The rest of you may go, but Mr. Neely, I would like to discuss your patients with you." An hour later, I emerged from the conference room browbeaten and one hour behind.

I entered the room of my first patient and started gathering items for her morning care. Miraculously, the little girl with spina bifida appeared as though she had already been bathed. She had a fresh diaper and powder and the sheets were changed. I turned to the doorway just in time to catch a glimpse of a fellow student as she passed by. She gave me a big, secretive wink and then went about her business. I was tickled beyond belief, because I now might be able to finish my work on time and avoid the wrath of Ms. Stark. I also became aware of an acceptance from my classmates and their understanding of the swelling harassing behavior that was taking place against me, and they appeared willing to help as needed. The harassment continued until two weeks prior to my graduation.

I will not go through every grueling moment of my two years at the university but will highlight the eventful ones. I once believed that my clinical training counted as some of the best and worst days of my life. Little did I know that things could become much, much worse. Strange how we think that the situation of the moment might be the best or the worst forever, when actually, many memories of them slip into obscurity as time passes by. Maybe our minds protect us so that we always look forward to something better or are aware that something more horrible is always possible.

My psych rotation was my favorite, mainly because of my instructor, Ms. Key. She was gorgeous and the only one of my four instructors who appeared to have sprung from the loins of a recent, normal generation. Also, she did not hate me, and from the beginning, I believe she took a liking to me.

The classrooms in which the instructors taught were quite puritan and sparsely decorated. All of them had wooden floors and a stage-like elevation of about one foot from the student seating level. The instructors either spoke from a podium or sitting in a chair up on that platform. Ms. Key taught, nearly always, sitting in that chair, and from my self-assigned seat in the front row, she nearly drove me crazy with crossing and uncrossing her long, slender legs. I know she caught me wandering from the text on many occasions. But she never reacted negatively, and at times, I thought I might have detected a small smile. I must say that Ms. Key was a high point in my educational experience there. I looked forward to her classes, and I always felt totally fulfilled after our sessions.

I had always enjoyed my studies in psych and had taken twelve additional psychology credits prior to coming to Philadelphia. I likewise enjoyed my sociology and philosophy classes and was able to see the interactions of the three disciplines in many of my daily experiences. It was my philosophy that we were all afflicted with some degree of psychosocial anomaly; the method by which we handled it made the difference whether we were accepted, shunned, or locked away—in other words, crazy or not crazy. My interest was such that Ms. Key chose only me and one another student out of our entire group to do home psychiatric health visits on patients that, for one reason or another, did not fit the mold for office counseling. Our activity scripts were very tight and limited. Ms. Key consulted with our patients immediately after every visit so our ventures would cause as little trouble as possible. I was amazed, however, that I received little criticism.

Ms. Key's evaluations of us, held in her office after each of the patient visits, were stellar, although unusually long and time-consuming. They were so good that Ms. Key announced my achievements at a quarterly meeting among all students in the class, all instructors, and the dean. The other three instructors were dumbstruck. I could see a variety of reactions and thoughts going through their heads, and I loved it! After all, these three witches were probably going to send me off to Vietnam on the next plane after they failed me, and I would be lucky to finish any type of education, let alone return home breathing and walking on my own.

The remainder of the psych rotation went very well, and I received the highest grade of the entire class. I do think Ms. Key disliked the other instructors nearly as much as I, but she made her point without openly exhibiting any malice toward her coworkers.

My rotations through medical and adult surgical nursing were pretty similar to the pediatric surgical rotation. Continuous questions came in machine-gun-like fashion, putting me hopelessly behind in my assignments. I might say that I have since been a fast worker and finish tasks expediently. Without this subskill and my silent, behind-the-scenes helpers, I would never have finished my patient assignments by the close of shift, as my multi-patient assignments continued through all of the rotations while the others rarely got more than one patient at a time.

Ms. Stark was particularly sneaky. She would often stalk up on me, and I wouldn't know she was there. One afternoon, I was getting a dose of Maalox—a chalky, thick, sticky, white medicine—from a multi-dose bottle. The person before me had left the cap just barely seated, but I didn't realize it. I pointed the bottle over my left shoulder as I always do and shook it vigorously. The cap came off, and the liquid shot over my shoulder and all over the front of Ms. Stark's face and chest. When I heard her yelp, it was only a second or two before I realized what had happened.

I turned around to find her covered in the white, sticky goo. I broke out laughing. She showed no humor at all and stomped out of the room. I didn't see her for the remainder of my shift until I reported off. She looked daggers at me as she handed me my study sheet for the next day. I had learned, however, from experience that all of the diagnoses she had written down for my patients would be different the next day. When I arrived for work, she would have me assigned to different patients just to stress me out. This would require me to study my ass off whenever I could while on shift so I could give my patients the best care possible.

As I took the assignment sheet from her hand, I noticed remnants of the Maalox clinging to the tips of her hair and a dried puddle of the stuff lying in the hollow of her left ear. While I walked away, the whole episode replayed for me. For at least that day, I left her shitty company happy and laughing.

My final rotation was to be obstetrical nursing, the rotation that I had feared since the beginning of my nursing education. I seriously had no idea of how my prejudiced instructors would approach the very delicate dilemma of deciding my role in this nursing specialty. As the first day approached, I didn't just suspect them to be prejudicial toward men entering the nursing career; I was downright sure of it. The instructors, with the exception of Ms. Key, had assured me in one form or another that I would never get a graduation certificate from the program at the university. Ms. Key, being somewhat of an intermediary for me, shared her doubts that the remaining instructors would ever relent and allow me to finish the program.

So the first day of my OB rotation was anxious, to say the least. What a perfect time and place to drop the bomb. We all gathered in a large conference room at the hospital awaiting the outline for the next eight weeks. The unit, which we later learned was the postpartum unit, had a myriad of smells that were very strange. Everyone was dressed in these wraparound, over washed cotton gowns and strange hats, not too unlike the ones I saw worn by the operating-room personnel during my surgical nursing rotation.

Our large group, composed of a collection of the surviving students from all of the smaller groups, was now awaiting assignment to prenatal and postnatal classrooms, labor, delivery, and finally, postpartum nursing. As names were read and specialty assignments were filled, the in-house charge nurses led their assigned student groups out of the room. Soon, no one remained except me. I stood in the room, feeling certain that I was going to be cast down and out. I wondered how I had remained in the surviving cadre this long anyway.

Soon, Ms. Stark, who I think fought for the chance to deliver all of the special, abusive news to me throughout my time there, said to me coldly, "We had a very difficult time deciding on what role you might play during the next eight weeks and decided the least offensive to the patients would be to place you in the gynecological-obstetrical surgery suite for four weeks and the gynecological outpatient clinic off-campus site for the remaining two. We will decide on the last two weeks later." I was actually relieved since there was at least a place for me. Maybe I would benefit from not having the constant pressures of the enemy looking over my shoulder for the next eight weeks.

My first exposure on my new assignment was an outpatient OB-GYN clinic on the edge of the slums in the worst part of Philadelphia. I was taken down to the clinic for my introduction, surprisingly, in Ms. Stark's private car. I noticed some extraneous objects in the car that told me a little about Ms. Stark and her private life. I will not divulge names or facts descriptive enough that it would put me in a courtroom, but I will say that Ms. Stark was married to a high-profile person. He was rumored to have a very exciting life parallel to his profession that kept him traveling and in the company of much younger members of the opposite sex. This was spoken of in lowered voices in some of the more prestigious watering holes, and it became somewhat public.

Later, I learned that Ms. Stark's attitude toward men was not uniquely for me but was routinely shown in her behavior toward most other males during school functions. She was outright rude to some and frequently openly criticized some of the male speakers after their presentations. Yes, after nearly two years with Ms. Stark, I had a slight sense of pity as I realized that loneliness might well be a big part of her psyche. Her life was about to get much worse.

Ms. Roberts was the clinic's nursing director. As I watched the secretary make her phone call to Ms. Roberts, I did not realize that Ms. Stark had simply just left. When Ms. Roberts came into the waiting room from the long hallway leading to the exam rooms, she asked me what my business was with the clinic today. I think she must have thought me to be a salesman or such. I told her that I was a student at the university and that I was assigned here for two weeks to work in an OB-GYN outpatient clinic.

Ms. Roberts appeared stunned and asked me to come with her to the office so we might look into the matter in a more private setting. We weaved our way through nearly fifty waiting patients, some sitting in chairs, some on lounges, some on window ledges, and a few huddled in a corner on the floor. The place was packed, and there was also a line at the registration desk across from the secretary with probably another ten people waiting.

When we arrived in her office, I found it very small and cluttered with paperwork piled in stacks. A multiline telephone that had every light blinking with calls waiting was ringing incessantly. Ms. Roberts just picked up the receiver and put it back down. The floor on one side of the room was stacked halfway to the ceiling with patient records with red tabs on them, and the other side of the room had supplies in boxes stacked nearly to my height. I started to get the picture. This was likely a mostly free clinic, and they were horribly understaffed, overused, and, more than likely, underappreciated. It turned out to be the case all the way around.

Ms. Roberts dug around in a bunch of folders and piles of papers and eventually pulled out a letter, yet unopened, that had my university's graphics on the envelope. She said, "Oh, shit, I've really got to start getting to this mail sooner. I really am sorry, I wasn't expecting you." I was kind of stunned as she silently scanned the letter. As she put it down on the desk, she said, "Well, don't feel badly. They don't think much of us, either!"

I have no idea what the letter of introduction for me actually said, but I am certain it wasn't too favorable. Ms. Roberts added, "Don't worry, you won't have any problems with us. We are glad to have the help." I liked her from the start, and she was the first lady of power, other than Ms. Key, who seemed to have manners, politeness, and goodwill toward others.

I was introduced to the doctors and the doctor assistants, and she made me promise to look her up at lunchtime so we could go to the deli across the street. She would fill me in on some important details that might help out over the course of my work there. She assigned me to a middle-aged nurse who had worked at the clinic for some time. Ms. Roberts felt she would be best to teach me established procedure and how to get things done in a free clinic that didn't have a lot of funds to work with. The nurse had me observe the first several patients and her interactions with them. I took some procedural notes but mostly noticed how natural and personable she came across with the patients and how much information they would tell her without her really asking for much at all.

The majority of the patients appeared to be in need. Some were teenage girls, and there were many ladies of the street. The complaints ranged from urinary discomfort, pregnancy, vaginal infections, and severe abdominal pain. At that time, intrauterine devices (IUDs) were a very popular birth-control measure, and we saw countless women with pelvic inflammatory disease (PID) secondary to terrible infections caused by the intrauterine devices and the neglectful way in which they were used. The street ladies found the IUDs perfect, as they could be inserted, left in place for a long time, and pretty much forgotten. However, given their high traffic, most often unprotected by condoms, many of them became infected early, and the device soon became threatening and dangerous.

I remember seeing several ladies, after removing their pads, having foul, yellow drainage dripping to the floor from their infected devices. Some of them had worked until just a couple of hours before coming to the clinic. So, pretty much, the typical standard operating procedure was a gynecological exam, a culture sample, removal of the IUD when possible (some were embedded so far into the uterine tissue that they could not be removed without surgery), a huge course of antibiotics, a brief education, and a scheduled follow-up in ten days. The education included a recommendation of abstinence, but that point was rarely acknowledged or followed. Many never came back at ten days but would return weeks or months later with the same ailment.

We attempted to keep the younger, more, innocent females in a different setting, away from the street ladies to help replenish the absent or diminished self-esteem they often suffered. It was sad to witness that most of the unwed teens had no support at home, and their hopes and destinies were as dismal as an old, distressed, sailing ship lost in the fog. Many were despondent to the point of being suicidal rather than face family and friends. It didn't seem fair that all of the support they might expect to receive came from strangers during their brief visits to the free clinic.

Aside from the usual nursing activities I did over the four weeks, there was lots of social contact with the clinic staff. They were a great bunch of professionals, and I was happy to attend several get-togethers after work and even a couple of parties. The staff seemed to have a need to help others and took every opportunity to do so, even for me.

When I finished my outpatient rotation, I was given glowing evaluations by all of the charge nurses that I had worked with and also by the supervising nurse and the physician in charge of the clinic. I am certain that the excellent reviews created a myriad of problems for my hostile instructors back at the main campus. After all, they had been crafting mechanisms to oust me from the program for nearly two years, and now they had to confront another impediment to their effort. With just six weeks left in the program and graduation scheduled for June 18, I lay awake for a good part of the weekend wondering what their final, destructive move would be. It was a horrible weekend.

Monday morning, and we were once again herded into a large classroom. A few more faces were gone that apparently didn't make the muster to continue. The staff at the School of Nursing was famous for allowing students to go through nearly the entire program and then booting many of them out at or near the very end. I felt that they most likely had reserved a special slot for me in this category.

The choices for my final six weeks, according to the instructors, were labor and delivery, postpartum, and surgical obstetrics. The nursing supervisory staff and instructors retired to another room, and after about an hour, they made their decision. I would spend four weeks in surgical obstetrics, and finally, two weeks in a segment of the course that was actually tested on the state board exam: labor and delivery. I guess they felt they had to demonstrate some level of fairness. They probably figured that labor and delivery wouldn't work out, and even if it did, I would never pass the boards in OB with the anemic exposure they permitted me to have.

Labor and delivery was not fun for me. Husbands and boyfriends seemed to hate it also, as they felt helpless and totally responsible for the pain and suffering that their loved ones experienced. I am a huge advocate of equality and fairness, but the whole process of childbirth, as lovingly as it may be discussed, is a test for every partner in attendance. It certainly isn't pleasant for the patient either! This is an event that is so far from the erotic, sexual experience that created new life that it takes months to erase the images from hubby's mind so that he quits using his hand and thinks once again of approaching the baby maker. He will always remember the screaming and the swearing! *Who is this woman screaming obscenities and threatening me with my life should she survive?*

It often takes hours of painful work and culminates in being rushed to the delivery suite to endure even more pain. The experience is highlighted with amniotic fluid, poop, urine, and other unknown fluids coming from a place that was so special for her partner not so long ago. That space is now managed exclusively by a screaming, "out-of-her-mind" woman in pain. When the rapture is completed by the expulsion of a purple, cheesy, mucus-dripping, screaming little person who is Mom and Dad's future, all of the terrible things about the delivery are pushed to a recess of the mind and replaced by an unexplainable connection of love and attachment.

Upon looking down at the new life, the realization of being responsible for that offspring for the next eighteen-plus years comes into focus, and the mind is dizzy with feelings of joy, relief, fear, and accountability. The rearing part adds years to the parents' boilers as they lead the child through early life and young adulthood until such time as they feel the joy and the grief of giving their offspring up to someone who they pray loves him or her as much.

Although many of the female nurses enjoyed labor and delivery and seemed to look forward to coming to work, I could not imagine ever becoming enchanted with that department. The whole process is repeated twenty or more times for each student before the rotation is over. Definitely, that is way too much emotion for me. But surprisingly, I endured, as did the majority of my very accepting patients.

—m—

The last four weeks of my nursing education was akin to an old-time steam train chugging up a mountain, pulling way too many cars. After using every ounce of its strength and power, it looks like the top is in sight, only to realize it is at rest on a small plateau and success may only lie at the end of a long series of unseen hills yet to be traveled. The real zenith seemed never quite to appear, yet the anxiety of being so close to it was unbearable.

Two years of brutal scrutiny and endless hours of study, along with the realization that most of my instructors had taken a vow at the onset never to allow me to leave their sacred halls with anything even resembling a diploma, depressed me deeply. Even if all of the hills were accomplished, new responsibilities that a "real" nurse assumes by default upon graduating would then be in play. We would have responsibilities that could affect the very existence of life. I and others were unaware that the future would be wrought with such extreme emotional successes and failures that they would leave deep imprints and change lives forever. Would it all be worth it?

My fatigue was nearly overwhelming at that point. I felt disliked and prosecuted. I felt discriminated against. I felt that given any sort of obstruction, I would just say "Fuck it, I've had enough. I'll just take my chances with Vietnam." I had never had such negative feelings in my entire life, and I felt myself questioning my self-worth and the loss of the image I had hoped to show my father so I could say, "See, I made it. I'm not worthless after all!"

Students who did not succeed in passing and graduating the programs sponsored by the military were routinely processed into active service. In the medical field, that meant training as a combat medic for the nasty mess taking place in Southeast Asia. I had always hoped to go to Vietnam, but as a nurse or a doctor, not a combat medic, whose life expectancy was of the lowest of all military occupational specialties (MOS). As I would later learn, this was a meaningless concern. There really were no safe zones or combat zones or battle lines in Vietnam. Everyone there was vulnerable in one arena or another. If I had taken time to learn more about Vietnam, I might have eliminated a large source of my worries long before the two-week sprint to my graduation—or failure.

The surgery department at the hospital was a very busy place. The surgeons fought with each other daily to secure time slots to perform their backlog of surgeries. This did not surprise me, as there were a lot of OB-GYN doctors in the greater Philadelphia area. The malpractice boom had not quite yet exploded. There were still strong doctor-patient relationships, and physicians were among the most respected professionals, which is not always the case today. The surgical-suite director was a tough lady who took no crap from the doctors and had most of them, especially the older ones, eating from her hand while some of the younger ones still attempted to challenge her until they realized the futility of it all. If they persisted too long, they would pay, one way or another.

The senior residents or staff physicians would have them doing microscopic studies on surgical drainage (that was, in fact, Ivory soap or mayonnaise). First-year students were often sent to central sterile supply and told not to return until they had found a dozen fallopian tubes (which, of course, are part of every woman's anatomy). The newbies usually got the drift early on, and if not, they received harsher punishments along with non-physician apprentices like me. Vaginal enlargement or reduction procedures were a big part of the surgical board each day. The good stuff, like cystoceles and bowel repair and bladder suspensions, were saved for the favorite sons.

One section of the surgery suite was reserved for OB patients, generally C-Sections. In 1967, Caesarian section was not done nearly as often compared to today. It was done mostly when things were not going well with either the mother or the infant or both. It frequently included an exciting, adrenaline-pumping event and a premature or over mature newborn. Some did not turn out well. Neonatal nurseries were not yet prevalent, so the smaller hospitals did their best with underdeveloped neonates until they were stable enough to transport to one of the few centers fortunate to have modern equipment.

My time in the surgical department passed remarkably fast. Before I realized it, I was making good-byes with all of the wonderful people who worked there. They had certainly turned a potentially tense, difficult situation into a very pleasant, educational one that moved me one more step toward graduation.

My last afternoon was an exit meeting with the surgical director, surgical chief of staff, chief of anesthesia, and head nurses from the OB unit and general gynecological unit, and, of course, Ms. Stark. All went well, and once again, she was embarrassed by the blank looks she received after asking if I had committed all of the cardinal sins of nursing that she had accused me of in the past. I received a glowing report from all and was assured a written report would be available before my graduation date in June.

I nearly bit my lip with pride as I was reminded that since the first week of classes two years ago, the instructors, spare Ms. Key, had promised each other that I would never graduate. Even though I still had reasonable doubt that I would share the space on stage with my classmates in June, I was one step closer to success upon finishing my OB rotation.

The after-party was great, and all of the remaining students as well as the instructors had cake, ice cream, and plenty of civil socialization for a change. Ms. Stark left right after the business part of the meeting, so she missed out on all of the frivolity. Ms. Key stayed until the end, and she and a few of us visited a little bar frequented by the hospital group that we used for rest and recreation following bad days. We drank until closing.

We all had a great time, and Ms. Key danced nearly every dance, whether with a guy, a girl, a chair, or sometimes by herself. She was really quite drunk and appeared not to have much drinking experience. She was definitely not safe to drive. Some of us tried to talk her into a cab, but she flatly refused, as she needed her car early in the morning and did not have time for the nonsense of retrieving it. After a bit of discussion, I was nominated to drive her home, as my classmates at the bar stuffed bills in my shirt pocket to cover my return cab ride home. I was quite affected by the alcohol as well but didn't really show it.

We tried to load Ms. Key in the backseat but she would have none of it, claiming that she got sick riding in back. I was fearful that she would be sick in the front seat—more specifically, on me. At any rate, she was loaded in, her door locked, her lap belt secured, and off we went on a set of directions compiled from the info given by some of the partygoers who had been to her place before. Ms. Key changed those directions about every other block, taking us right across the North Side, which is not a good place to be for a white guy and a good-looking white girl at 3:00 a.m. on Saturday morning.

Remarkably, about an hour later, we were in Ms. Key's long, circle drive. She lived in the suburbs. The properties must have been at least an acre, and the homes were arranged so that there was decent privacy. Ms. Key, by this time, had loosened her seatbelt somewhere around the North Side and had nestled her head against my right shoulder. She was sound asleep with mouth agape, dripping saliva down my arm and onto my leg.

When I awakened her, she was very embarrassed at the mess she had made, and not yet really knowing where she was, she wiped some saliva from my shirt with her finger and put it back in her mouth. She wasn't happy with that and began to lick the cloth of the shirt until all of the sloppy spit was gone, leaving just a wet spot. She then noticed the large, wet spot on my right upper thigh and immediately dove down and buried her head in my lap, licking up the saliva and goop left from the beer and bourbon until, once again, only a wet spot remained.

At this point, I was hitting the roof with sexual anxiety, and it wasn't until she lifted her head toward me that she saw the expression on my face, a mix of arousal, anticipation, and disbelief. She gave me this wry little smile, clutched my thigh nearly at the groin, pecking me on the cheek and saying, "Maybe another day."

I helped Ms. Key to the door, and after fumbling with her keys and cussing like a sailor, which was way out of character for her, she stepped inside and tilted her head down, looking at me with a pouting expression on her face. She said, "If this weekend were only game over, huh?" She then called a cab for me. I felt destroyed and unfulfilled.

Well, I kept that little memory in my head for several months after leaving the university, and whenever stuff was going bad or I was getting a bit homesick, I recalled her very alluring dark eyes, her long, black hair, and her overwhelming sex appeal, and that memory helped keep my self-esteem alive.

—w—

A bright day on a Sunday in June and it was graduation day. Yes, I was standing as the odd one among all of the traditional, white-capped graduates of the School of Nursing. The dean even joked with me concerning the possibility of wearing one of the caps and the traditional apron as well. As I received my degree on stage, I was never so surprised and disbelieving. So many wrong turns with so many Indians waiting to arrow you, spear you, bludgeon you, kill you, and finally, in defiant victory, scalp you.

This scenario would not have taken place if it were not for the Saturday afternoon just prior to graduation that I was summoned by phone to the dean's office. After Friday night and the alcohol, I certainly wasn't mentally prepared for one of the biggest failures imaginable and all of the horrid, bad things that would follow. First, there would be the terrible news to my parents that I had failed to make the grade and would not be the first of our entire family to attain a college degree. Second, a chance to fulfill a lifelong desire to work in the medical profession would be gone forever. Third, I would be inducted into the army as a medic at a time when their life expectancy was about that of a fruit fly.

Most important, however, would be my own disappointment at failing again to accomplish something very difficult that required a long-term, extended effort. This had always been the problem Dad had with me and I felt crushed that I still couldn't change that. I had accomplished many things as a boy and as a teen, but none had had much real meaning, and most had involved collateral consequences that my folks would rather not have dealt with.

As I waited outside the dean's office, I stared into space and wondered about my alternatives. The secretary then summoned me in and on into an adjoining room that held some faces I recognized and some I didn't. There was the dean, of course, and Ms. Key—and, remarkably, not a single one of my other instructors. The president of our student body, Jan, was there; our student administrative liaison (a go-between for the students, instructors, and administrators of the nursing program),

Maria; and a few older folks I did not recognize. *Holy shit, I really expected something grave.* I sucked in a deep, irregular breath, awaiting my execution. The makeup of this group was so overwhelming that my mind had no idea which direction to take.

The dean commenced: "Mr. Neely, on behalf the university, the university's School of Nursing, the faculty, and the directors, I wish to offer to you my deepest and most sincere apology for the path that you have been made to follow over the last two years. It is more than difficult to endure the rigors of our nursing program. It is meant to be that way so only the best represent the school following graduation. But to survive what several of my staff instructors required of you is not only a tribute to you, but an unforgivable admonishment for them.

"I, the president, and your class officers came here today not only to offer apologies, but to commend you on your endurance and tolerance of what must have seemed at times insurmountable tasks and expectations. I have reviewed all of the material provided by your classmates and your instructors and I have shared it with the university administration. It is agreed that you succeeded in meeting and, in some instances, exceeded the requirements of the program, and we wish to have permission to highlight your accomplishment of being the only male graduate of the university for the class of 1967. Most of us will see you tomorrow afternoon. Thank you."

As I left the office, the air was much easier to breathe, and the weight of my body seemed negligible. I pretty much flew out of the room. Ms. Key was not far behind. She grabbed my arm and told me she would like a few minutes to talk with me.

Ms. Key and I went to the bar. I wondered what it might have been like to go through the program without the stress that followed me each and every hour of each and every day. Maybe it would have been worse. I have problems applying myself, especially when the issues that occupy me are not very demanding issues. Maybe I wouldn't even be graduating. Maybe...

Ms. Key looked somewhat tired and challenged as we shared a pitcher of local beer. She told me that she was really happy about the way everything had worked out and was proud of me for enduring the challenges of the previous two years. I believe she was trying to gain assurance that I did not perceive her stern and specific directives in class similar to those of the other instructors who had aimed at destroying my chances of graduation.

Before she traveled down that path very far, I stopped her and told her that I truly appreciated her firm guidance and her standing up for me as a good student. I knew her position with the other instructors was not the best. She told me that monumental events had occurred over the past few days involving my fellow students, the instructors and the dean. It so happened that many of the classmates that I had worked with, after complaining to the deaf ears of the instructors, began keeping dated notes of every incident in which I was treated differently or more severely than the rest of the students.

I had wondered why a good friend in class had asked me nearly daily what my home assignment was for the evening. I thought it was just a habitual thing with our friendship. At any rate, along with Ms. Key's testimony on my performance, all of the info was shared with the dean of nursing. Ms. Key said the dean was livid when she received the news and demanded to talk to each of the instructors immediately. Ms. Key heard that all but one had professed their motivations. I was speechless. Ms. Key had a half grin on her face, and as she finished the last of her beer and headed for the door, she blew me a short kiss as she left my sight for the last time. On Sunday, I graduated.

With my diploma in hand, I wrote my National Board Exam in July of 1967 and received my failing grade about a month later in August along with suggestions on how to improve my performance on the next and last chance to pass, which would be held in November. I had failed obstetrics by three points.

For nearly the next year, I served at my local hospital as a graduate "male nurse". There actually was no job description for such a creature, so it was fabricated by my sponsor-mentor as we went along. She was pregnant and uncomfortable. She was not keen on my being there, openly stating that men should not be nurses. Things worked out, however, and we eventually became quite good friends on the busy medical-surgical floor.

November exam time finally came around. One other person from the hospital school of nursing had also failed the state boards, someone I didn't know. We decided to drive to Harrisburg together, which was a couple of hundred miles east of our homes, and on a Saturday morning, we embarked with little money and even less of a plan. After seemingly endless hours on the road and finally finding the motel we were to stay at, we could not afford to get separate rooms.

The night was very uncomfortable, as neither of us had interest in the other. We hadn't planned on staying in the same room, so our sleepwear was fairly inappropriate for our two-night stay. She wore a very short pair of baby-blue bottoms with matching top, and I wore my usual scrub pants that were two sizes too large. We finally said the hell with it, climbed into bed, and actually talked to each other about our lives.

We studied almost every moment on Sunday and hit the sack early for the exam at 0900 on Monday. The test only took about two and a half hours, and Harrisburg was before us. Neither of us felt inspired to see the city, and we were both sick to our stomachs at the thought of possibly flunking this test again. I was extremely worried, as I had received no instruction on postpartum at all, and that is the area in which I had missed all of my questions on the first test. Beth felt more confident and was smiling once we convinced each other that we had passed. The drive home took forever. I actually looked forward to going back to work to keep my mind off of the State Board exam.

About a month later, I received a plain, white envelope from the State of Pennsylvania Licensing and Regulation. I nearly tore it in half out of anticipation. *I had passed!* Beth came on duty the next day, and when she appeared in the break room, she just shook her head in a very sad way. I needed no further information. I did not see her again, as failing for the second time revoked her privilege of working as a graduate nurse. She would have to reenroll for classes and repeat the whole curriculum in the failed subjects before writing the exams again.

Within two weeks, I received orders to attend medical officer training school (OTS) at Camp Bullis, San Antonio, Texas. I had a second set of orders to then proceed to Walter Reed Army Hospital in Washington, DC as my first duty assignment. It was a huge disappointment, as I had volunteered for Vietnam and wanted to get it over with. My previous concern about going to Vietnam was vested in being there as a medic and not an R.N. My motivation was never to avoid the war but to have a reasonable sense of survival while serving.

I worked at WRAMC until March 5, 1969, and gained a lot of experience. The new technical abilities under my belt would help tremendously in Vietnam. I treated and cared for many patients at Walter Reed. One of the more memorable was a boy from Georgia by the name of Ray.

Ray's Story

—⚮—

RAY SCRUNCHED DOWN ONTO HIS duffel bag to make his seat more comfortable for his skinny ass on the big C-130 transport plane. He had been looking forward to this trip for six out of the twelve months of his second tour here in the Republic of Vietnam (RVN). This tour for him had been a ballbuster. It was so much different from the first. It had dragged endlessly until day 365 finally arrived, and after waiting for three days in Da Nang, he was finally on the first leg of his journey home—home to his new love, Jeannie, and a son he had yet to see. It was only a short, thirty-minute flight to Bien Hoa Air Base, where he would board a big commercial aircraft that would take him home to Georgia.

His thoughts took him back to the end of his first tour after returning home, feeling gratified and proud of the job he had done as a field medic with the Fourth Infantry Division. He was awarded the Bronze Star with the V device for his service under enemy fire and was admired by all of his fellow platoon members as a happy-go-lucky guy that would do most anything to give aid to a fallen comrade.

Upon his return home, things there were just not the same as when he had left. His old friends had found new haunts, and they weren't that friendly toward vets. He would have thirty more days in the States before his second tour. A lot of his old buddies who had escaped the draft were adamantly opposed to the war on all counts and really didn't give him much of a stage to spill all of the toxins that needed to come out. Foreseeing a young life spent in that negative environment, Ray

re-upped and volunteered for a second tour in Vietnam based on a zealous recruiter's promise that he would be assigned to one of the hospital
units. He would not be under direct fire for returning to Vietnam. It
sounded like the perfect solution, and Ray jumped at the chance of a
promotion with a resulting raise in pay, another R and R that he had
hoped would be in Thailand, and to be back among comrades who felt
as he did about the war.

Into the story came Jeannie, a new graduate from high school, a
three-year, lettered cheerleader and salutatorian of her class. She just
happened to be at the same Labor Day weekend party that Ray's brother
had invited him to. Ray swept Jeannie off her feet the moment they met,
and after just the second date, they became sexually active. Ray waited
nearly until the end of his leave to tell her that he had opted for more
military service and another yearlong tour in Vietnam. Jeannie was devastated and felt she would never see him again in spite of his promise
that he would be back regardless of what he needed to do to make it
happen. Ray shares the rest of his story:

Over the rumble of the plane's twin-prop engines and the rattling of
the rivets of the old C-130's skin, I looked at the other guys on the plane
and wondered where they were headed—somewhere here in country, or
maybe home, like me.

God, I couldn't stand to spend one more hour in that fucking place!
I'd been on a tour from hell that had sent me to a field hospital where
it took a month to fit in with the established reserve-unit guys who had
already been there for nearly eleven months. I had just begun to melt
into the group and form some decent friendships when almost all of
them, being from the same reserve unit back in the States, DEROS'd
(date eligible for return from overseas) and left for home. The few
medics that were left, rather than adjusting to the new recruits coming
on staff, were reassigned elsewhere.

Guess where my remaining ten months would be spent? Out in the bush with a new platoon from the Fourth, and this time in an area that was as hot as all hell, real Indian country. Contact was made on a daily basis, and the casualties in our company were heavy. My platoon seemed to have a guardian angel however, as we had no KIAs but lots of WIAs, with only a handful going to Saigon and probably beyond for further medical care. Even at that, every single day of the ten months I spent in the field was hell on earth. I felt that I would never make it back to see my Jeannie, and that is what drove me each and every minute of every day.

Jeannie was great with her letters. After the first month, however, her expressions changed about the passion that we had shared and that I had hoped to continue when I returned. I assured her at that time, and truthfully so, that I was relatively safe stationed at the field hospital. It was only after several letters begging her to come clean with what was causing her change of emotion that she told me that she was pregnant. She was two months along when I received new orders for a platoon-medic assignment with the Fourth near An Khe, and I could not bring myself to tell her.

After about a week in the field and after some really hairy close calls, I said to myself, "What the fuck are you doing, lying to Jeannie every time you write? What if you get wounded, or worse yet, killed, and she learns you were dishonest with her? Is that what my son is to hear?" So, nearly three months into my tour, I finally told her that I was back in the bush, and she immediately became terrified. She spoke of raising our child on her own and not knowing if she could cope with me not at her side. I tried to reassure her in every letter, but it seemed that she never really believed I could honestly promise her of my safe return—and she was right.

As the big C-130 banked hard to the right and seemed to drop from the sky, I slid kind of cockeyed onto the straps and rings of my duffel, and since we were landing at Bien Hoa, I decided to take one of the many vacant sling seats, thinking that their pendulum-like connection to the top of the cargo hold would buffer the lefts, rights, ups, and downs that were so common on these lumbering old workhorses.

It seemed that all of the airfields in Vietnam were placed between two mountains, and most often, the runways seemed barely long enough to accommodate safe landings for a small plane, let alone a passenger jet or C-130. All of the aircraft landing at the airfields came in very high and then suddenly dropped altitude at the very latest moment to avoid ground fire. Most often, this worked out—at the cost of leaving your stomach in your mouth and a feeling of dizziness for a good time thereafter. The rapid decent over the end of the airfield just past the triple-canopy growth of the mountain was usually too difficult a target for Charlie and his rustic weapons. Unfortunately, this time, that was not the case.

There was a huge boom and the heavy sound of metal hitting metal, and I was thrown against the wall of the aircraft while it tipped violently, the wings now suddenly perpendicular to the ground. There were sparks and blue splashes of light all through the compartment. Small, pencil-sized chards that appeared red hot and lethal ricocheted back and forth off the metal walls in a death dance followed by a screeching noise and rumble that nearly deafened me. I reached for the harness above me that suspended my seat to get leverage so that I could reposition my weight and get out of the sling seat, but I never made it.

I felt a strange pressure sensation sweep across the back part of my thighs, and within the short time it took for me to look down, both of my legs were completely sheared off below my knees. A large pool of dark, sweet-smelling fluid puddled on the metal-grid floor. With the cargo hold filling with dark smoke and rays of sunlight coming through many small fragment holes in the aircraft's skin, I was dumbstruck, thinking this was a dream and that if I waited awhile, I would wake up and we would be landing in Long Binh.

I had no pain, but I did feel a sudden rush of energy to my head, an overwhelming feeling of me spinning and being helpless. Then a strong, bright light blotted out my vision of everything. Then there was nothing at all. Just before the nothingness, in a split second that felt like several minutes, I watched the bright light over my head, having no idea of what it might be. The light was large at first, about the size of a manhole cover, and there was total blackness around it. It very quickly became smaller and smaller until there was nothing. As it became smaller, I became very sad and felt extremely vulnerable. I felt robbed of my special reward at the very last moment after traveling far down a long, long, hard road that went nowhere. The light felt so wonderful that I wanted to be a part of it, but it became smaller and smaller. I know it sounds crazy, but it was probably the most pleasant feeling I had ever had in my life. I still feel its warmth and the comfort it gave to me that day. I reached out for it, but in a moment, it was gone. The darkness closed in on me, and I was cold.

I awakened three days later in a hospital near Saigon. I had no memory of the date or the days that I had apparently spent in coma and had to rely on my nurses' accounts of what had happened on the plane. I did not know at first that my legs were gone, but I had the strangest sensation on my backside, and I was positioned in a strange-looking bed on my stomach. I hate lying on my stomach, and when I reached around to try to turn myself, I felt the dressings on my butt. I joked with the nurse, "What, did Charlie shoot me in the ass when we were landing?"

She lowered her head and in a quivering, nearly tearful voice, she told me that the plane had been nearly halfway in its descent to the runway when a rocket propelled grenade (RPG) had hit one of the engines. The engine had exploded, and a large portion of the propeller became a projectile that went spinning through the belly of the aircraft at me and exited the other side. The hold had been riddled with shrapnel, and several passengers were killed or injured. Unfortunately, I had been in the path of a large section of the prop. Nearly two feet of hot, spinning steel had hit me just below the pelvis while I was still sitting in the strap seat.

The nurse explained that a lot of damage had been done and both of my legs had been traumatically amputated below the knees. She tried to continue, but her voice became choked. She turned midsentence and left. Soon, a doctor came to me and apologized for the nurse and explained quite dryly that the propeller had come through the plane at high speed and amputated not only both of my legs but my entire buttocks and perineal area, including my testicles and penis. It had also severed all of the muscles and tendons from the back of my upper legs, and he was quite pessimistic whether I would walk again, even with the use of the latest prosthetics.

I wanted to die. At first, I was in total disbelief, waiting for the nightmare to end. But it didn't end, and soon, the reality of not only the injuries but the remainder of my life as a cripple flooded my brain. It was overwhelming. Much too much for me to carry. I thought about how to get a gun into here. I thought about saving up strong pills and taking them all at once. Mostly, though, I thought about how anxious I had been to see Jeannie and my new son and how I now detested the moment it would happen.

I thought about how I had planned to sit on the porch swing back in Georgia on a warm evening and sip tea while the crickets helped lull our young one asleep as I rested Jeannie's head on my shoulder and we whispered to each other how very happy we were and that nothing would ever change. Well, fuck all of that! She won't want to look at me. Christ, she was just nineteen when I left her. She hated my going for the second time, and soon after I got there, I knew she was right. How could I ever fuck up so badly and ruin my chances for the only happiness that I had known since childhood?

Soon, I was sleeping. Whenever I became anxious or uncomfortable or had pain, or felt obsessed with killing myself, or didn't want to take any shit from anyone, the same solution was forthcoming: morphine, pretty much every two or three hours. I soon became very good friends with it. It didn't expect anything from me, and I didn't cringe when I looked at myself and the mangled, half-rotting tissue on my ass and upper legs. But could Jeannie ever look at it? At me? I didn't think I should give her that responsibility. I'd just tell her to go away, forget me, and get her folks to help take care of the baby. Maybe she would find some other guy smart enough to stay out of the fucking military and be a decent husband to the most wonderful woman in the world.

—⚍—

It is November, 1968 at Walter Reed Army Hospital and ward thirty-two is now my new home. I met Lt. Neely today. He is assigned to me and a couple of my bunkmates, but I don't know how he stands it. We are putrid with infection that we brought back from the Nam, and it reeks to the point of making the whole ward smell dangerous and dirty.

The LT, however, is dauntless in his assignment, which is pretty much to meet the beck and call of five patients here on this side of the ward—supplying us with morphine, dry dressings two or three times each shift, morphine, help with our ones and twos, morphine, making our beds with us still in them, morphine, and making sure we get just the right amount of food and water that will help our utterly disgusting, fucking wounds heal, and, finally, morphine. He is at WRAMC getting experience for his future assignment in Vietnam. He volunteered to be assigned there as soon as he graduated from OTC at Fort Sam Houston, Texas.

As most things go in the army, he is still awaiting his orders while all of his friends that went to school in Texas with him and did not volunteer are in Vietnam on their fourth month. We talk a lot among us on the ward, to each other and the staff. We learned that the LT, after eight weeks of training at Fort Sam and two weeks of paid leave and thus far here at Walter Reed, has not been paid one red cent by the army since he graduated from nursing school. Somehow, his records got lost, then found, then sent to the wrong place, and then lost again. At that point, he had lost all hopes of ever escaping Walter Reed, or getting paid, for that matter.

Fortunately, he was invited to stay with a fellow Fort Sam graduate, Lt. Sam G., along with his newly wedded wife, in their small, one-bedroom efficiency in Maryland. When the LT refused because he felt they needed this time to be alone, they strongly insisted. He lives on the few dollars for gas and food that his parents send every couple of weeks. The lieutenant takes tremendous care of us, and we will hate to see him leave when his orders are finally cut. I think he feels the same about us.

When I arrived at Walter Reed, no fewer than seven doctors and surgeons visited my bedside to examine me and my records and to explain the possibilities at hand for my future. I examined each of their faces to read the shock and horror they showed upon seeing my pitiful body. From the belly button up, I appeared quite normal, while the rest of me amplified the horror ten times over.

Even though it was tough going through all of these really stressful reenactments, having to explain the details of my injuries, there was some ground to be gained for me as well. The gastrointestinal specialist explained that although all of the muscles and nerves were gone in my buttocks, the intestine was intact all the way out to my anus. It was, however, slightly damaged and without total circulation and nerve supply. They were going to attempt to transpose some tissue to fix that, and hopefully, with a little luck, passing shit from the right part of the bowel would be possible in the future when my wounds were all healed.

I have a colostomy, and it makes me hate myself completely. The urologist explained that both testicles were gone, as well as 90 percent of my penis. I had a little stub that protruded from my otherwise normal-looking front profile if you didn't look below my knees. There was a tan rubber hose that came from the center of it and then went on to a clear plastic tube that went to a bag hanging on the edge of my circus bed to collect all of my piss. The medics religiously collected and measured all of it at the end of each eight-hour shift change. It seemed they measured the value of the day's work by the amount of the golden, smelly, musty urine they collected. I later learned it was out of concern for how well my kidneys were working.

The doc told me that they were planning on inserting a copper tube into my bladder and out of the little stub as the groundwork for some plastic surgery. They would take some soft skin from my abdomen and wrap it around the tube and connect it to the little stub, and eventually, after several surgeries, they would make me a fake penis. I asked him if I could do anything with it afterward, like piss when I wanted, or maybe even fuck with it. He said no, it would only be for appearance and self-image, and I would still need the catheter going to the bag on my circus bed. He also explained that my body and sex drive would be different and that my interest in physical sex would probably never be the same. I told him, "Fuck that. I don't need something that doesn't work that's no better than what I have now. I'll stick with my stub."

"Circus bed" was my name for what the nurses called a circle-electric bed. It looked like a piece of circus equipment. A couple of people were required to change my position each time. My friends on the ward and I played with the bed when no one was around, and we could make it do things that would make the staff gasp. A good amount of humor was appreciated when the new nurses and medics were brought to my bedside to learn how to use the contraption. After I had been spun in a circle a few times by each of them, they would leave, feeling satisfied that they had mastered this miraculous contraption that I both hated and loved.

A bed training was also the first time that I met Lt. Neely, but he didn't leave like the others after the education. He pulled up a chair and sat and talked with me for quite a while. It might have been a short time, but it felt much longer to me because not too many people ever lingered around my stench too long. He apologized for him and the others putting me through all of the maneuvers and felt bad that it seemed callously impersonal. I could tell, in this first contact with him, that he had not yet been across the pond.

One of the first and most obvious characteristics of Viet vets, especially those "who saw a lot," was to pursue no personal attachments for fear of deep and painful emotions due to the nature of war and its destruction. This horrific baggage was carried back to the States, and it stayed with them for a long time, sometimes forever.

The psychologist was my most depressing, bothersome interview. During her very first visit, she leaped into discussing the image and relationship problems that I should expect. She seemed like a cold bitch inside who was acting out a part in a stage production or something. I asked her to leave my bedside after only ten minutes and that she not return until I called for her—and that would probably be never.

I had already started to think about how I would end all of this horridness and my nightmarish existence by my own hand. Even though I so wanted to see Jeannie and my son and my blood family, I detested the thought of it and delayed the possibility on each occasion that the staff tried to arrange one. Since it involved travel from Georgia and necessary emotional and psychological preparation by the staff before they actually saw the injuries they had heard about, careful planning was in order. At the point that Lt. Neely sat at my bedside, I knew that I might be able to lean on him a little to help me with some of the difficult social issues.

Ray amazed me each time I came on shift for my brief, informal visits before my actual shift started. Even though the weight of the world was on his shoulders with his memories, his pain of healing, and the absence of his loved ones, he always smiled and went along with the burdens of his care and recovery. His dressing changes were extremely painful, as he was afflicted with a horrible pseudomonas infection while still at the hospital in Saigon, and it was taking over what little viable flesh remained on his buttocks and posterior, upper thighs.

We used a special, open-weave gauze dressing that was put on just slightly moist with a bactericidal solution, and we changed it about every six hours once it dried. When the dressing was removed, it pulled away a good amount of the greenish, purulent ooze that was typical of pseudomonas, and eventually, in the areas that were responding well, bright, pink, bleeding granulation tissue appeared. The goal, of course, was to defeat the infection entirely with this procedure, along with antibiotic therapy, which had a very limited scope in the late sixties.

Pseudomonas, a gram-negative organism found normally in the soil, our intestines, and also in our feces, was not very threatened by the usual antibiotics, so the course was long and difficult.

Ray seemed to do well in tolerating his daily care until one day one of his ward mates died unexpectedly. He had happened to have the same infection as Ray, but he was overtaken with it, and it killed him of sepsis. Ray, for the first time, seemed to realize his vulnerability to death other than by the route that he considered nearly daily. At any rate, he seemed to wilt at that point, and his attitude toward the hospital, the army, his care routine, and willingness to survive seemed to plummet. He frequently asked for his pain meds long before they were due, and it was clear to me that a storm was on the horizon.

He was not coping well with his life, and he frequently refused important care measures such as his PT and respiratory exercises. Many patients with overwhelming injuries frequently die of pneumonia or pulmonary emboli (blood clots to the lung) simply from the lack of mobility forced on them from their condition. Regardless, Ray needed to have a redirection in his course, or he would certainly succumb to his illness.

Christmas was about ten days away, and everyone who was able was hoping to spend it with family, either here in DC or at home. I could sense that Ray was struggling with the idea that he might not have family members here to visit, as he had yet to allow them back into his world.

At break time, I made my way to the free phones in the small union room of the facility and called the number I had copied from Ray's chart just minutes before. The phone rang several times, but finally, a female voice answered. "Hello, is this Maxine?"

"Why, yes it is. Who is calling, please?"

"This is Lieutenant Dennis Neely at Walter Reed Army Medical Center, and right up front I want to let you know that my call is personal, and it is not to tell you that Ray is worse or in crisis. I am one of Ray's caregivers on the ward, and he frequently speaks of you and his sister, and he speaks of both of you so highly. He also talks a lot about Jeannie and his son, who he has not yet seen. I am wondering how you feel about coming to Washington around the holidays to see Ray? Even though he has been deciding not to see you and the family and Jeannie, I think it is because he doesn't want you to see him in his condition.

"But, honestly, Ms. C., I believe, although it breaks my heart to say this to you, Ray will never progress physically much further from where he is now. He has worked very hard and endured unreal obstacles and has bravely fought his battles, but even after the wounds are healed, there is not a whole lot more that the doctors will be able to offer him. He more than likely will require some sort of skilled or home care for the rest of his life, and his family members must play a huge role in that undertaking.

"His mind is young and clear, and if he can get over the physical and psychological hurt, he has the opportunity to find pleasure and success with those resources that he still has. He is terrified with the idea of your seeing him for the first time and needs to get the 'discovery' off his chest. He bemoans the issue daily, and it is so vital for the family, especially Jeannie, to face his condition, because he also knows that he is not going to improve much. He wants her to understand that and appreciate her acceptance or non-acceptance.

"A lot of responsibility is attached to a matrimonial relationship with him. I believe that he would greatly benefit from having this one devastating burden resolved for him, because his progress has stalled to near zero. I know a visit might be hard in several ways for you, and it certainly will be terribly traumatic for Ray, but after all settles down, I believe he will achieve peace of mind, and it will allow him to find real motivation toward improving. What do you think about that, Maxine?"

"I'll talk to my husband and see what he feels. I know what you are saying. I have noticed when we talk on the phone, he has been very depressed and dark and talks of nothing in the future. He has asked us please not to come there until he is ready. I will speak with Jeannie. There are, of course, a lot of hurdles to clear. Georgia is not close, and it's winter, and our family has never been blessed with a lot of money."

"That would be great, Maxine, if you and your family would just consider the possibility. I'm going to give you my personal phone number where you can reach me. I may be receiving new orders in the near future, but I will keep you posted on my new number as needed. Thank you for your time, Maxine. Good-bye."

Only six days until Christmas. Ray still is not speaking to me and I have not heard from Maxine about the family's decision to visit him. Ray has been royally pissed off at me since the day I told him what I had discussed with his mom. He was infuriated, and actually the most animated that I had seen him in weeks. At least that was good. He was threatening to ask for a new caregiver but did not. He didn't speak with or to me, although he would yell out, "Shit!" or "Fuck!" or some other expletive when I hurt him changing his dressings.

I didn't push him but spoke to him as though things were just fine, a one-sided conversation at best. One afternoon, Ray did not get his pain med when he was due, as the doctor had not made rounds and the ward master couldn't find any other doctors. They were in some kind of staff meeting. Ray's order had expired after his morning dose, and someone had slipped up on getting a reorder.

When I went into Ray's room, he exploded. Not about his pain med but about how fucking brazen I had been to contact his family against his wishes. He said he would never expect that behavior from a "true friend." He had never used the word *friend* before, and he knew immediately that he had slipped, confessing that our relationship was closer than he'd wanted to admit. I told him that I understood and the reason I had called Maxine was that I was his *friend* and wanted the best for him. I thought our plan was the best, although difficult for everyone. His mood changed almost immediately, and after a short while, our relationship was back to where it had been before.

—⟋⟍—

Today was a very special day in my life. Finally, after nearly sixteen weeks, I was called by the paymaster early and was asked to come to his office on post before my shift started. I was very excited. I knew that it had to be a payday, finally! I was worried to death, thinking I might have to leave Washington owing Sam and his wife money, as well as a ton of gratitude for their hospitality. But now, two days before Christmas, and it seemed that I would be looking for an apartment instead.

About 1:00 p.m., just after a short lunch of a ham and cheese on white rye, the mailman dropped my mail through the door slot, and the doorbell rang immediately after. I peeked through the view hole, and the postman was waiting outside. I opened the door. He had a special-delivery letter for me to sign, and I could see by the size of the envelope that it was from the army. I signed for it and was so excited about opening the letter that I left the door open and went to the kitchen table. There were two sets of orders in the packet. The first set granted me leave from March 5, 1969, until April 22, 1969. The second set was travel orders:

> 22APR69: report to SEA-TAC, WA. at 1800 hrs. for FLYING TIGERS AIRLINES, Flight 6970Y, arriving ANCHORAGE, AK @ 0100. NO DEPLANING, Continue on Flight 6970Y, FLYING TIGERS AIRLINES to YOKOTA, JPN, NO DEPLANING, Continue on Flight 6970Y to arrive in LONG BINH, BIEN HOA, R.V.N. on or about 24APR69. Report to 90th Replacement Battalion, Long Binh, R.V.N. for deployment and/or assignment.

I had finally got my request fulfilled, after nearly a year had passed. It was time to spread the news to my family, friends, and especially, my patients on ward thirty-two. There was also another letter with my mail from the Department of the Army, postmarked from San Antonio, Texas. I discovered that it was a paycheck for the eight weeks I had spent at Fort Sam Houston, plus my travel and leave time between Texas and my leave period in Pennsylvania.

At the paymaster office, I was paid fifteen hundred dollars. I discussed the matter with the paymaster about paying me again for the same back pay period. He said that they were processing so many people that army routine would require me to turn in all of the money from both paychecks, and they would recalculate from the beginning again. He suggested I keep the money, and the army would contact me as discovery necessitated. I waited anxiously until a week before leaving for Vietnam, during which time I received one more check, but nothing was mentioned about the overpayment of nearly ten weeks. I felt rich and said, "The hell with it, they can work it out."

—⚏—

Christmas Eve: When I arrived for my afternoon shift, the curtains around Ray's bed were pulled, and I was terrified that something might have happened. The curtains had never been pulled at this time of day. The worst-case scenario came into my mind. I then heard talking and laughing, also something I hadn't experienced around Ray for some time. I eased up to the yellow curtain and said softly, "Ray, are you OK?"

"Oh, hell, I'm great, come on in!" I stepped through the curtain, and Ray's family was there! There was Maxine, fussing over Ray's hair; Ray's sister, who was cleaning his fingernails; and Jeannie, who was at the head of the circle bed, nearly nose to nose with Ray. At times, although I tried not to look, they kissed, and believe me, I could tell that they were in love. They seemed to melt into each other, and their time together was beautiful. An aunt had the little one in the day room, and Ray was promised that he would be pushed there in his circle bed so he could see his child at last.

Before I was able to excuse myself and check on the other patients, Maxine grabbed my arm and pulled me aside. She said, "Thank you for the money. I promise, Ray will hear nothing about it." The family spent the day together, Ray saw his baby, and I completed most of what I needed to do before my trip home for my four-day holiday with my family back in Pennsylvania.

At the end of my shift, I bid farewell to Ray and wished him a happy holiday. I rushed back to my place at Sam's and Carol's, packed a few things, made a thermos of coffee (my lifeblood when I was tired), and left for Pennsylvania. I felt exhausted.

With my Christmas break over, back to Washington, DC, and about two months remaining until my leave in March before going to Vietnam. Sam and Carol tried to convince me to stay in their apartment rather than rent, but I knew deep down that Sam might well be getting orders also, and they needed some time alone. I paid Sam and Carol back generously and found a new month-to-month lease in a brand-new apartment in Silver Springs, Maryland. It was just an efficiency but all I needed.

I visited one of the furniture-rental stores and rented just enough to make life bearable: a kitchen table and two chairs, a sleeper sofa, and a recliner. I had 1 stainless pot for soup and such, one frying pan, and a coffee percolator. I had tableware for four, and that was about it. I spent little time in the apartment, so any more conveniences would have been a waste.

I received good and bad news today. Ray was being transferred to a VA hospital closer to his home in Georgia and much closer to his wife and child and his mom. But I was deeply concerned about the level and quality of care he would receive there. It would be difficult to meet the level of attention that Ray was accustomed to and needs at WRAMC, and I was well aware of how quickly a condition could slide into the shithole if things aren't done right. Maybe I was just a bit selfish in not wanting to lose a friend, a close friend. Ray and I had a special bond on so many levels. We both loved to hunt and fish, we both were crazy about cars, and we both had very close connections to our families.

I met with the family and Ray and made them promise that they would keep in touch with me on his condition. This was the only immediate comfort I could achieve in my worries about him and his care. I am sure his family would be his caretakers and insist that he received the best. They were just that kind of folk.

It is January 29 and Ray left this morning. A cold, rotten day in Washington.

I had just come back from possibly the best party ever, thrown by the folks from my ward. Oh my God, am I ever drunk. It's 3:00 a.m., and I must get some sleep, as they are coming for my furniture at 10:00 a.m., and I have to get all my stuff packed and ready to roll.

I received a call from Maxine today. She was sobbing in a low, heartbroken moan that I have heard so many times, and much of her conversation was hard to make out, but it was clear that she was devastated. I knew what news she carried before she was able to tell me. My friend, her son, "was taken up by God" at seven o'clock this morning, Thursday, March 28, 1969. He had made a turn for the worse a few days earlier when the infection took over his body and he became septic. His condition worsened, but while he was still lucid, he and his family requested that no further heroics be done.

Maxine took pains to assure me that Ray was without pain and talked to her right to the end. As she cried with long sobs, she said, "He wanted me to call you because he wanted to tell you that he loved you and that you had made his life meaningful during the short time he spent with you. He said that he would save a place for you and that 'hopefully we can go fishin' when you decide to give it up.' He said that you truly are his friend and he is going ahead on a scouting trip to make sure everything is OK." I was shattered.

I spent a short period trying to console Maxine, but I was so devastated that, after an hour of seemingly making things worse for her, I couldn't utter another word and said good-bye, put the phone down, and crashed on the bed. Too much input. Leaving parents, leaving home, and now, I had lost a good friend forever. I sure as hell hoped tomorrow would turn the corner.

The next two weeks were very sad, hectic, and confusing. Trying to figure out what to take to a third-world country for a period of a year was very difficult. The army really didn't provide a list of what they supplied except that we would be issued our uniforms once in country, and we would be issued a side arm. So I packed about one of each bath thing just in case they didn't provide it, some Bermuda shorts and a couple of summer T-shirts, and a dozen pair of underwear and socks. Turns out, I could have gone there with nothing but the shirt on my back and survived quite well, as they supplied everything, including sunglasses and a wristwatch. Not the best quality, mind you, but a fair representation of everything. I wish I had known of their generosity, as I would have taken a lot more of my records and some sporting equipment—soccer balls, mostly.

The remainder of my time stateside was spent with parents, family, and friends. I must say, I received a ton of attention from them just before leaving, and it made me feel somewhat uneasy, as their attention seemed to be based on their not knowing if I was coming back home. The most appropriate advice I received was from my dad as he hugged me and said, "You make damn sure you come back now." He was very serious, and I could see he was troubled.

The night before I was to leave, my dad came into my room and sat on my bed. He never did this. He was not an outwardly affectionate man, but I knew that he loved me and that he would do anything in the world for me. He did have difficulty expressing emotion with me. He proceeded to talk to me in a tone of voice that I had never heard him use before. He said he was so very proud of the son he had raised. He choked out his words. "I have been so very proud of you for several years, but I didn't want to pour it over you, thinking that might be enough for you and you would slack off. I know that young people crave attention from their parents, and I'm sorry now that I didn't give you more when I was able. Now, later in your life, it might not seem nearly as important as it may have felt when you were fourteen or fifteen."

He praised the way I carried myself with my peers and elders and while playing on the high-school varsity baseball team and third base for Quaker State Oil in the Pony League. He explained that he had never had the opportunity to be socially polished as an adolescent. He had been bartered out by his parents when he was nine, as his family had had difficulty feeding all of their children.

It turns out that his family had been dirt poor and could not come close to putting ample food in nine kids' mouths. There were local farmers who needed help; they would take kids and raise them at their homes and feed them in exchange for very difficult work. Dad did such labor until he went into the service at age twenty. I had always known that Dad had had a terribly hard life and that my performance and contributions paled and often didn't meet his expectations or his needs on several occasions. I tried very hard to be the man he had wanted to raise, but his strict habits and work ethic were so very much beyond what I was able and willing to put forth, so all I could do was "my best."

I used to often see him shake his head in disgust, not necessarily with me, but with the circumstances. This happened in the summers when we were laying brick past dark. We were behind critical schedule because I could not haul two heavy, concrete blocks plus the mud (cement) fast enough to keep up with two master bricklayers. I tried hard and refused to give up, frequently riding home in a stupor from fatigue. The next evening, after baseball practice, which my dad insisted on my attending, we would repeat the whole process all over again on a new job site.

Yes, my dad loved me, but I don't think that he could bridge the challenge of working three jobs and participate with his family as he wished. It had left little time for his children and his wife but certainly met our survival needs.

But now, my dad was different, and it was scary. It brought me a true sense of seriousness that I should have felt much earlier, much younger. I was feeling naked and alone with the realization that my life was moving from a bunch of disjointed, unrelated activities of youth that meant little into a much more focused, serious, purposeful existence. Any failure or less than perfect work from here on out would have the most serious of consequences. *God, what if I am not ready for this? This may be the last time I see any of my loved ones.*

Dad assured me of my strength and said that given the need, I could endure anything. He then buried his bearded face in my neck and held me there for an eternity. We cried. We said, "I love you." When we stopped, I finally knew my dad felt that I was a man. And because Dad thought of me as a man, I knew I could make it. It would be all right!

There's Nothing to Fear

—ɯ—

I NEVER QUITE AGREED WITH the old FDR proclamation, "The only thing we have to fear…is fear itself."[iii] It often just doesn't ring true. I believe its root meaning is that we are capable of accomplishing most anything and that the only thing that might impede our success is the fear of attempting the feat in the first place. This is very motivational, especially when you are asking thousands of young men and women to risk life and limb in conflicts and causes that many of them do not understand.

It also implies that fear is a nasty-ass emotion that degrades the character of those who allow it in. It implies that if we choose not to have fear, we will be a lot better off, and, more important, productive. While the end product of deployment can certainly please those sending us into harm's way, most frequently, it is not so great for the soldier. Ironically, after the heroic posturing of the Roosevelt family in World War II, only a very small number of the offspring of those important enough to make such proclamations and the life-and-death decisions that follow them end up being asked or ordered to participate in the effort of war. It is much too dangerous!

That the wealthy and the famous should be excused from participating personally in conflicts has been present throughout our warring history, but more so in the days from the Korean War forward. Controlled selection through the draft was discontinued after the Vietnam Conflict, and psychological and economical brainwashing took its place, again leaving out the wealthy and the famous. Their recruitment interviews somehow rarely take place.

A few things stick in my throat regarding FDR's old saw. It is much easier to proclaim that fear is a controllable emotion that overtakes only the weak and untrained if the one proclaiming has never personally experienced real fear—like in the fifteen to twenty seconds when your car is pushed over the rail of a bridge by a semi and you are plummeting into the darkness toward the water below, or watching your child chase a ball between parked cars into the path of an oncoming truck, or being found in bed with your wife's best friend.

How about being flown to another country, half a world away in the middle of the night, and landing on an airstrip hardly long enough to stop a Piper Cub, let alone a militarized 707 Flying Tiger jetliner? While the pilot dodges newly created mortar pocks in the concrete-asphalt mix runway at 125 miles per hour, you are told to deplane immediately while mortars, rockets, and small-arms fire are all around you, and you're sure that at least one is going to take off a leg or maybe an arm, or maybe just kill you outright on your first day in country.

You are directed into a sandbag-and-steel-barrel bunker that smells of mold, sex, and pot and told that you may be in there all night with no food, no water, and no latrine. The big plane that never came to a full stop while you deplaned has made a 180-degree turn and is tearing ass down the runway with all of the baggage that holds everything you were to own for this, the first of 365 days in South-fucking Vietnam.

As you take in the expanse of total darkness interrupted by flashes of light and sounds that are unfamiliar, some distant, some close, you suck in a deep breath of super humidified, hundred-plus-degree air that smells like a pot of cabbage your grandma left on the stove a week ago. That odor competes with the unmistakable stench of raw sewage. You gulp to keep from barfing while you attempt to mop the sweat before it flows into your eyeballs, red and exhausted by the day-plus flight. All of this floods your senses a little more than twenty-four hours after leaving the comfort of your own bed, hugging your loving family, and heading off to the airport with a stop at IHOP along the way for the biggest breakfast you have ever eaten.

As you sit in the bunker, studying the faces of unknown others, you wonder if the extent of your fear is visible to all. You wonder about their fear and how they might respond to it. Upon settling down a bit, you immediately start to question your sanity in asking to come to this place and wonder if you will ever leave the same. You immediately start to hate those who sent you here. Your feelings will never change.

Flying the Friendly Skies
of Southeast Asia

—⚏—

DURING MY YEAR IN VIETNAM, I went on occasional dust-off operations on an as-needed basis. Most of my time was spent at the field-hospital level: six months in Qui Nhon near the South China Sea and six months in An Khe in the Central Highlands, supporting the Fourth Infantry Division. Throughout my tour, I continued to carry on in the spirit I always had—being adventurous and taking the more difficult assignments while understating my activities in my letters to my parents. I took every opportunity to volunteer for helicopter evacuations needing to go to the next level of care in Saigon or Qui Nhon. It was very strenuous and tiring, but I enjoyed the excitement immensely.

At Camp Bullis in San Antonio, some of us learned field measures that, in addition to emergency medical procedures, taught us about the meaning of the different smoke colors and how to jump from a low-hovering helicopter. Medevac choppers and medical personnel were not supposed to carry weapons, but I soon learned that it was actually the exception rather than the rule. Both WO pilots usually carried side arms and often a carbine between them. On most dust-off missions that I was involved with, a gunner was present, but most of those flights were on "slicks" (a Huey without weapons pods) and carried no Red Cross as they fulfilled multiple duties of carrying in grunts and supplies and carrying out dead and wounded.

Being trained on just the M16 and the .45 (which was removed from my person early in my Central Highland tour), I was introduced to the M79. It was a wonderful little weapon that looked like a large-bore (40 mm), single-shot, sawed-off shotgun. It fired several types of ammo, including explosive, illumination (white phosphorus), smoke, flechette, and buckshot, to name a few. I preferred the buckshot and explosive rounds, as they both covered a considerable target area, and I had little time to practice on my "thumper."

Many times, Charlie would surprise you, either with a full volley of ground fire, RPGs, or a mortar barrage—or, on some rare occasions, a full-on frontal assault. As a medical noncombatant based on my MOS, the M79 grenade launcher with antipersonnel rounds seemed the likeliest for me. Most times, you never saw a face or a form, only a muzzle blast and sound. That was your enemy.

Some of the most dangerous flights were when we traveled to and from parties. This was by helicopter, many times at night in the fog. We followed the taillights of deuce-and-a-half (two-and-a-half-ton) trucks to make it through the An Khe Pass, a treacherous passage in the mountains on Highway 19. With our rotor dicing off large branches of overhanging trees and spraying them through the open cabin doors, those of us sober enough to have evaluated the event then are more likely to be revisited by the terror of it all to this day. This was, at the time, perceived by all of the drunken participants as great fun, spare the pilot and copilot.

Only one or two of these joyrides were offered to each of us during our one-year tour as a method of brain cleansing. Everyone talked incessantly of the drinking, the meal, the drinking, the dancing, the drinking, the wild sex, the drinking, and other unspeakable good times for months after their gauntlet through the pass. We literally lost soldiers for days at a time on these parties due to weather but would cover it up with the XO, as most everyone detested him, and the rest of us were the best of friends. We would frequently kid each other about the parties being the most dangerous part of the tour and assured each other that had we been sober, we would have most likely taken only that one free party ticket through the pass. One was sufficient to create a near-death experience.

The TDY Fiasco

—ɯ—

DAY 1, MAY69: *THE FORM, cloaked in camo BDUs, lying so still, with only a slight rise of the chest, subtle like the breeze moving the elephant grass, dancing with it, playing with it. All appear to blend into a surreal picture: a monotonous din of sounds and motion, the moans and screams, the wash of the chopper rotors, even the pings and whooshes of the small-arms fire. Nothing appears real, yet all is so distinct and morbid that a swell appears in your gut, nauseating you, making you want to run from this place.*

His eyes are vacant and lackluster with a stare toward the top of the jungle canopy, nothing focused, nothing fully perceived. With lips pursed and teeth tightly clenched, the eighteen-year-old FNG (fucking new guy) *is quickly approaching an arena unknown by the living. He curses his journey there so soon, ending his adventures as a man. Nonresponsive to any of my questions, he has accepted his destiny though still clings to the last, precious vestiges of life.*

Respirations four to six per minute, deep and agonal. The life air is forced through flaring nostrils, and his clenched jaw shows outright disgust with his fate. Pulse rate 136, heart attempting to provide oxygen to an otherwise youthful, healthy body while, in actuality, pumping his life fluid onto the flora of the jungle floor. A pool of crimson envelopes his torso from the three small but deadly entry wounds in his chest. He may have endured the one, maybe even the second, but the three together were overwhelming to him and his chance to survive. Now, left only with his thoughts and the waiting, the pain is probably nonexistent as his miraculous machine attempts to fix the hell laid upon him.

The morphine will help. It will take away the anguish and the anxiety of this premature trip into another realm, and it will help the pain, if any remains! It will help me. After plunging the first syrette through the pants and deep into the meaty flesh of the right thigh, I realize that the material of the BDU pants is not soiled and still has the stiffness of fatigues newly issued. It couldn't be more than a day or two since they were issued at a base camp far away from this mountain.

It is obvious to me now that the FNG's ultimate life experience in this stinking, fucking country had started and ended within the time it takes to attend a senior prom and the after-party. I open the second syrette without hesitation and, without looking at the face, plant the needle to the hilt while squeezing down on the plunger so energetically that some spills onto the pants before the needle meets flesh. Already, the breathing has become more shallow, and the eyelids, once wide and disbelieving, are now tired-looking and slowly and rhythmically closing, taking on the trancelike cadence of this fucking place.

The third syrette finds its course into the left thigh, and soon things will be all right for both of us. After ten minutes that seem like hours, respirations zero, heart rate twenty, eyes closed to all earthly visions—it's over, for all practical purposes. I stand and walk away, not looking back.

About twenty yards from the cherry, I can walk no further. I am stricken with the sensation that I am hopelessly lost in a jungle on my first day on the side of a mountain that I know nothing of, and it is over 20,000 miles from the safety and assurances of my home. Holy fuck, what if I get left here? What if they forget me? Worse yet, what the fuck do I do if the gooks show up?

I have enough ammunition to maybe last ten or fifteen minutes at best. Then what? I don't have a fucking clue where to go or where friendlies might be. My medical bag is empty save the few syringes of the God drug that remain in my pouch. I may have to stay here all fucking night. It is really cold at night, especially up on this godforsaken hill. I don't think I should build a fire. That would be a big mistake. I tear through the cherry's rucksack and find the ground cloth and then the camo poncho liner and a few MREs that don't need cooking. Best get started. It will be a long night.

I am my own security. I'm scared shitless. I finally move up on some higher ground with a slope behind me that is quite steep with several undestroyed trees and a good vision of an open area carved out of the triple-canopy jungle. No sleep tonight. The cherry's eyes haunt me, and I feel ashamed of what he was dealt compared to my self-pity and what I had been left with—being alive.

—⚉—

Day 2, May69: I was awakened at 0600 to begin our second day's work of evacuating soldiers off another part of the mountain near the border of Laos along the course of the Ho Chi Minh Trail. Yesterday had opened my eyes to one of the many horrors that I would witness in this godforsaken war in this godforsaken country. My *dreams* of being abandoned on the mountain overnight prevented me from beginning the day with any sense of optimism, but it was the vision of the cherry's eyes that actually haunted me.

Without the help of the generous, brain stimulated doses of dopamine that had rescued me the day before, I now felt inept and helpless. Only when the chopper lifted off and cycled into the radical bank toward our destination was I rocked to my true senses as small doses of the drug began to save me from myself.

The temporary duty personnel (TDY) assignment was intended originally to break the boredom of waiting in Long Binh for orders that would eventually send me to the 311th Field Hospital in Qui Nhon. Now, on our third mission of the day, I was sure I was to die as the skid of the Huey grated into the slope of the mountain. The main rotor, spinning just a few feet from the sloping edge of the mountain and fewer feet from the charred, smoking flora and the bare earth, hurled grass, dirt, and pieces of bark throughout the cabin of the chopper.

My eyes were nearly useless from the wash of the blades and the debris that came with it as I reached blindly downward. Teetering on the grid on my knees, grabbing one corner of a poncho liner while the gunner grabbed the other, we dragged a wounded soldier on board. We repeated the process twice more, and we soon had three patients loaded. The heat and the humidity re-liquefied the jellied, spilled body fluids that had accumulated on the deck grid from earlier trips. The slimy goo soon covered the entire backside of my fatigue trousers, creating a nauseating, sick smell, and what was worse, a very slick ass to sit on.

Just as I was beginning to dig my knees into the rough surface of the metal-grid floor, the chopper tipped violently away from the hill. We seemed to rocket upward off the ground as the pilot poured the juice to the engines, pulling us up and out of this hellhole that still held living, wounded, and dead soldiers. I pitched toward the other side of the chopper, grabbing wildly for something that would keep me from tumbling out of the open door on the other side. It happened to be the trouser leg of one of our wounded. How ironic!

As we reached the top of the trees that had surrounded us, I secured the wounded to avoid any further possibility of them being shifted or ejected upon any sudden maneuver. My attention was then diverted to their wounds as we seemed to fly at jet-like speed across the top of the canopy. It felt like we had entered another world, risen up from beneath the shroud of the triple canopy into the light and into breathable air. Our nirvana was interrupted only by the music of this miraculous machine that had brought us here safely and was now taking us away. It was analogous to being plucked from the throes of hell and being lifted into the gates of heaven, a wonderfully pleasant place of safety. The memory of how it was back down there was filled with the sound of explosions, the smell of gunpowder, fire, burning wood and flesh, and the screams of men from both armies. We are sickened with the thought of going back again...and again. But we must.

Two of my patients had serious chest wounds. I checked the chest dressings that had been applied by the medic on the ground, and both seemed effective, keeping just enough tension on the wounds to keep the air and blood from building up inside and restricting breathing. Had I only found the cherry early enough yesterday, I might have retained a future for him, but it was not to be. The third patient was a double amputee, with the left leg gone below the knee and the right just below the groin. There were tourniquets and a pressure compress on the left and a bulky pressure dressing over the right femoral artery and very small stump. There was a tremendous loss of blood from the right, and the wound needed attention.

I checked the IV status and the vital signs of the other two patients and then dug handfuls of dressings out of my field bag to stabilize the dressing on the double amputee. I rolled the patient up on his left side and propped him there with a rolled-up wool blanket so I could access his backside and secure the tourniquet. I cut away what was left of his BDU bottoms so I could assess his femoral pulse and found that he had a large part of his penis and both testicles shredded and mostly missing. I jammed two large abdominal dressings between his remaining left upper leg and the small stub remaining near his right hip and bound the stumps and the hips with Kerlix with so much pressure that the gauze tore twice.

When I laid the soldier on his back, the dressings seemed to hold a little more of his precious life fluid inside. Hopefully, there would be enough remaining within the arteries and veins to prevent collapse until we got him to an OR table back at the field station. I started another huge, sixteen-gauge IV site and put up a liter of saline. I dug out a couple units of albumen from my bag and started them in each of the two IV sites. Upon checking on the other two patients, I found them to be pale, and one was moaning loudly, causing the copilot to look back over his shoulder for an indication of how things were going.

The grid was getting increasingly covered with clotting blood and body fluids, and I was very pessimistic about the survival of any one of our three wounded. I briefly thought about the shock and horror that the news to the parents would cause and how young each of these guys appeared to be. Probably all fresh to Vietnam and to battle. They might not yet have experienced adult life but got catapulted far ahead into facing its final stages at eighteen to twenty years of age. My heart wept for them, but I said nothing except that we were not far from the hospital and that I promised to get them there.

One of the chest patients gripped my hand and said, "Thanks, Doc." I will remember his face forever. His own forever lasted just another ten or fifteen minutes. Conditions in the compartment were gaining on me, and when the copilot looked back one more time, I gave him a hand signal and expression that alerted him that things were not good. The engines whirred, and we climbed well above the trees. Rather than flying visual, the pilot took a directional course, using the instruments to lead the way.

Most pilots were well trained to "fly instruments," but it was avoided except in select circumstances. They were more vulnerable to ground fire from the big guns at the higher altitude but were a possible trophy to rifle fire at top speed just above the towering forests. Those factors were far from my mind as we climbed higher over the heavy, triple-canopy stuff and started to see the flatness and bright-green patchwork of the rice paddies and farmland.

From previous trips that day, I had come to recognize the landmarks, and I knew we were not far from "home." I had peeled off my microphone and helmet as soon as we had loaded patients, as it was very difficult to care for them with the flight helmet on. The ER triage doctor wanted a report, but our engine was whining loudly, making communication difficult. I put on my helmet, and as I fumbled, looking for the plug-in mic wire, the copilot handed me his, and I gave report.

I asked that they have one surgery room immediately available for the amputee and at least two chest-tube sets ready to go. I alerted them that intubation would be necessary for oxygenating all three. They acknowledged my call, and I fully expected all to be set up as requested.

I watched a small detachment of medics gather at the helipad with stretchers and blankets as we approached. We finally sat down on the pad, this time with both skids securely on level ground. The patients were off-loaded quickly, and I stayed in the compartment, checking each as they left the aircraft. It was only after all were taken into the ER that the helicopter crew and I huddled for a quick smoke break and a huge release of anxiety that each of us carried but never spoke of.

I took only about six power puffs and headed into the building. All three patients were lined up on ER stretchers. They looked terrible in the artificial light of the ER. The staff was somewhat blunt, commenting offhandedly on how the dressings were so filthy with leaves, dirt, and soot. I bit my tongue, knowing they hadn't the slightest fucking idea of what we had just been through. I attributed the remarks to just plain ignorance of the realities of combat medicine in the field versus at a hospital or field station.

It was always important to value the team effort, and almost everyone was aware that circumstances rule. Forty-odd years later, my awareness has been tweaked, and I have come to understand that variations in behavior are many times just outlets for the pressure. It's the kind of pressure that builds up in your chest and pushes out at the veins in your neck. It causes your cheeks to go numb and dumps so much adrenaline into your system that you feel too weak to stand at first, and then you become superhuman. When it's over and you are no longer "that way," you wish for it again soon, not giving a thought to the necessary prerequisites. A strange, morbid addiction indeed.

The pilot got in touch with me and said we would be going back in as soon as we were refueled and the bird was checked over to assure the small-arms fire hadn't cut pressure, hydraulic, or fuel lines. There was a huge deficiency in medevac choppers and crews in this operation, and the reason for my presence here now seemed clear. Even with the fact that I had little experience as a nurse, minimal experience in trauma, and a stateside crash course in combat medicine at Camp Bullis, I was here in hour-by-hour on-the-job training (OJT) with the very highest of consequences for slow learning.

As I was walking out, the major doc yelled, "Lieutenant!" I turned and saw he was standing over the gunshot wound (GSW) of the chest who had thanked me. The doc grimaced as he shook his head regretfully and pulled the sheet up over the deceased's head. Oh, fuck. What else could I have done? We had so little time, and doing anything really tricky in an open compartment of a chopper is near impossible, but there might have been something.

The situation weighed on me heavily as we climbed into the bird, its floor still covered with blood and filth. As we took off, I cried quietly to myself as I swished the shit on the grid out the open door with my hands to clear as much as I could as well as the memories that went with it. I laid the wool blanket down on top of the mess until I found that it made perching on the metal-grid floor way too slippery. That blanket might still be hanging from some tall tree up near the mountain along with the stench of battle and its crushing emotions.

—⁂—

Day 3, May69: This day found us near the base of the mountain as the ambushes that the NVA had mounted earlier were now broken. They had since returned back up the hill into their caves, tunnels, and spider holes. Those grunts that had been trapped halfway up the hill with gooks above and at both flanks fought their way back down and cleared a decent landing zone (LZ) that caused much less stress on the pilot. The wounded had been moved to this more stable area, which had been cleared of the few remaining trees on the scorched, reddish-brown earth that was pocked with rocket, mortar, and bomb craters. It reeked with the smell of napalm, burned dirt, blood, and death.

One PFC nearly put me over the top in the compassion and helplessness categories. He, according to the only two of his squad members that remained alive, had charged a bunker that was dug into the side of the mountain and connected to a tunnel system. Throwing his two grenades and then firing clip after clip of sixteen rounds into the bunker, out of which the NVA were firing continuously, he ran straight on against machine-gun fire and RPG rockets, making it to within twenty feet.

In full view of his comrades, an RPG had slammed through his gut, unexploded. The impact threw him several feet back and to the side, and he lay there for twenty minutes before the last gook in the bunker was taken out and his friend arrived to help him. His friend told the story of himself retching and vomiting in view of his buddy's open eyes. He had observed his friend's still-attached, mangled, and destroyed bowels quivering on the ground like giant earthworms while oozing green, yellow, and brown bowel contents. It had created a putrid stench in his nostrils that made his stomach cramp into a tight knot. He had wanted to run away.

Instead, he quickly removed his poncho liner from his pack and placed it over the huge abdominal wound. He cradled his friend's head in his lap until the medic responded to his calls. The medic needed his assistance to care for the horrible wound, and I'm sure that if PTSD could be forecast with certainty, the two of them would be at the head of the line. They had very little water left, as water was critical on the mountain, but as the medic cradled the PFC's bowels carefully in his hands, his buddy sparingly rinsed them. This was repeated several times until much of the red-brown dirt was removed and each cleaned section was gently tucked into the huge, gaping hole in the abdomen.

The medic then placed a large abdominal dressing over the huge wound and poured the remainder of his water on the dressing. They gently carried the PFC to the LZ, where we secured him in the best position on the floor where the pitch of the chopper would be less evident. Fortunately, I had brought several liters of normal saline on this run, and after fumbling with my pocketknife was able to uncap one as we weaved up through the trees, escaping the base of the mountain and climbing to a high altitude for a fast trip to the field hospital. I dumped the entire liter of saline onto the dressing so it pooled in the wound cavity underneath (it is necessary to keep exposed bowel moist, as it is very fragile, and dryness will cause the tissue to die). Before long, we were setting down on the pad of the field hospital.

Good fortune followed, as the hospital had an OR prepared for him and were at the ready in the ER for the other patient we had on board. My only news concerning the private is that he made it through surgery that day after removal of a large portion of his small and large intestines. I still wonder to this day if he rejoined his loved ones back home or became another entry on the solemn black wall to be. God be with him in either event.

By the end of the day, we had transported eight more WIA and three KIA out of that wretched place. All of the wounded that afternoon were transported alive with some chance of survival. Like most times, we would never know if they pulled through. There were also three choppers lost along with an entire crew, but there was never an inkling of any pilot and crew waiting until the LZs cooled down to do the extractions and medevacs.

The army helicopter crews that I knew never questioned the status of the LZ and many times, against orders, went in regardless of the situations at hand. "We're going to get you out of this fucking hellhole alive, soldier." That was the goal above all else. The ship did not matter, the crew did not matter, and the CO with orders to abort on the radio before the touchdown did not matter. Fuck all of it. We were there. They were not! We were the masters of our own self-made, surreal universe, and what happened there was solely ours. We did our job very well, or we did not. It was ours to own all the way, and that's the way it had to be. My deepest admiration remains with my comrades.

After a few more days' experience on the mountain, the procedures had become routine, and we carried out our jobs with little communication required. A great number of soldiers were evacuated out of there, and depending on our jobs, each of us saw the picture in a different way. I didn't really realize this until after we sat back, sloshing down our poison, and the recollections started rolling. At times, I didn't think I had been on the same bird as the pilot spun his tale versus what I remembered about the trip. It made me realize that the same event could legitimately be interpreted in a totally different manner depending on your position and where your senses were directed or confined. As we tied our recollections together, I believe we were impressed with ourselves, but mostly, we were a bit more fearful as we realized the extent of the adversities we all had experienced and survived. This was one time that the liquor did not make things better. Not then, and not now.

Goin' Up the Hill

—⟨⟨⟨—

Day 7, May69: For reasons unknown to us, it appeared as though the progress up the mountain was to be relinquished, and we were ordered to vacate it with expectations that the operation was over. However, on day eight, orders directed a repeat of the previous assault. Attention was given to resupply and locating the grunts into position on the hill. The concern that everyone had for the level of sanity at the command level was no secret. Regardless, the next assault on the hill began on day nine, and halfway to the top, all hell broke loose once again.

Dirt filled my ears, and my eyes were inflamed with stinging sweat and debris that the rotor lifted off the denuded ground that only several days before had been covered with lush flora and living things. We were left there alone on the doorstep of hell, trying to snatch hapless grunts from the clutches of a regiment-plus-NVA force that was dug into the merciless fucking mountain so well that it took a direct rocket hit just to disturb their tea.

I could hear the scream of the turbo engine of the slick leaving us and an occasional moan or weak yell. Then it was gone. I and two others had been sent to this LZ to assist getting wounded ready for evac so the choppers would not remain on the ground longer than necessary. New sights and sounds took the place of the departed slick. I was standing here in this place in the dirt, with a smattering of light that made strange patterns all around me on the ground. Dancing shadows and sprinkles of brightness appeared and disappeared as the wind blew the tops of the remaining trees around the LZ, painting an abstract canvas on the ground.

A hundred yards ahead and above me on the next ridge, I could see the figures of men climbing inch by inch up into what they aptly called "Charlie's Place." The machine-gun fire up there was so continuous that it sounded like a musical score written for each inch they struggled upward, hoping to find a rift or depression to protect them. It didn't turn out that way for many as I watched men fall, some hurled through the air like rag dolls. The rifle fire dancing in between seemed more distinct because there was a beginning and an end to each series of the reports, and they cracked with their own signature, more specific and decisive.

On frequent occasions, the figures would come down toward me. In most cases, upon crawling to them, there was little for me to do. The damages were horrific, beyond what I could ever have imagined. Was this to be my job today? Crawl on my gut for forty or so yards, check out the wounds, realize they were mortally wounded or already fatal, help with their pain, and then crawl back with just the imprint of the scene on my brain? That's all these poor grunts got for now. What a hell of a job. I had to be crazy for causing myself to be anywhere near this place.

Very soon, my mental unrest abruptly ended with an influx of ambulatory and carried patients from the hill, all of them heading toward me. In this already surreal situation, all I could think of was a black-and-white movie I had seen years before in which all of the zombies arose and walked toward the viewer out of a fog. I was immediately ashamed of myself. As they came closer, I bumped hard against the edge of reality and said to myself, "Holy Christ, they all need me?" I treated over thirty-six walking or assisted wounded, many of which could return to the battle with only minor injuries. It was a tough call on whether they could fight or be a detriment to the others and needed medevac.

The wounds ranged from wood splinters, small frag wounds, small flesh wounds, and destroyed nerves. Then the litter patients started coming. This would be the third act, the one that always proved to grab you by the balls and make you want to go to your knees and hide your face, but you couldn't. Just as the litter bearers broke the edge of the trees, two F4C Phantom jets made a treetop run across the remaining jungle in front of us and just beyond from where these grunts had just escaped.

Their engines screeched and vibrated my eardrums to the point of near deafness while their payload of bombs warned of the coming holocaust.

Then it happened. After their bombs were dropped, they each also dropped huge doses of napalm that took paths about seventy-five yards ahead of us, about thirty yards into the tree line. The explosions slammed our eyelids shut, and we had to squint when we opened them, as they burned from the brightness of the world in front of us. The heat seemed to wrinkle our faces on contact. The fire was so intense that it sucked all oxygen from the air, even that in our lungs, to completely satisfy its hunger for destruction. Softball-size fireballs flew into our area, splashing like water balloons before erupting and spreading even more evil around us.

Then came the coup/countercoup caused by the explosions and the huge fireball that affected one's whole body. Vessels and blood, skin, and fat responded to the great changes in pressure created by the scientific experiment carried out just in front of us, seemingly pounding against each other like demons trying to escape the containment of the body. It lasted but a few seconds or so, but we would never forget the feeling. Your belly and your chest feel it most. The smell of gasoline ruins what oxygen is left for you to breathe. The grunts called it "snake and nape," and it was devastating.

It was beyond real. It was extreme. It was intense. It could not be understood by anyone who wasn't there. Who the fuck would listen? It's nauseating. You are taught to care for and attempt to save even the gravely injured men if they have a chance to live. Otherwise, medicate for pain and go to the next. The numbers needing treatment seemed overwhelming, and the short supply of medical equipment that could be stored in our bags usually ran out in the first fifteen or twenty minutes. We would hope for a drop along with the ammo that could validate our purpose for a while longer.

Everything seemed impossible. We were expected to be highly successful while working in hundred-degree heat and 70 percent-plus humidity, filthy conditions, and the extremes of combat. We had to find something to cover raw, burned flesh as we had only one burn pack left in the bag while three victims with skin and flesh hanging from their faces and arms from the napalm all deserved it. Everything was filthy with sweat and dirt, so fabric from anything worn or carried into that place and not under cover was unusable.

There was a PFC cradling his intestines in both hands with a weird look of satisfaction on his face. I believe he was smiling because he was able to find and retrieve his own guts, making him feel once again whole. A sergeant leaned on a tree stump with a horrid, bleeding neck-and-shoulder wound and a shattered arm. By the time I reached him, his color went from ashen to nearly white, and by the time I got the fluids going, he was dead. I tried CPR but was exhausted after the first minute, rolled over on my back, and squinted my eyes at the sun. The filth dissolved in my sweat ran into my ears and eyes and mouth and tasted as I imagined death to taste like.

I was mentally and physically depleted to the point that I considered a self-inflicted wound to the head to be much better than enduring this for another eleven months. But then I realized what was expected of me, and my pain in being there was trivial compared to that of all of these poor souls. They deserved everything that I might muster and then more. Do what you can, get them on the fucking chopper. Get them all out. After that is done, canvas the KIAs and help gather their info, tag them, and wait for the trip back on the next available bird.

After what seemed like hours awaiting extraction, my mind was crazy with feelings of danger and remorse. The waiting times were the worst, as nothing was off-limits for your mind and where it took you. As the hum and then the rotor whump of the next chopper was heard, we would nearly explode with feelings of relief, and after the last of the wounded were aboard, we would help load the KIAs. As I rode back in the last bird, sitting on the floor with the bodies, living and dead, I watched the blood and other body fluid once again drift back and forth on the deck within the intricate little metal channels of the grid, sometimes escaping out in a thin string onto the jungle below. It was like a symbolic exorcism representing the purging of evil from the soul and back into the clutches of the horrible monster on the ground. It must surely be the trickery of hell down there in that black hole within the green, lush garden from where we had risen. High in the air, it looked so peaceful and beautiful. But I knew that it was not.

Arrive back at base camp, help unload the KIAs. Vomit once or twice. Try to remember their faces. Can't even remember coming back here! Use one quart Jack Daniels Black on ice until it's gone. Go to bed. Remembering faces really well now! Awaken at 0500. Shower, eat breakfast, shit, and meet with your assigned crew. I was a TDY, and with each new crew, I needed to listen to the flight plan and any special rules of the ship (all had their own special, little rules and habits), and then go do it all again, just like the day before. Maybe this time, they would make it to the top.

I was to repeat this routine each of the ten days I was there, and with mixed emotions, I was returned to the Ninetieth. As we flew over the command post (CP), the gunner and I pulled out our Johnsons and pissed on the palm leaves atop the bunker. That felt really good.

Days later, I learned that the mountain had been breached and captured, but someone sitting back in a command bunker earning decorations and accolades pulled them all off the hill. The slicks would transport the remaining grunts to their respective base camps, and others would remove the equipment and supplies that needed to be salvaged. The bloody battle had appeared to accomplish little.

The Enormity of Napalm[4]

A New Mission, a New Beginning

—⚏—

As I SEE IT, THERE is an arena in which each of our fears are based. One could be a distant mountain with dangers unseen; another could be within you in the form of the haunting faces of those you have failed. Each of us carried fear, some more than others, and some not admitting it to this day. Most of my fear back then stemmed from my responsibility to perform under extreme and ever-changing circumstances.

With my TDY assignment completed, I hoped for a less stressful time at my new assignment at the 311th Field Hospital in Qui Nhon. Fortunately, for nearly five months, it was almost like having a regular job "back in the world." We had our meals on time, we were able to keep groomed every day, and we played volleyball on our off shifts when we weren't getting trashed at the club or in our hooch. Other than the near-nightly red alerts, the majority of which turned out not to affect us, our lives at the 311th were embarrassingly comfortable. It was very weird for me after spending time up north on the mountain from hell and then coming to this nearly country-club setting and enjoying "the good life." That was soon to change.

October 1969 was an intense period of physical labor and necessity for all of us at the 311th Field. The mission of our unit was changed from care of POWs at the 311th Field Hospital in Qui Nhon to opening a fully capable combat field hospital near An Khe in the Central Highlands. I believe all of us felt a great relief at no longer providing care for POWs and anticipated giving all of our efforts to our troops.

We worked feverishly to prepare the POWs for transfer to the Republic of Korea (ROK) camp, and it seemed like an endless job.

All had to have fail-proof personal identification, medical records, and hard-copy diagnostic data matched to them while not permitting them to physically possess their records. They required all types of transport, since they ranged from ambulatory patients to litter patients who had to be carried by the MPs. All of them were very apprehensive, as they had heard about the reputation of the ROK camp from those who had been there and sent back to us due to medical necessity. The ROKs were very aggressive and had a low opinion of all Vietnamese. They had even less love for the Vietcong and NVA, and that was a primary reason for us providing their care in the first place—to keep them alive for valuable information that could help the effort. Nevertheless, all were transferred to the custody of the Republic of Korea troops, who were our allies in the war.

Transfer day for all patients at the 311th Field Hospital

Our assignment required us to pack up all moveable equipment and supplies at the present hospital, load it onto a convoy of deuce-and-a-half trucks and tractor-trailer rigs, travel a long distance on Highway 1 to slightly north of Qui Nhon and then west to An Khe. This was all to take place in the heat of one day, as convoys did not travel through the An Khe Pass at night.

Part of the 311th Convoy Ready to Move to An Khe

The trip was at a snail's pace, as army trucks are not known for going fast anywhere, and their drivers are often slower yet. As we passed by villages and expanses of countryside, we were flanked on both sides by acres of rice paddies. We observed several dead, decomposing Viet bodies lying along the roadside while villagers on bicycles and motorbikes zipped by, seemingly unconcerned and disregarding. We later learned that if anyone paid attention to the corpses, it indicated that they must know the person and would be hauled off by the ARVNs for interrogation and probably imprisonment or worse.

Highway 1 would then lead us to Highway 19 into the mountains and through the An Khe Pass, one of the more treacherous places in the country. It had many steep inclines and steep embankments and was laced with extremely treacherous curves. Some were hairpin curves requiring the trucks to move even slower. Breakdowns and overheated engines would disable the entire convoy and invite the Vietcong or NVA to an easy turkey shoot. We were escorted by Cobra gunships, but they were unable to fly as slowly as we were traveling, and they had to circle back continuously to pick up the trailing truck of the convoy. They moved forward on full alert, watching for enemy activity and for any action on the hillsides adjoining the road. Much of the roadside foliage had been retarded and destroyed by fire and Agent Orange. Fortunately, we made it through the pass with only minor delays.

Upon finally arriving at Camp Radcliff in An Khe in the early evening, we were to have an eight-hour period to make a rudimentary, temporary camp and then sleep. Overnight, our CO was to evaluate what buildings and structures left by the First Cavalry remained salvageable and then give us orders to off-load and set up the hospital. Most of us, after working in the heat of the day for sixteen hours, were really looking forward to a good rest and a bite to eat. We all grabbed hospital mattresses and looked for some kind of shelter in one of the tin or wooden shelters.

An hour later, we were mustered from our sleep with the message that we must be set up and fully operational within twenty-four hours. The surprises of An Khe began and did not end until I returned to the (continental) United States (CONUS) in late April of 1970.

Highway 19 Winding toward An Khe Pass

Slow-Moving Tankers in An Khe Pass Were a Favorite Target

(An Khe Pass photos courtesy of SP4 Wayne L. Robbins)

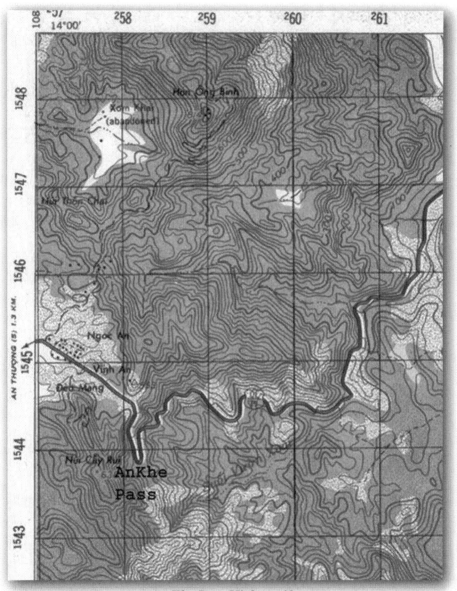

An Khe Pass, Highway 19[v]

Camp Radcliff

—ᴍ—

Aɴ Kʜᴇ ᴡᴀs ᴀ ʟᴏɴɢ-ᴋɴᴏᴡɴ hot zone, having being a past or present loca-tion of the 173rd Airborne, 1st Cavalry, 238th Aviation Company, and a few artillery units. The Fourth Infantry Division was newly relocated to Radcliff and operated from around An Khe and west to the Cambodian border. The area was known as a major ingress route for NVA troops and supplies from the Ho Chi Minh Trail, and casualties in these missions were common.

The Seventeenth was not unique as a field hospital. It was composed of folks from all over the United States and Central and South America, all patriots who, for the most part, had their own special reasons for wanting to serve. A large number of our medics and medical support personnel at the Seventeenth came as a single unit from a reserve group in Ohio. They brought a real family-like atmosphere to our little operation starting out in Qui Nhon and then moving as a new unit, the Seventeenth Field Hospital, to the Central Highlands. They finished up their one-year tour at An Khe after about four months and then were sent back to CONUS as a whole unit.

Our hospital would take over the few vacated buildings, mostly Quonset huts and wooden hooch's located at the very base of Hon Cong Mountain. We eventually remodeled the buildings into functional medi-cal facilities. From outside our ER, the canopied jungle was visible in the near distance just at the edge of the no-defoliation area around our pe-rimeter. The enclave, known as Camp Radcliff, was also home to an air-port that fielded a large contingent of UH-1 (Huey), Cobra, and Loach helicopters. It had achieved the nickname of "the Golf Course" from its previous exposures and history and in recognition of the fact that the terrain had been leveled completely by engineers to accommodate aircraft.

A military-police headquarters also occupied a large base that served an expansive area around An Khe, including Highway 19, which traversed the Mang Yang Pass (a wicked pass between An Khe and Pleiku) and the An Khe Pass. The Fourth Infantry was very active in the area and had a ranger unit, the K-75 Rangers, Airborne, that did frequent long-range recon patrol (LRRP).

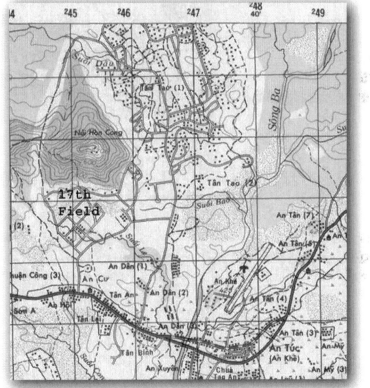

Seventeenth Field Hospital at the Base of Hon Cong Mountain[vi]

So, the Seventeenth Field Hospital, as a "noncombatant" component of the conflict and protected under the Geneva Convention, was perched among some of the enemy's most hated units: the Fourth, the MPs, the Golf Course, and several large fuel depots and firebases. The Fourth Infantry needs no introduction. They are a kick-ass division that strikes fear in any enemy, regardless of the location of the soil.

The airport, with its rich endowment of Cobra gunships, slicks, and the miniscule LOH (light observation helicopter, a.k.a. Loach) provided reasons enough for the enemy's hatred. The Cobra, with its mini-guns firing at six thousand rounds per minute, terrified the bad guys, and it was a real prize to put one down or destroy it on the ground. The Loaches were small, mostly observation aircraft that resembled mosquitoes and frequently were used to seek out enemy deployments and to direct aggressive fire. Often, they would go in low over elephant grass, and the rotor wash would part it like a hair dryer, revealing all of the lice (bad guys) within. The Cobras would be close behind with the terrible *brrrrrrrrrrbrrrrrrrrrr* of the mini-guns lighting up the sky with tracer rounds and striking terror into those below. It would often be capped off by a rocket or two, and there were usually no survivors. So, the personality and presence of these terrible aircraft, along with the slicks that carried the grunts into the most godforsaken places imaginable, were plenty of reason for the gooks to take aim at the airfield at Radcliff on a regular basis.

The MPs were very instrumental in curtailing the black-market activities of the Vietcong and civilian supporters of the NVA. Much of the money that supported the Vietcong in the South came from black-market "dollar changing" as well as procurement and resale of stolen US military property—vehicles, ammunition, metal, uniforms, everything. Anything they could steal brought a price from someone, usually inflated hundreds of times with conversion to illegal currency, the MPC, and the American dollar.

The MPs were also the biggest deterrent to prostitution, except when they were the customers. The civilians hated that, because a whore in Vietnam had a gold mine between her thighs, and that gold, once earned, would be spent at several of the local business'. If she managed her money well, she could move from the cardboard-and-orange-crate shack along Highway 19 to a really nice place that had maybe two rooms, some plaster on the wall, and some semblances of furniture. The pimps, usually madams (mama-sans), really had it nice. They had several-room houses complete with furniture and a small TV, or at least a radio. I knew of one who had a full-length mink coat. She used its softness and comfort to sleep on, as it was way too hot to wear a mink coat in Vietnam. It was her most prized possession, as she had learned that all wealthy women back in the world had at least one of them. Oh, yes, prostitution was the second most profitable business in Vietnam, and its purveyors did not like interference from the MPs.

But why would a field hospital that treated civilians on site or in villages at a level of care never seen by any living generation in the RVN be attacked? At times, lifesaving care was even unknowingly rendered to Vietcong or NVA soldiers. It is thought that the Vietcong considered assistance to the South as a sort of "hearts-and-minds" trick that the United States had cooked up to make our effort look good to those who were not quite yet convinced of unification. They were exactly right. LBJ thought it was a sterling plan to show the people of South Vietnam how supportive the United States was, even though the population suffered heavily every day from our presence. Winning "hearts and minds" was his new tactic.[vii]

The Vietnamese civilians were always extremely thankful and looked forward to our med-caps many days ahead of our presence. They frequently formed long lines in the village awaiting care. The medical exam was brief, with chief complaints related to us by the interpreter. If feasible, we dealt with the complaints right there with them standing before us or lying on a wooden bench. Sometimes, treatment was as minimal as dispensing an aspirin or a penicillin tablet; sometimes it was more complicated, such as pulling teeth or giving wound care. The patients were always so very thankful.

We learned, however, that some were saving the drugs and giving them to the Vietcong. Thereafter, medicine was administered as a load of PCN in the ass or the witnessed swallowing of pills followed by an oral check of the toothless, horrid-smelling nuoc-mam (fermented fish sauce) tainted mouths. We did many of these med-caps, regardless of the setbacks and unseen dangers.

I think that the Vietcong correctly recognized the visits to be a sort of a repatriation for those on the wire, and, in fact, that was exactly what was intended—not by us, but by Johnson and Westmoreland. Upon the enemy figuring this out, we soon became the enemy as well, and we were an easy hit. Hell, the permanent buildings and helipads of the field hospitals frequently flaunted the big Red Cross outlined in white, which then represented a good sight-in landmark for mortars rather than a safety zone not to be fired upon. Hence, the attack on the Seventeenth Field on November 15, 1969, was neither incidental nor accidental. One wondered about the sanity of the war planners. Lunacy at best!

Medical personnel have long been considered in the "noncombatant" ranks, antiwar folks who enlist in the military wanting to serve their country—but not in combat. Actually, a large number of the soldiers in the medical corps were members of the Reserve and were moved as an entire unit to Vietnam. Granted, a considerable number of the COs had been drafted and then chose the medical branch of the effort. They had not realized that many combat medics ended up in the thickest of the shit and would never see CONUS again. The survival rate of combat medics in Vietnam was atrocious, making their duty the third most dangerous of the war.

The second most dangerous was the helicopter-door gunner, and the most likely MOS to kill you quickly was the radio telephone operator (RTO). My hat is off to all of them. I only hope most did not go to duty unknowing of the peril, as that would mean they were terribly deceived. Most of them were surely enlightened shortly after arriving in country, getting grim news about those they were replacing.

Naïve ignorance of the war was the case with many of the under-twenty age group as well. Too much family history with Grandpa's and Dad's war stories to live up to and too many war movies watched with your best gal in your arms. What was a young fellow to do but corner himself into joining one of the fighting forces? All very wrong reasons to join an organization that sends you to war. It teaches you how to kill and makes you believe you don't care about it—maybe even like it. Drafted or a volunteer, you soon learn it is your ass only, not those of any who caused you to be there, that sticks out above a mosquito-infested depression in the ground filled with stagnant water in hundred-plus degree heat and oppressive humidity while carrying nearly a hundred pounds of gear. You curse all of them while thinking of how your once clean, groomed body and slick hair made you feel perfect while cuddled up with your sweetheart. That was now far from your reality as you fought the urge to scratch the yellow-white fungus that invaded your crotch, your balls, and your feet. All of this while some little slant-eyed, four-and-a-half-foot-tall bastard shot at you relentlessly, wanting nothing more than to render you dead. If you were lucky enough to survive, Uncle Sam paid your ticket back to the world, but I hope you didn't expect much else because this was an unpopular, "criminal" war, according to most.

Most dust-off units early on in the conflict were not weaponized other than with the pilot and copilot's personal weapons. The dinks gave no quarter to medical personnel whatsoever, and the big, hovering birds proved to be easy targets, especially on the hoist missions. Later in the war, more deviation from Geneva Convention was evident and we were in for more surprises.

Many of our personnel were combat qualified on several weapons of one type or another. All officers, doctors, nurses, and medical service corps (MSC) were required to qualify with the .45-cal. side arm. It was optional to qualify with the M16. The medics and noncoms were qualified for the M16 as well as other weapons. It so happened that many in our unit, coming from Ohio and the Midwest, had a history of wild-game hunting back in CONUS, and those skills were certainly a big plus in protecting our asses in South Vietnam.

I personally carried an M16, an M79 grenade launcher, and a .45-cal. semiauto. I was never able to hit a bull in the ass from the inside out with the .45. The slide on this weapon was so loose, it could be moved about thirty degrees side to side when the chamber was loaded and the hammer cocked. The sights are on the slide, so it is not difficult to see how easy it is to miss a softball-size target at twenty feet.

While in An Khe I had to borrow my CO's personal .45 to requalify, and upon returning to my hooch, I tossed mine in my locker and hid the ammo from my mama-san just in case she might be moved to shoot my ass someday. It remained there for months under dirty underwear, gathering all the mold and corrosion imaginable, until one day we were blessed with a surprise weapons inspection. I knew what was in store for me, so when it was my turn, I presented the .45 and hung my head in resignation to the chew I was about to receive. The pistol was taken from me, and I was asked if I had any other weapons. I presented my spotless M16 and my M79 grenade launcher. They both passed with flying colors, and I was left alone without my .45, thank God. I might have been tempted to use it someday. I reached for the M16 on the red alerts, as it was surgical in accuracy. The M79 with the antipersonnel rounds and grenade rounds was what I chose to carry on dust-offs.

Armed as we were and with two perimeter wires surrounding our compound, we felt quite content with our level of safety. We shared the huge camp with a number of different units, but each had its own perimeter and its own guard posts. We were to learn, however, that Victor Charlie was well trained in insurgency and guerilla tactics and unfortunately, we would experience his expertise firsthand.

Hon Kong Mountain, a very large, high mountain with heavy foliage requiring frequent, heavy doses of Agent Orange, was laced with tunnels, bunkers, and spider holes, making the area around the mountain a very dangerous place. Some of the entrenchments had been there since the French had fought on the same ground. The mountain was highly favored by the enemy, and Camp Radcliff was the recipient of frequent mortar, rocket, and sapper attacks (sappers were gooks carrying satchel charges—any receptacle filled with metal, glass, stones, gunpowder, and some C4 used to detonate the rest) whether intended for the MP compound, the Golf Course, or the Fourth Infantry.

I don't know if they held a grudge against us beyond the psychological reasons discussed earlier, but we were incidental participants in every Code Red event, and they were frequent. Many times, we were used as a diversionary tactic with some mortar or rocket rounds into our perimeter. Once additional protective forces were sent to the hospital compound to help in defense, heavier stuff was then directed toward the other, more valued targets.

Our structures were mostly Quonsets and they were old and filthy dirty. They resembled halves of fifty-five-gallon steel barrels bolted onto concrete pads, resembling barns or coops, and we soon found that they served their purpose very well. Without too much effort, they could be emptied and cleaned and hosed down in a short time. The concrete floors took the bleach quite well and dried quickly with the help of the huge, aircraft-size propeller fans that ran constantly at each end of the open huts. Temperatures inside were relentless during the day; the fans were necessary for cooling and for ventilation, as there were no other openings. Wide screen doors served as the only portals.

Ironically, as stifling hot as it became during the day, patients needed their poncho liners and sometimes wool blankets to keep the chill away at night. Only a couple of the huts were served by air conditioners, and they were of the small, apartment style that hung through holes cut in the metal walls. Surgery, recovery, and ICU were of the few to have such conveniences in an effort to cut down on the myriad of organisms lifted from the orange, contaminated soil outdoors and carried on the wind by the huge fans.

Our routine at the Seventeenth, if I dare to call it that, consisted of working one of two shifts, 0700 to 1900 or 1900 to 0700, six or seven days per week for 365 days. This was if all went "as usual." But nothing really was usual there. There was no fresh water, no sanitation, no modern equipment, and, at times, limited medical supplies, requiring careful scrutiny on wastefulness and rationing. Most of the food started out dehydrated and became quite palatable through the skill of our unit's cooks.

There was no hot water, only that created by the hot sun beating down daily on the giant drum that held a mixture collected from somewhere that had a little less water-buffalo shit, piss, and rotting flesh mixed in. It was made somewhat safe by a concoction of chemicals that made tiny, red pustules on our skin that itched and burned like fire until our bodies gave up reacting to the mixture. The chemicals were intended to buffer all of the nasty shit. But each time we stood under the shower with the water running down over our heads while keeping one eye trained on the door in case Charlie decided to visit, it was difficult to keep away the images of buff excreta and the many corpses rotting along the roadsides.

Most GIs who showered regularly were on a standard prescription of two to six grams of vitamin C and a stiff dose of Benadryl daily for the first couple of months until their immune systems just gave up fighting the foreign shit that doused their skin. Constant sweating that soaked your socks and the front and back of your fatigue shirt after just minutes of exposure added to the overall misery of the place. It was an advantage to allow the legs of your fatigue bottoms to blouse so that cooler air inside would keep them from pasting to your legs. It wasn't terribly stylish, however, so many ignored the advice.

There was a standing joke that the Sgt. Major used with the new female recruits during their orientation to the unit that involved wearing fatigue bottoms that were loose and not skintight as many of the ladies preferred, especially in the company of the helicopter pilots at the officer's (O) club. He would tell them, "There was once a new female LT that wore her fatigue pants so tight that one day at the mess hall, she farted, and it blew her jungle boots off into the soup pot."

As for the food, we frequently could not make the usual mess times due to high work volume or other emergencies. This was, in a way, a gift, because it was at the noon mess that you were forced, under observation, to take your CP pill and Dapsone tablet and other drugs that were recommended. CP antimalarial drugs were lethal on the stomach, and even with as much effort as the chef made to make the dried shit taste decent, it was ruined by the reflux of the chemical solvent mixed with the acid-laced, dried food. The Dapsone pills were an altogether different story. We were told that they were for a special type of malaria and they were vital to our safety while in the Nam.

Years after the war, however, much discussion was held on the use of GIs as the white rats of the late sixties and early seventies, and Dapsone[viii] was at the front of the list of questionable items. It had early promise in preventing leprosy, the old biblical abomination that struck those who were full of sin and deserved to lose a digit or two, a nose, or possibly a whole face. Vietnam had its share of leprosy, and we did several medcaps at a beautiful, Eden-like garden built by the French during their share of the war. It was still run by French nuns. It was a haven for those with leprosy and their family members only. It seemed that, once one family member was afflicted, it scared the bejesus out of all who didn't have it, and the entire family was exiled from its home with no place to go. The nuns took in all of them, and they actually lived in a much better and much safer environment than they had been expelled from. Sometimes the meek do inherit the earth, or at least the best of it.

Housing at the Leprosarium

November 15, 1969

—ᴍ—

NOVEMBER 15, 1969, SEEMED LIKE most any other evening at the Seventeenth Field. I worked until about 2015, made rounds on all of the surgical floors to assure staffing was OK, and then made a quick trip through the ER to assure all was under control and that no dust-offs were reported to be coming in. I had a nice steak at our makeshift, outdoor O club and my usual three fingers of JD Black on ice, times three, and made my way to the shower, the third one today.

Upon becoming accustomed to the chemicals and rashes, showers were divine in Vietnam once the (fuck you) gecko lizards, occasional snake, and the majority of insects were evacuated from the shower room. Of course, we just had the tepid, chlorine-laced liquid trucked in from an unknown source and stored in an open, solar-heated receptacle. It was filled about every three days by some guys we bought drinks for on about the same number of days so they would keep our showers running on a strict schedule. That's how things worked here. Despite the source of the showers and the mental images produced, they were one of the few semblances of civilization. Three showers were a real treat; I usually only had two, one in the morning and one after work. The short ten minutes after each brought you the best feeling until your next one, and however brief that feeling of being clean and human was, it was sacred.

When I returned to my hooch, it was about 2200, and my roomie, Lt. Al S., was intently studying the PACEX catalog, dreaming up the perfect stereo system that could be purchased dirt cheap and shipped anywhere in the free world. I was pondering which of the newly arrived female nurses I should approach to offer a guided tour around Camp Radcliff while I sipped on a BJ on the rocks. We chatted on the merits of Pioneer versus Sony for a time, and Al was refueling his scotch on the rocks, when we heard the whistling, vacuum-like whoosh of what on first thought seemed to be outgoing artillery, which was commonplace on a near-nightly basis from one of the units nearby.

But, microseconds after that sound settled uncomfortably in our ears and brains and before we both had a chance to say anything other than "incoming," the tin on our roof crackled, and the ground shook. A familiar *whoomph* seemed to suck out all of the air around our heads for just a split second. The tin roof was peppered with rocks and debris. Al said later that it shook badly enough that it spilled his scotch, but I don't think that's the way it was, especially with the brown spot that appeared on his white cotton undershorts. I grabbed my helmet, flak jacket, and M16 and exited the room at low level just in time to see a second round blow the roof off the male crapper.

In seconds, that corner of the compound lighted up like the Fourth of July as several other rounds soon followed. Al was right behind me, and after turning the lights out in the room, we took positions behind the sand-filled fifty-five-gallon barrels with two layers of sandbags on top that allowed us to carefully peek over to get a full view of the situation. Several mortars followed, along with the sound of a gazillion rounds of small arms and .60-cal. machine-gun fire directed out toward the perimeter where the dinks might be in hiding.

Our hooch was one of eight in barracks style—four rooms on each side, housing sixteen doctors and male nurses. As the others filtered out of the hooches, they were directed one at a time to cross the exposed dirt roadway to the safety of the bunkers next to the ER. The back of our barracks was on the edge of the first perimeter with a steep bank of mud and knee-high grass that flourished into elephant grass about six to seven feet high at the bottom. The grass jungle melted into a ridge upon which some old, dilapidated, vacated buildings abandoned by the

First Cavalry stood in ruin and then extended into a fairly thick bush of heavy vegetation.

Facing to the west, it was an eerie sight each evening watching the skeletons of the old, vacant cavalry buildings backlit with fading sunlight. We had always expected action to come from that direction. Al and I kept watch on the perimeter area while all of the men made it across the roadway. Suddenly, a barrage of small-arms fire opened up with the familiar *ak-ak-ak-ak* crack of AK-47s coming from out in front of us in the tall grass. We could hear the swish of rounds passing by us in the air and heard structures and trees being hit with a whack, showering debris all around us.

After Al and I had used up about three clips each in return fire, we covered each other as each crossed the roadway. We watched three of four of the enlisted barracks explode in the night with large pieces of burning wood, metal, rocks, and dirt flying and ricocheting all over our compound. Al and I looked at each other in amazement and surprise that we were both unscathed. Small-arms fire was really heavy, and it was difficult to tell its origin or its destination. Once on the hospital side of the compound, we took defensive positions around the ER until a few enlisted guys arrived to watch the front as we worked our way to the back of the ER through the Quonset hut to see what damage may have been done and to assure that no sapper activity was in progress.

Small-arms fire continued zipping through the air and at times hitting or ricocheting off the metal huts. Al and I returned back through the Quonset to the front of the ER just in time to see two rockets, probably RPGs, hit dead onto the roof of the female nurses' quarters. Little did I know that this event alone would affect my life for another forty-four years.

Almost simultaneously, two more enlisted barracks seemed to collapse, followed by the horrible sound of explosions a second or two after. I knew we were in deep shit if this continued, as there was also intense fire further to the west of our compound near the MP compound and also near the airport (the Golf Course). The ground fire continued with tracer rounds and .60-cal. machine-gun fire. Huge areas of real estate just outside our perimeter were lit up with illumination flares, and all of our perimeter guard posts now seemed to be manned. Soon, the sky lit up with an onslaught of red tracers as if coming from a black hole opened up in the sky, and we knew that the dreaded mini-guns of Spooky (a.k.a. Puff the Magic Dragon) were at work. Hopefully, they would end this shit real soon.

Puff the Magic Dragon[ix] (with a Fire Rate of 18,000 Rounds per Minute)[x]

Shortly after setting up some canvas stretchers in addition to the usual ER carts, plugging tubing into saline IV bottles, and supplying the care and triage areas with boxes of bandages and other emergency supplies, our fellow wounded comrades began to appear as well as those not wounded but not quite sure what to do. Al and I and Gary sent most of the unwounded to the bunker, as it was still a hot fire zone and there was not a need to expose any more bodies than necessary. We assured all of them that we would call them as soon as we needed help to care for patients.

We snatched a few of the doctors and our CO, a brilliant thoracic surgeon, was there overseeing the action. He was a tall, well-structured Spanish man who spoke the romance language as smoothly as in the wine and liquor commercials. All of the women loved him, and maybe some of the guys. He was an excellent fit as the CO of our medical unit. His wing man (hit man) XO was Scottish and most of the time a prick, a stiff-collared lifer and huge womanizer. He got engaged to one of our OR nurses, but soon after he left country at the end of his tour, she hocked the ring and became engaged to a very nice, young enlisted guy. (Excuse me for wandering off the subject, but their stories were memorable.)

Our first patient this evening was a sergeant major who had been pulled from the flaming NCO barracks. He had multiple second- and first-degree burns on his upper torso, face, and thighs and had strands of skin hanging from his forearms. He also had a few superficial frag wounds from a satchel charge. It appeared that he had been very fortunate, as his hooch was hit with satchel charges and a rocket, and after collapsing, it had burned to the ground. After he was worked up (thoroughly examined) and his burns crudely debrided (dead tissue and debris removed down to viable, living, perfused tissue) and carefully dressed, our chaplain chatted with him at his bedside. They were very good friends, and the sergeant major attended his Mass every week.

After a short while, the chaplain came and told us that the sergeant major had said that he had some pain in his jaw and his left shoulder. We brought him back to triage and found him pale and diaphoretic (sweaty). He seemed very anxious and fearful. It was not his nature at all. We immediately suspected heart problems and did an EKG, which confirmed a posterior-wall ischemic heart event was taking place. We had no monitors or any type of clot-buster back then. I don't recall if aspirin was used as a deterrent to clotting in 1969.

Our anesthesia nurse, Ken, was not yet predisposed, as we had not yet taken in any casualties needing the OR. He dragged out a relic of an oscilloscope that he had as a backup to the one he actually used in OR. It simply gave a green EKG pattern going across an oval screen as big as a grapefruit, and once the tracing was gone, you couldn't bring it back to examine it or keep any kind of record on the machine. We were in a pathetic dilemma. We had a field hospital with very little equipment, a medical and trauma victim who happened to be someone we all knew and respected, and in the midst of a mortar, rocket, and sapper attack, that was all less than ideal.

Capt. S., one of our super combo medical docs who also spent a lot of time at the surgical table, was current and up to date on treating myocardial infarctions and more or less took over the care. He was already in contact with the Sixty-Seventh Evac Hospital in Qui Nhon, planning a transfer. The decision on the transportation was mind-boggling. The sergeant major, even though a seasoned veteran of the Korean War with combat nerves of steel, was a very emotional, supersensitive Hispanic gentleman who wept inside for every patient he had contact with. At times, he would weep over a whiskey and water while talking about his family back home and relate how much he looked forward to retiring from the army, just several months ahead.

With all of this considered, we struggled with whether a heart-thumping chopper ride at truck-top level through the An Khe Pass in the middle of a rocket-and-mortar attack was better than being in the back of a slow-moving ambulance bumping through the Pass, again with heavy enemy activity all around it. The medevac chopper won flat out. CWO Bill and his copilot had just come in with a GSW of the right hand and had plenty of fuel for a fast trip too Qui Nhon.

Capt. S. stabilized our patient with a load of morphine and a touch of phenobarbital for the nerves and climbed aboard with him in the chopper. The doctor and sergeant major were a little stunned that they were lifting off with both rear doors open, but the choppers nearly always flew with the side doors open, keeping the target as small as possible. Off they went, and thirty minutes later, we received notice that they had arrived safely without incident. In another hour, Capt. S. was back in the ER, up to his ass in trauma patients from the attack on Camp Radcliff and the Seventeenth.

Gradually, more and more patients were showing up in the ER, most with minor wounds, scrapes, and burns suffered from the attack on their quarters. A group of MPs were coming down the road in front of the ER with some of the female nurses (MPs guarded the female barracks 24-7 against the enemy and amorous intrusion by male Seventeenth members) when, just then, a mortar round struck dead center in the middle of one of the few remaining NCO billets. The MPs double-timed the nurses to the ER Quonset, almost dragging them by the wrists.

Just two of the nurses were wounded, and the remainder were in a state of fear and disbelief as their contingent had only been in country and at the Seventeenth for less than two weeks. Less than a month in country, and already you're nearly blown out of your bunk by mortars and rockets? Not a good start for the next three-hundred-plus days. The male contingent of the Seventeenth had hardly even made acquaintance with any of the female nurses. The assignments always seemed to void any social time, and the CO made it clear that the nurses would be off-limits for friendly visits and the like for at least thirty days. Duty assignments kept them quite segregated on certain ward units so that gradual integration could take place.

I believe the CO felt the policy was critical to the women's survival because all the males greeted each chopper and jeep that arrived with them with whoops, hollers, and cheers. Most of us had not seen a round-eyed woman in months. I thought the CO's rule was silly at the time, but I now understand the sage position he chose. He wanted the women who came into this shithole of a place in this shithole of a country to create bonds with each other before being ogled, fondled, and overwhelmed by the males of the Seventeenth. Since it was in the midst of extremely heavy activity with red alerts nearly every night and high patient loads on both shifts, contact between the sexes was incidental at best.

The first nurse we saw, Jackie, had taken a header coming out of her hooch and had a large abrasion on her forehead and scraped elbows. A more serious insult to Jackie was the direct mortar hit on her used, brightly blue-painted refrigerator for which she had shelled out about $200 just days before. These small fridges were like gold, and we were lucky to get one at any price. Her wounds were cleansed, antibiotic was administered in the form of an ungodly amount of penicillin, and her forehead was dressed with a head bandage resembling that of the flutist in the Revolutionary War painting.

Jackie was escorted to the bunker along with Major J., a large woman who, on of all nights, chose to wear a pink, diaphanous nightie that left little to the imagination—and she had a lot! To this day, I tend to hysterical laughter imagining the five-foot-two-inch woman of about two hundred pounds wearing a pink, see-through nightgown, a steel pot (helmet) on her head, a flak jacket, and jungle boots. Put that in your mind, and tell me you don't chuckle at least a bit.

The other nurse wounded arrived in ER with several fragment wounds from a mortar that had hit the concrete in front of her as she was exiting through the open courtyard of her barracks. Lt. Carole DeCovich said that she was awakened from a deep sleep by the sound of explosions. The MPs had been shouting, *"Get out! Get out now!"* She said that she had rolled out of her bunk in a fog and grabbed her pants and fatigue shirt, her helmet, and flak jacket, and ran out of her room into the open, concrete courtyard toward the only exit in the fenced and gated compound. Just as she had entered the area, a mortar came slamming into the courtyard, exploding several yards in front of her.

Actual Impact Photo of Rocket that Wounded Lt. DeCovich

The concrete had splattered in all directions along with the metal shrapnel of the mortar. She had sustained wounds on her face below the eye, on her forehead, and a few puncture wounds on her chest and abdomen. The MPs had recovered her and led her down the hill to the ER, where she was quickly triaged and rushed off to X-ray to determine the location of the fragments, as no exit wounds were found. Miraculously, none of the wounds had penetrated deeply, and by procedural routine, the docs began removing those that were close to the surface and opening the deeper ones to allow drainage and prevent infection.

We had all learned that everything that penetrated the skin was likely to cause infection, so we treated all wounds at the onset as if they were already infected. Open them up wide, scrub them out with Betadine, leave open for three days of observation and antibiotics, and cautiously do delayed closure on the deeper ones, letting the superficial ones granulate in (scab over and heal). All received huge doses of IV penicillin in the millions of units as well as plenty of IV fluids and lots of attention.

On completion of the nurse's care, she was taken by stretcher to one of the patient bunkers, as we were still under red alert. To this day, Carole remembers little from the time of the explosion to the point she found herself in the bunker after her ER care. She spent that night in the bunker in the company of Johnny Bench, catcher for the Cincinnati Reds, who happened to be in An Khe with several other celebs with a USO tour that was entertaining at another compound. After the attack took place and all the celebs were gathered up, they were hurried to various unit bunkers that had space available. The whole process was quite organized and effective, and all who needed shelter were housed in an orderly fashion. To this day, I kid my wife, Carole, that she spent the night after our first date shacked up with Johnny Bench in a bunker, and it still tends to tick me off a little.

November 15 was my first blind date with Carole, and our next five months were exclusively about getting to know each other. It didn't take nearly that long, however, for us to make a life decision. We each had R and

R coming, so we traveled to Hong Kong, where we formalized our engagement to be married. Chaplain Liteky pressured us on nearly a daily basis to allow him to marry us in front of our Seventeenth Field Hospital family, but I was certain Carole's parents would not think well of it, so we declined. We celebrated our forty-fourth wedding anniversary in October 2014.

First Lt. Carole Ann DeCovich
Wounded by Mortar and Rocket Fire, 15NOV69

As more of our personnel clambered from their destroyed hooches, rescuing their bunkmates, and encountering an ongoing assault by the sappers, our vulnerability soon became evident. At first, we really had no idea how much damage had been done to our compound, how many of our patient-care areas were still usable, and how much of our blood store had been destroyed. Our best information for several hours was just word of mouth from folks who had seen or heard about something elsewhere in the compound.

Our CO kept a careful mental log of all that was reported damaged or destroyed. With no lights in the compound except some emergency, low-level lighting inside the Quonsets and on generators for the OR, it was an eerie, unreal, scary environment. We quickly realized that any defense for our hospital unit would have to come from us. Medical-unit personnel were not usually trained to perform maneuvers that combat units would have to make. Other than with the help of a few hard stripe sergeants and a couple of captains and lieutenants that were MSC, the medical officers were in charge of the whole show. We would have to use common sense and prudence, carrying out our medical roles while also safeguarding those we cared for, those who worked with us, and, most important, ourselves! It was the only time I can remember in a hospital setting that I did triage, dressed wounds, and started IVs with an M16 slung over my shoulder.

After a considerable period, we once again heard the familiar *brrrrrrrbrrrrrrrrrr* bursts in the near distance from the mini-guns of the Cobras mixed in with small-arms fire and an occasional *woomph* from a mortar or rocket. Tiny, little parachutes that floated illumination flares lay all over the place, and some remained lit as they drifted in with the breeze toward our Quonset. We quickly posted someone at our ordnance bunker just outside the ER to assure none of the flaming drifters found their way into the highly explosive storage of weapons and ammunition.

News of the events from the rest of the camp was somewhat like hearing about what had happened in a different country. No bit of information was related to or associated with the last, like news about a large disaster affecting several different cities. We considered ourselves far downstream of good information. The rivers upstream were receiving lots and lots of rain, and as they swelled into larger torrents, the information they brought became more confusing and unreliable. From what we gathered, after report after report on the damage, the destruction had been widespread and included many of the units at Radcliff, including several helicopters.

After expending a huge amount of concern and a good part of your energy on the good people of your own unit and everyone's safety, your mind begins to connect it with forthcoming misery and death. You have been in that position before, and, after seemingly endless hours, you feel genuinely guilty for just wanting to go to sleep.

For many hours, the carts and stretchers were full with two or three patients each waiting to vacate. Triage was vital and stressful. Most of the wounds were superficial, like frag wounds that needed to be opened and small lacerations that needed irrigation and scrubbing down. However, there were several serious cavity-penetrating wounds needing exploration, some burn wounds, and a few fractures during the first several hours, but all were handled smoothly.

As the hours rolled on, during short idle periods, I thought about how easy it was to focus selfishly on oneself. In such a restricted, confined, dangerous area about the size of five football fields, many emotions slid in if you let them. Fortunately, they vanished as soon as the switch was flipped and the adrenaline started pumping. Some in our midst struggled with considerable issues, mostly outside of our unit but not all. There was excessive use of alcohol and sometimes weed, and much worse, some of the heavy hitters used LSD, morphine, heroin, or benota.

The very worst effect of this was explosive behavior erupting without warning from normally quiet, controlled individuals; that happened fairly frequently, especially when alcohol was used to top off the other substances. These folks were almost always armed, so these events were not considered minor, and occasionally, serious wounds were inflicted. Several required transfer to a more tranquil, social location with environments more similar to that back home, while some were sent to Long Bien Jail (LBJ) if they behaviors had tipped the scales. When I saw these experiments in the human psyche, it made me think of the very different ways everyone carried their burdens. Unfortunately, I apparently did not discover the best way myself.

Years later, fictitious trips back to that place haunt me with a cold sweat in the middle of the night, and I tremble at just the thought of it. This dream that I am back there and must endure all of those things over again visits me too frequently to this day.

When we realized that we were a party to the happenings only at the little camp at the base of Hon Cong Mountain and that hundreds of similar events were occurring not only in Camp Radcliff but all over the Central Highlands and Vietnam, we felt an overwhelming sense of futility. It captured and restrained us until we overcame it by recognizing our importance in that place and the roles we played. All that we experienced, good and bad, became a permanent part of each of our lives, making each of our existences unique.

Existence is purpose, and purpose is born out of necessity, and there has never been a scarcity of necessity—not then, and not now. I realized, much later than I wish I had, that I was a very small part of a huge plan, yet my part in caring for the wounded made a monumental difference to hundreds of GIs, each one at a time and place of his or her greatest need.

I recall, in the midst of the very height of activity inside and outside the ER, we were visited by the CO of the Fourth Infantry Division. He strolled down the concrete aisle of the ER, nodding to everyone and giving a huge smile of approval in spite of all the carnage he was seeing. Most patients were his own men of the Fourth. With his troops spread all over An Khe and the Central Highlands, his responsibilities were huge, but after having a brief chat with our CO, he moved on to some of the patient bunkers to give his best to others who were wounded.

On his way back through the ER, he praised everybody for taking on the huge responsibility of continuing the full services of a field hospital while providing our own security. He thanked us and said that he was sending a couple of squads to our compound to relieve us of the latter duty. He said, "I just can't believe it. Your caring for the wounded, many that are your own, your buildings under attack and in flames, and you have the awareness on top of all of this to assure your own safety. I just can't believe it."

NCO barracks. One Died as a Result of Wounds.

NCO and Enlisted Barracks, Destroyed 15NOV69

I didn't realize the importance of that brief visit until forty-two years later when I was researching matters for this book that my senility had permitted to go adrift. I found that the CO of the Fourth Infantry had been very instrumental in recommending the Seventeenth Field Hospital for the Presidential Unit Citation for its performance while under attack and suffering considerable material and manpower damage.

I stumbled upon some thirty pages of the recommendation that was finally rejected in 1972, three years after the actual event and long after all of our unit had left the country. A few numbers didn't match regarding the WIAs and KIAs and the size of the enemy force as reported by our commander and several other unit commanders' mission-activity reports. By 1972, no one was left in Vietnam to answer for the discrepancies. Once microfilmed and declassified, it became public record. Unfortunately, the award appears to have been denied based on the very issue I mentioned earlier—the ability to report an event reliably when information is communicated from the vantage points of many different storytellers.

See:
(Appendix A for a copy of the DOD report (declassified))
(Appendix B for official recommendation for Presidential Unit Citation for Seventeenth Field Hospital)
(Appendix C for Map of Sapper Intrusion on the Seventeenth Field Hospital)

NCO and Nurses' Quarters, Seventeenth Field Hospital,
Destroyed by Mortars, Rockets, and Sappers on 15NOV69

Billy

—∿—

I VIVIDLY RECALL A YOUNG man by the name of Billy. He was burned over 80 percent of his body when a large pool of JP4 helicopter fuel leaked in an area where he had decided to rest and have a smoke. One flick of the Zippo, and his life changed forever. Billy was brought to us with all of his clothes burned off him and with long strips of skin hanging from the muscles of his arms and legs. He was a mass of second- and third-degree burns, with first-degree burns in most other places.

A burn that encompasses 80 percent is nearly always fatal. It takes extreme vigilance and determination just to keep up on the right type and amount of fluids to replace. Any breach in technique lending to infection could have sent Billy home in a body bag. A lot of attention also had to be given to a major complication of severe burns: gastrointestinal stress bleeding, more commonly known as stress ulcers. This medical complication was substantiated after studies of the high number of severe burns seen in Vietnam compared to complications encountered in their recovery. A lot of new medical technology resulted. Billy had even less chance of survival because of moderate obesity, nicotine addiction, and the fact that the filth of Vietnam had already imbedded itself in his open flesh.

The first order of business was to get adequate IV access to the tune of three sixteen-gauge intracaths. In Billy's case, this involved two antecubital cut downs to access large venous sites and one jugular IV access. After fluids were started, his pain was addressed with morphine and the cooling down of the burn areas with sterile normal saline (NS). Blood and fresh plasma were administered according to a formula calculated on his body weight, extent of burns, and other factors. The formula was developed at Brooke Army Medical Center in San Antonio, Texas, and appropriately called the "Brooke formula." It remained the standard in military and civilian life for many decades thereafter.

After hours of fluid therapy and pain control, antibiotic administration, tetanus booster, and positioning, Billy was prepared for the OR, where his burn wounds would be debrided and our wonder drug, Silvadene (sulfamyalone) cream, could be applied without pain. Bulky, protective burn dressings were applied over the cream, necessitating lengthy dressing-change sessions two to three times per day.

Upon Billy's return from OR, he was placed in the cleanest, least accessed area we could find in the intensive-care unit. For two weeks, Billy received the attention and care of our staff with the determination that he would make it back to the burn center at Brooke in San Antonio with a better than 50 percent chance of survival. We were able to keep our promise to Billy through meticulous fluid and pain management as well as the highest level of sterile technique outside of the OR that I had ever witnessed in Vietnam.

Even the slightest breeze coming through the doors on either end of the Quonset huts carried red dust laced with bad organisms, the most feared being the gram-negative Satan of burn management that proliferates in the soil from human and animal waste. There were no sanitation systems in the whole country, and we established a stringent routine for each dressing change. It involved closing all of the doors and limiting human presence to the two caregivers changing the dressing and one to care for the remaining two or three patients at the opposite end of the intensive-care area.

The caregivers would gown in sterile paper gowns, masks, gloves, and caps before the two-hour procedure. Even though heat, lack of ventilation, and the production of quarts of sweat were at times nearly overwhelming, some of the best jokes were shared during those two hours. Unfortunately, I can't remember a one! Every couple of days, Billy would be taken back to the OR for more debridement and a super dressing change under sedation.

On the fifteenth day following Billy's injuries, we all gathered at his bedside as he was awarded his Purple Heart. After the ceremony, we prepared him for his trip to Saigon, where he would then be prepared for the long trip to Japan and finally his DEROS trip to Brooke in San Antonio. As we loaded his stretcher onto the Huey, all of his caregivers from the Seventeenth gave him applause and saluted his strength and willpower.

Bill, our helicopter pilot, started up the engines for our transfer to Saigon, and I attended Billy on the trip. We spoke little, as it was nearly impossible to hear anything with the turbine engine whining and the *wump, wump, wump* of the rotors. We shared a special friendship and respect for each other and didn't really need to speak anyway. Billy was one tough dude, and he had endured a ton of misery, but through it all and during the tough times, we would smile at each other and the connection was there. I left him in Saigon in the care of the burn staff and really didn't expect to hear of him again. We rarely got reports on any of those evacuated out.

A month later, as we were finishing up another grueling day with multiple casualties and a full hospital requiring evacuation of some of our more stable patients to Qui Nhon, our communication operator, who ordered up our choppers to transport patients, came to let us know the ETA of our birds and casually said, "By the way, I heard through division that the burn guy you guys sent to Brooke died. He was doing well but suddenly had a stress bleed that required a bunch of blood. He developed DIC, and they couldn't keep up with the loss and he bled to death. Sorry, boss." We were crushed. We wondered about the number of our patients who actually recovered after our care, their future care, and then their convalescence. We rarely got the end of the story.

It was a dark day at the Seventeenth, and we all worked six or seven hours over our designated shifts to catch up and try to understand the seemingly cruel nature of it all. Diversion would help heal our personal wounds and mend our minds until it was safe to numb them with alcohol. Even after the extra-long day, lots of adrenaline was left over, and sleep that night was impossible as I remembered the frightened, innocent, schoolboy look in Billy's eyes as we flew to Saigon. *This war is fucked! I don't want to do this anymore.*

Steak and STD

—ɯ—

ANOTHER OF THE MOST BEAUTIFUL sunsets imaginable, and at 1900 I was imagining tasting not only the thick T-bone steak and a Black Jack on the rocks but looking forward to a couple of hours with my fiancée, Carole, at our makeshift O club. Our O club was nothing fancy, nothing like I had known at Walter Reed or at Fort Sam Houston. It was just a bunch of salvaged lumber and some tin thrown together over a discarded BBQ pit. It was built and left un-demolished by the First Cav. when they were here in An Khe. It meant the world to most of us.

Chow time was frequently inaccessible or, at best, interrupted when we were on duty in triage and urgent care. Our meals cost only a few hundred piasters, less than a few bucks, at the club and were the highlight of the day. Another drawing card of the open-air club was the fact that our unit chaplain, a Medal of Honor recipient on his second tour in Vietnam, was responsible for the special food there. He had a gold card of sorts for acquiring food on barter and trade with some navy officers. Through the spread of his good and godly word to other units by invitation, he had befriended some navy cooks while serving in Qui Nhon. He had impressed them so much that they established a year-long supply and delivery system of T-bone steak and shrimp. What did he barter? Clap cards.

Turns out, in time of war, three visits to the infirmary for a load of penicillin for clap (GC) got you three punches on your "clap card" and some disciplinary action leading up to an Article 15. The same trouble arose if you were seen at sick call with three episodes of sunburn or being too drunk or too drugged-up to do your job. Odd association, but the army needs to preserve the fighting strength, and if you are tearing limbs off trees while pissing because of pain or can't wear your fatigue shirt because of sunburn, you're not much good to Uncle Sam, and you had best not get drunk to forget about it. It could cost you money and rank. Unmarked cards were like gold in Vietnam, and the chaplain, in a respectable, Christian manner, helped himself to blank ones from the medication cabinet on a regular basis. No one ever muttered a hint about this—not even our CO. He loved steak too!

For the seven months I had spent to date in Vietnam, I felt guilt on many occasions. Most of it was prompted by the frightened gazes and unbelieving faces of those I and others had failed. I also felt guilt for sampling the local economy and its special offerings downtown for a mere handful of pocket change in piasters, but I never did feel guilty about the wonderful food at the O club. As one of my two best experiences there, I ate T-bone steak, cooked to medium-rare perfection, as often as I wished. Occasionally, there would be a side of shrimp of a size I have not seen since, and the choice of a huge baked potato slathered in sour cream and chives or a huge pile of French fries done just right.

Just as my steak came off the grill, I could feel the vibrations of the rotors as they chopped out their space in the air. The pink evening sky now punctuated with the red and green lights on each of the three dust-off choppers seemed out of place in the peace and quiet we had enjoyed just minutes earlier. Shortly, the clerk came trotting across the street from the communication shack with news of five WIAs and one KIA.

I carved a huge triangle of the wonderful beef, crammed it in my mouth, and worked on it like chewing tobacco as I ran to the care area and began setting up the stretchers and care equipment at each workstation. The CO waltzed in to check out our situation, and upon seeing him, I bent over like I was picking something off the floor so I could keep relishing the three ounces of beef in my mouth. He just nodded to me in his familiar, assured way as he walked by. He left in as little time as it took me to swallow my steak.

I had assigned three stretchers to each medic and three urgent stretchers each to an RN. The triage doc and I would first see the patients as they entered the ER while getting a quick report from the field triage tags and the dust-off medic. We would do a quick visual and assign our own triage categories while a designated recorder wrote down all we told him or her as we worked through the exam. It was a great system for dealing with the number seen today, but in a mass-casualty situation, we would need three or four times the staff, pulling medical people from the other care areas. The lab tech would be summoned to collect the one or two tubes of blood we would draw upon starting the intravenous.

We rarely did a lot of lab right away during multiple-casualty situations. What we were really interested in was a baseline hemoglobin/hematocrit (H/H) to compare with a later one after we had replaced some fluid or blood. At times, we would get a chemistry profile if the wound was massive, the patient had burns, or problems were expected later on.

We did not cross-match blood. Most times, we just used type O. The need rose to 30,000 units a month in 1968 and 38,000 a month in 1969[xi]. From 1966-1970, 1,087,994 units of blood were made available[xii], and it was treated like gold. As valuable as it was, there was about a 30-50 percent wastage rate, and over 600,000 of those considered wasted by military standards were used in the treatment and benefit of Vietnamese (ARVN) soldiers and a small number of civilians. The blood was perfectly good but was close to expiration[xiii] and could not be sent countrywide due to its remaining, short life span. Real wastage was due to obvious wartime complications such as heat, transportation, storage, and weaponry damage.

X-rays were done stat for head and neck and chest injuries as well as a handful of others, such as a pelvic injury with massive bleeding or cavity entry wounds without exit wounds. It's not that all of these diagnostics would not be done later on a timely basis; it's just that in mass-casualty situations, you cannot physically do all of these things at once in a small field hospital the size of ours. It is much more efficient to provide minimally required emergent care and then send the patients to the urgent area where chest tubes, more permanent airways, catheters, and whatever other life-preserving medical equipment could be provided.

Amazingly, statistics proved that if patients arrived alive at a field hospital following a traumatic wound, their chances of survival were about 80 percent. Our record at the Seventeenth was over 90 percent—and we counted all patients, even if the chaplain was giving last rites as the dust-off chopper medic was bringing the patient through the door. That means that we were 10 percent imperfect.

That 10 percent remains uppermost in your mind forever. It awakens you from sleep forty-five years later or deafens you in the middle of a conversation when something said vaguely reminds you of it and the memories pop into your head. You frequently see the faces of that 10 percent and feel the grip of their hands as you stood with them at the litter and looked into their tired, tearful eyes as they asked you for permission to die. It seemed many times, if they were to die, that they did so more peacefully if you told them it was OK to go. Sometimes, they would apologize for dying, wasting their last breaths on their caregiver: "I'm sorry, Doc."

As the pain of the body and the agony of the mind defeated the fear and they went on to the peacefulness and stillness of death, you many times wished that you could go with them. You suddenly felt like the "sin eater" of the Dark Ages who was hired to come and feast on a wonderfully prepared meal served on a corpse, supposedly assuming all of his sin soaked up with the food. But that sin was to remain within you forever, and you would never be worthy of passage through the pearly gates.

Once you assume a part of the consequence of death, then what? That remains the question. Then what? There seemed to be no limit to the amount of misery and agony offered and needing to be shared and absorbed in wartime. The understanding remains very sketchy of what happens to all of those toxins once taken in, digested, and circulated through one's body and mind over the course of several years. One thing is for sure: the outcome is never good. It stays with you and becomes a part of you. Little or nothing can block it from your mind. That's the way it is. For all of those wonderful young men and women whom you touched with a helping hand, you become aware that in the course of their long migration home and to healing, they must overcome many obstacles, and each could die if there is just the slightest complication. Those already dead kind of had it made. Their anticipation and fierce, frightful emotions climaxed quickly, and that was it. It is then your pain to own and remember.

From day one, standing on that cement floor in the triage area of the ER, I thought that as time went on, all of this would become much easier as the routines became established and I became seasoned to the absolutely horrific, unimaginable trauma and the extremes of human emotion. As I waited for the latest flurry of patients, I felt no different and admitted to myself that I really didn't have the answers even yet. I wondered what the fuck was in store for me today and if I would be able to do it.

Coming closer, they get louder and louder. The drone of giant bumblebees overtakes all other sounds as they line up to set down with their precious cargo. Zero hour has arrived.

A Reluctant Servant

—∞—

IN THE BIBLE, ANANIAS WAS a disciple who was directed to travel and meet Saul, who had history of jailing and sometimes killing Christians. Ananias was hesitant, realizing his low stature and weakness compared to a powerful and hate-filled man like Saul, whom God had caused to be blind as punishment for his sins. A reluctant Ananias traveled a long distance and met Saul with great fear in his heart: ACTS 9: 17-18

9: 17 *"And Ananias went his way, and entered into the house; and putting his hands on him said, Brother Saul, the Lord, even Jesus, that appeared unto thee in the way as thou camest, hath sent me, that thou mightest receive thy sight, and be filled with the Holy Ghost."*

9: 18 *"And immediately there fell from his eyes as it had been scales: and he received sight forthwith, and arose, and was baptized."*

Acts 9,17-18 King James Version (KJV)

Ananias as the Reluctant Servant overcame his fear and went forth to give new life, even to his enemy.

—∞—

When dust-off visited us with special cargo, everyone felt it and hated it and loved it simultaneously. We got an empty, jittery feeling in our guts that most times made us want to vomit, but we knew we couldn't do that. A whole lot was expected of everybody—the medics, the docs, the lab guy, the x-ray guy, and even the cook. When you finally admit that you must stay and be a part of whatever carnage is coming to you, you embark on the highest of highs, adrenaline pumping, your heart at a hundred-plus, and your brain on full alert.

This must be the part that you love—but the chemical that enables you and somehow provides the ability to function at the highest level is the same one that leaves you empty and feeling guilty when it ceases to flow. Deep within your soul, you love this high but won't admit it because of all the gore that accompanies it. Mangled legs and arms hanging by a tendon or bloody piece of flesh; tiny or gaping entrance and exit wounds, so important to identify; missing fingers, ears, noses, feet, eyes, skin, brain matter—all candidates for the horror you label as the worst ever, until the next time you hear the *wump, wump, wump,* and then it's the start of a whole new game with anything possible. Will you do everything right? Will this be the one that tops them all? Will the "special chemical" be enough?

The first bird set down on the helipad like a butterfly on a delicate flower. The pilots, WO Bill and WO Don, were assigned permanent dust-off for the Seventeenth, and they were part of our family. Bill, in fact, became engaged to one of our superstar OR nurses. I'm sad not to know how that romance turned out, as I left country before the final act. This was so frequently the case in Vietnam, not ever knowing the end of the stories, actions—or anything, for that matter. When you left, you were gone, no longer part of the whole, and all went on without you. You went home with horrendous memories and experiences needing to be told. Not going to happen back in the world!

Mass casualties may be summed up in a couple of words: organized chaos. The ingredients are an overwhelming number of young bodies with wounds of varying severity coming at the same time into a very small arena, all requiring meticulous examination within a very short time. Each one's proper place in the queue must be assured; any error, and the gravest of consequences are probable. Add to this the limited availability of caregivers, who themselves are at the height of emotional and physical exhaustion, and things can get up tight very quickly.

Such an event often repeats several times a day, with the days running into weeks. Chaos is easily achieved and difficult to curtail. We learned very early on, however, that feelings of inadequacy and a loss of control sneaking in spoiled our "fixes." It was the job of the triage doc and nurse and the CO to keep the emotions functional. Their close observation of the caregivers assured us that we would receive this vital emotional support. We had learned that little things, such as sending us on short errands to get more blood, providing us with cold drinking water, or something just to get us the hell out of there for a bit, meant everything in keeping our resources effective.

The most overwhelming and defeating emotion during mass casualties, however, was the deep, unrelenting sense that we had an impossible task under even the best of circumstances. No matter what we did or how we did it, the workload escalated. You can't imagine that anyone endured it before you and neither could anyone survive it after you, but they have, and they will. Then, as you are so absorbed with the environment and the needs surrounding you that you are on auto pilot with your senses shut down, a sudden realization finally occurs that it's over. One more episode in your purpose on earth has been fulfilled; yet soon, another new group of awestruck young men with new problems and needs emerges so quickly that solace and satisfaction is never granted. Sleep won't fix it; alcohol and weed might fix it briefly. But the restless, gnawing feeling never goes away as you wait for the worst day of your life.

At a field-grade hospital, our surgeries were, for the most part, palliative, quick, with the intention of saving life and limb. Field-hospital surgeries gained the nickname "meatball surgery," which kind of demeaned the miracles that were performed several times over. No neat, little suture lines—many times, the wound was left open with just a few retention sutures to keep things from spilling out during the next chopper ride.

The ABCs, then stop the bleeding, and then assess for more aggressive intervention while replacing all of the red stuff that splashed under our boots onto the cement floor and running down little chiseled channels there just for that purpose. How clever, yet so morbid and sick that someone had thought of that. Some got saline, some got plasma, some got albumen, some got blood: all was determined by what was available and the degree of the wound. Many requiring intubation (a tube placed in the trachea for breathing) then needed continuous attendance, as there were no respirators or monitors, just hands and minds.

Some of the caregivers became very adept with the Ambu bags (bags used to breathe for patients with artificial airways) and could do two patients at a time by placing the stretchers just so, allowing each hand to attend a patient. All the time, the chaplain made his rounds among the misery. He healed in his own special way and "sends on" those who are ultimately healed and do not have to fear injury or pain again. He quietly gives his support and his trust in what we are providing, and his presence is monumental to our efforts.

Most of the doctors are now gone off to the OR to do the magic that is only seen in wartime, and you realize that all of those coming in fresh will be yours alone for some time. I had been taught how to deal with all of this. Mentally and physically exhausted, I dozed standing up and worried that this would all happen again too soon. Would I succumb to this miserable, goddamned place that was thick with bugs and rancid with the smell of sewage and decaying flesh? I wondered if this was real or if it was hell or a vision of the hell that had been planned for me. Maybe it would be better tomorrow. Tomorrow is yesterday and today is tomorrow; it's all immaterial. There are 365 days, and you spend every fucking one of them in fear for yourself and for what you must do for others.

Patient one: an eighteen-year-old, blond E-2 grunt (foot or ground soldier) who was ten feet to the right of the point man when the point stepped on the mine. His name was Charles, kind of a dirty word in Country, but amusing under more innocent circumstances. Charles, Chuck, Charlie and Victor Charlie were some of the nicknames we used for the Vietcong.

Charles had been in country for ten days and had been assigned to the Fourth Infantry Division just three days earlier. This was his first patrol. His new acquaintance, Howie, someone he admired and looked up to, was brought onto the stretcher beside him. As Charles turned his head to greet his admired comrade, he gagged and twisted away, nearly falling off the stretcher. The corpsman immediately separates them, and Charles's attention is diverted toward his own wounds.

A complete trauma survey was quickly completed. Charles's most serious injury was a missing left foot just above the ankle. The jagged, yellow-white end of the tibia could be seen peeking out of the bulky, hastily applied dressing from the field along with a temporary tourniquet to stem the blood flow. The dressing was filthy with orange dirt washed into the air and onto the dressing by the rotor. The filth clung to the oozing blood like a magnet on the outside of the dressing, but the bleeding, for the most part, had ceased and was under control.

Vital signs were initially stable, even though not reliable given the psychological horror that this young man had just experienced. The BP, pulse, and respirations were checked, along with the nail beds for blanch, color, and refill rate in the remaining extremities, providing at least temporary comfort that the wounds were well managed and under control. His vital signs would be checked frequently when he moved to the next level of care.

The wounded patient usually has an aura of combined excitement, fear, and disgust. The absence of those emotions really worried us. Charles appeared to be appropriate to his situation, and he was given "yellow, delayed" status. "Delayed" patients received much attention throughout their stay while awaiting their turn for the OR and would suffer no adverse results if care was not immediate. Charles's info was recorded, and he was assigned to one of the stretchers in the "delayed" area manned by one of our premier medics.

The specialist and I had worked together many times under varying conditions, and we trusted each other without question. As Charles was wheeled by, he gestured by wiping his arm across his forehead and muttering, "Whew, I am so goddamned lucky. Thanks, Doc!" And his foot was gone!

Patient two: Howie, E-4, a blond, twenty-one-year-old redneck from Ocala, Florida. He had been the point man because he was the most experienced of his bunch, having been in country for about ten months. We know all of this because his buddy had told us. Howie would not spend another day alive in Vietnam. Howie showed no signs of life, and the cold fingers of his remaining left hand were stiffening. No apical pulse, no breathing. His right arm had been taken at the shoulder, with bits of his camo uniform twisted into tatters among stringy pieces of muscle, vessels, and cartilage. Blood was no longer dripping from any of the wounds. His left arm was yet attached, but a large portion of muscle and bone were missing below the shoulder, giving the arm a rag doll-like character.

The yellow marrow draining from the humerus had pooled on the stretcher. Both legs were gone, the left just above the knee, with the remaining upper leg peppered with shrapnel and frag wounds. The right leg was gone completely at the hip, leaving a large crater in the pelvis that exposed the large, white bone of the pelvic ridge under the high-power exam light. Bowel contents and urine ran out of the open wound onto the stretcher, over the edge, splashing onto my boots and onto the etched, concrete floor. The stench was horrific. I can relate the smell to nothing as bad or worse, not even that in Morrison's barn so many years ago when they had let the cow shit pile up in the rear concrete troughs for days and the cows urinated onto the shit, making a horrid stench that twisted at your stomach.

Yes, Vietnam was the worst. It was like nothing else on earth that one could envision. There, the human body was at its lowest state whether dead or living. Your own humility and sense of being nothing is amplified, as you can't imagine anything more horrific and repulsive happening to a human being. Thank God only "we" saw it. *Try to get over the shame for being horrified and repulsed, for God's sake. You are the caregiver and the only living savior in the eyes of these young men. They have given up on God for now because they have seen so much today. Their faith is now in you because you are there, and they have heard that you have created miracles. But you know that you are going to fail at this one.*

The chaplain was beside me quickly. He was always able to sort out those who needed him the most. With just a nod from me, he filled out the triage tag with Howie's name and other info off his dog tags and wheeled the stretcher back to the curtained-off area. The "black, expectant" area was the final stop on the journey for the KIA, those we had failed. We would not see the blond, blue-eyed features of Howie again.

Patient three: a twenty-year-old black male E-3, assigned to the .60-cal. Multiple small-fragment wounds to the lower extremities. Bleeding controlled. Vital signs had been stable since dust-off had taken over his care. Capillary refill and blanch was positive, and he was alert and talkative. We had stripped him down to the waist and found no wounds. We had opened his fatigues and searched his buttocks and privates and upper legs and found no wounds.

He begged us not to cut off his fatigues, as he had just gotten them broken in and said the new ones chafed the hell out of his balls and thighs. So that's what we did for him now. Even though the pants were peppered with ragged holes and they were blood soaked, we gently removed them in one piece and carefully examined his lower extremities. Minimal bleeding, good pulses, and no obvious broken bones were good signs. We tagged him "yellow, delayed" and congratulate him on his tremendous luck and his chances of spending some down time in Saigon at the evac hospital with all the round-eyed nurses, a soft bed, clean sheets, and three squares a day. He was elated and said, grinning, "Thanks, Doc."

Patient four: a nineteen-year-old Hispanic E-4 in his third month in Vietnam. Wounded in the firefight that ensued after Howie had stepped on the land mine. GSWs times two—abdomen and right chest. BP 88/40, HR 128, respiration 26, shallow and labored; paradoxical chest movements, abdomen distended and firm. Nail beds pale, blanch over three seconds. Awake and oriented, screaming, "Don't let me die!" Status: "red, immediate."

Emanuel was a young guy from Philadelphia. He had only four months left in his tour and was on a search-and-destroy mission with his platoon near An Khe in the Central Highlands. The day was hot, humid, and full of insects, and it had been boring until the last one or two clicks to the LZ where the slicks would pick him up with his team and return them to base camp for a fresh pair of socks, a dry bed, a decent meal, and a restful night of sleep.

His team had been approaching an old LZ partially re-canopied with new growth and came upon a wide stream that made a large horseshoe turn right in front of them. To stay on their heading, his platoon would have to either cross the stream twice or go a short distance to the east and around the stream altogether. Unfortunately, the platoon leader made the wrong choice. They went around the stream, and just as they reached the bend, the bush became very dense and visibility was minimal. As they squeezed through the gauntlet about ten meters wide, it brought the platoon into a tight group.

Just as though it had been planned, the point man, Howie, set off of a well-placed mine, and all hell broke loose. Milliseconds after the mine exploded, most of Howie was hurled airborne right onto one of his flanking men while some of his other parts scattered in the others' midst. As the team stood dumbstruck and repulsed for just a brief second, an RPG came spiraling out of the dense foliage just ahead of them, its tail smoke wobbling violently. It missed the entire team and slammed into the bush behind them, splintering pieces of bamboo, leaves, and dirt all over their area.

Machine-gun fire started up relentlessly from the front, and heavy small-arms fire was coming into their midst from the dense bush to their west. What a perfect ambush in a perfect funnel trap. What a perfect way to prevent a nineteen-year-old from returning to Philadelphia. Following three more RPG rounds that did no bodily harm and twenty minutes of small-arms fire, the RTO finally got through on the radio and requested close-in air support. In about ten minutes, a Loach and a Cobra gunship came sweeping in over the treetops, with the Cobra's mini-gun blazing at 6,000 rounds a minute, enough to cover every square foot of a football field.

The gooks were terrified of the mini-guns, and the course of a battle was often changed through their terrible destruction. The Cobra fired its rockets followed by another sweep with the mini-guns, and all became quiet for a moment until the pleas and moans arose from the grass around the unit's feet.

Emanuel wasn't going to die easily in this fucking place. The medic, Ed, was on him in seconds. A bulky wound dressing was placed over the pencil-sized hole with the dark, purple-black circle around it on the right upper quadrant of his abdomen. His bush jacket was opened, and his OD T-shirt, soaked with sweat and mixed with blood and dirt, was cut away to reveal another slightly larger hole midline, right chest, over the fifth rib. The area was gushing blood and bubbles, and Ed quickly placed a special chest-wound dressing and secured it with a handful of four-by-fours and hand pressure.

Seconds later, Emanuel became much worse, gasping for breath and choking and spitting up blood all over Ed's face. Ed, with his excellent training and experience (this was his third tour in Nam), knew the exact source of the problem and promptly removed the pressure and the four-by-fours. The chest dressing nearly blew off under the pressure, and Emanuel immediately improved. The bullet, or a fragment of a rib bone, had most likely severed or badly punctured a major air passage, a bronchial tube, or possibly even the bronchus. It more than likely had damaged a large area of lung, along with major lung vessels, allowing the air that Emanuel breathed in to build up an air pocket inside his right chest.

The pocket became larger with each breath, pressing on the remaining good lung and making it harder and harder to breathe. The wound not only prevented Emanuel from getting precious oxygen to his brain and heart, but the building pressure in his chest from the air and blood was pushing on the area separating his right and left lung (mediastinum). This reduced his lung capacity even more and prevented his heart from pumping properly.

Ed applied a small flutter dressing over the open puncture wound and tilted Emanuel just slightly over to the wounded side to make it easier for him to breathe. The dressing would keep blood from gushing, but when pressures got high enough inside the chest to cause problems, the dressing would flap open slightly to let out escaping air and blood.

Once the territory had been secured enough to move him, four of Emanuel's comrades had rotated turns taking Emanuel by fireman's carry to the LZ. It seemed an impossible task as they struggled ten to fifteen feet at a time through the tangle of grass and the hundred-plus degree heat and air infested with mosquitoes. Their noses and throats exhaled hot air in exhaustion and dehydration. They became aware of their own mortality through what they had just witnessed and what they carried.

Fear and anxiety turn to spontaneous exhaustion as soon as stressors are removed, the kind of exhaustion that renders the mind vulnerable and the soldier exposed to the elements in which he is trapped. Death witnessed in combat appears at times to be the peaceful solution, while the living wounded and unwounded are trapped in an unrelenting apocalypse of mental pain and deep suffering—suffering, it seems, that can be relieved by just running away. None of that was possible. Emanuel needed them to get him out of that fucking jungle.

So, Emanuel had been classified as "red, immediate." The chaplain gave him rites, standing beside him and calming him in the way that only a man of the cloth could do. The chaplain was a soldier's man. He was gentle, not pushy or driven in his spirituality, yet he gave counsel when needed. He offered God's word if asked and consoled without asking, regardless of the target's faith, and with a gentle, friendly touch.

He was just like any other regular, hard-drinking guy at the club. Most knew him just as "the chaplain." The CO called him Angelo.

His history ran deep; he had served two tours in Vietnam and then spent several years protesting the war back in the States after his tour with us. He actually served prison time for trespassing during an antiwar demonstration at Fort Benning, Georgia. Oh, did I mention he was awarded the Medal of Honor? Under heavy fire, he had rescued about twenty wounded men under the most extreme and dangerous circumstances, risking his own life and limb by repeatedly reentering the hot zone ("Indian Territory"), rescuing wounded soldiers. In spite of great danger to himself, he had been intent on saving the ground soldiers by carrying, dragging, and crawling on his back on elbows and heels, once with a man atop him, getting them back to the LZ that was also heavily under fire. In spite of wounds to the foot and leg, he continued this selfless rescue until the entire unit was cleared from the LZ.

The "immediate" triage category meant that if critical, urgent intervention was not exercised, death was imminent. The combat medic in the field had performed exceptionally well, and now it was our responsibility to make sure Emanuel returned to Philadelphia. The first order was to stabilize him sufficiently so that he could go to surgery and have a reasonable chance of survival.

Doc—Fritz—performed a double-chest-tube insertion into the right chest, one placed mid-right anterior to relieve all free air and one low lateral to drain blood, serosanguinous fluid, and wound debris. He expertly slipped the number-eleven blade between the ribs, which was followed by a whooshing sound like when you suck a sock up the vacuum hose. After the scalpel was withdrawn, he stuck his finger in the small slit and made it bigger and bigger, at which time he forced the number-twenty-four chest catheter through the hole with the help of the tip of the curved forceps.

The tube, once in the pleural space, was manipulated to acquire the best position, and once he was satisfied, he made several wraps of double-zero thread around the tube and through the skin, securing it to the chest. A Vaseline slit dressing was applied in each of three directions so that the wound was completely covered. A few four-by-fours topped with strips of four-inch tape provided protection from the filth.

The procedure was completed by securing the end of the chest tube to the skin with tape. Some doctors sewed them to the skin for an even better anchor, but Emanuel would be in surgery soon, and the tubes would be replaced there. Usually, the tube site would be secured with an elastic tape that covered a good portion of the chest area, and the tubing would be secured in a couple of places to prevent accidental movement or loss of the tube. This sounds excessive, but if the integrity is broken, you start back at square one, adding extra days to the patient's recovery and danger as well by creating a new pneumothorax.

With all of the moving necessary for these patients in and out of X-ray and in and out of bunkers during incoming red alerts on a near-nightly basis, and in and out of helicopters, no one wanted to deal with a badly placed chest tube. The second tube, a thirty-two, was placed just as the first, only to the side and in a dependent spot within the pleural space. The patient showed tremendous relief and finally began to feel that he would see the Phillies play again.

The abdominal wound was inspected, and it was decided that it would be best explored in the OR and to avoid messing with it here, where minimal invasive care was possible. Two IV sites, eighteen-gauge intracaths, were already in place, and both had NS up at two hundred per hour until we received the blood from the storage area. A lesson learned was that IV fluids should be monitored carefully to keep the blood pressure just above or at 100 systolic and the pulse at 110 or less. Too much fluid, and bleeders that had stopped bleeding due to lowered pressure would start up again and a see-saw exercise would be created to the determent of the patient. Too little fluid, and the patient would lose valuable oxygen to the heart, brain, and kidneys, causing more stress and the possibility of shock syndrome. These were all nasty complications that we wanted to avoid.

Oxygen had been running since Emanuel's arrival at ten liters per minute via face mask, and his nail beds pinked up just a bit. The lesson I had to remember from Fort Sam combat medical training was: enough fluid with enough red blood cells with enough oxygen under enough pressure make the heart, brain, and kidneys happy. That pretty much encompassed trauma care back then. At one point during the conflict, the "golden hour" concept was developed. It was simple enough: provide oxygen and fluid to establish viable vital signs and accomplish transport to an appropriate care facility within the first hour after injury, and the patient had a very good chance for recovery.

No fancy equipment. No heart monitors. No mechanical ventilators in the field hospitals. We had crude suction run by generators and oxygen supplied in huge cylinder tanks beside the beds, cots, and stretchers—not so great when the patient had to be moved during rocket-and-mortar attacks.

We finished up with Emanuel by inserting a Foley catheter into his bladder so his kidney function could be watched closely and decided against a nasogastric tube, as we were uncertain if fragments had injured his stomach. Each of us watched as the corpsmen wheeled Emanuel into the operating suite, which was adjacent to the immediate-care area by a large, open doorway with the rubber, flap-like doors resembling those of a meat-processing room at the local supermarket. This kept the conditioned air in the surgery suite and made it easy to enter without messing with a door.

Patient five: a nineteen-year-old black male E-3 grenadier (he used the M79 grenade launcher). GSW right wrist, through and through and wound right groin, appeared to be from small-arms fire, probably an AK-47. Leon had lost a lot of blood, and although awake, he was disoriented. His voice was very weak and his speech broken. In spite of our encouragement to rest and not talk, he kept muttering, "Motherfucking gooks, motherfucking gooks."

We had three teams of two each working with Leon, as his aura was worrisome. I felt he was barely clinging to the lucid side of his brain. His wounds appeared to be draining him of his life fluid and challenging his chance of hearing his mother's voice back in Mississippi ever again. He was tagged "red, immediate." Shock was gaining ground on him, and we needed to suspend it quickly. Two eighteen-gauge intracaths were placed in his left arm, and NS was hung at wide-open rate after we learned his BP was 60/30 and his pulse was working overtime to maintain it at 130 per minute.

Oxygen was started at fifteen liters per minute by face mask, and he was positioned flat on the stretcher with a small towel under his head. He fought the mask, but one of the medics gently held it to his face and encouraged him, assuring him we would get him out of the dark place he had stumbled into, that place between the awareness of life and the frightful, dark void where he imagined death to dwell. Four units of O-negative blood were on their way, and we had to examine the wounds that the field medic had dressed to assure that any bleeding had been controlled.

The wound to Leon's right arm had an entrance and an exit, and his hand was "floppy," according to the medic. Upon carefully removing the dressing and splint, we witnessed a pulsating flow of blood erupt just over the area of the radial artery. Nearly the entire anterior aspect of the wrist was gone, and a majority of what remained was badly damaged, with the tissue in tatters held together with dangling strings of clotted blood. The ulnar side was not bleeding, most likely because of low blood pressure. His hand was a grayish color and appeared cold to the touch. There was no blanch. A simple splint and light pressure dressing was placed back onto the baseball-sized wound, and we looked at each other, realizing that if Leon made it out of the hole, he more than likely would lose the hand.

The other team had been examining and exploring the wound to the right groin and were very disturbed, as there was a pencil-sized entrance wound just above the pulsating femoral artery but no an exit wound. It was impossible with the evidence on hand to determine the angle of the wound; we had to assume that if it entered the abdominal cavity, it could also have traveled through the diaphragm, causing a multi-cavity wound. One of the triage medics, while checking breath sounds in the left lung, felt they were absent in the base area, and after verification by the triage doctor, it appeared that there was a probable injury to the base of the left lung. This meant the bullet traveled diagonally from the right groin to at least the base of the left lung, injuring everything between.

A second possibility was that a fragment of bone and the bullet might have caused even more extensive damage to several adjacent areas in the abdomen and chest. These types of wounds were horrific. They caused destruction in major organs and structures and required extreme, time-consuming surgeries to save the life. Additionally, body fluids from one area are toxic to other areas and greatly increase the likelihood of infection.

Certainly, the expertise was available with the top-notch surgeons of the Seventeenth. Leon might require the orthopedic, the gastrointestinal, and the thoracic surgeons plus one or two medical docs as assistants—the pressure was on. Hopefully, an influx of additional patients would not push the limits of the team and require them to make less than ideal major, life-changing decisions. Though Leon's life would be in no further jeopardy, any more demand on resources might make the difference between a colostomy versus a bowel repair or an amputation versus precise limb-saving hand surgery.

Then again, Leon, the last patient in this small group, had to perform his role to the finest as well, as the stressors on the body were beyond imagination in this strange, dark place. The triage doctor placed a tube in Leon's left lower chest. As the stab wound was made and the air whooshed in, Leon gasped at the creation of the temporary pneumothorax. The number-thirty-two chest tube was forced between the ribs with the curved stats, and a gush of foul-looking, greenish-yellow, bloody fluid was siphoned through the tube and into the closed vacuum system. We verified that Leon had a very tough haul before him. Making it out of surgery would not mark the end of his battles here in the Republic of South-fucking Vietnam.

As we cleaned up the mess we had made in our spastic use-it-and-throw-the-wraps-on-the-floor routine, I realize the scope of what was happening in this for shit, fucking place. Picking up dressing-pack wrappers off the floor, dripping in blood and other body fluids, I know that, although our experience just then had been as climactic as one could imagine and had drained each of us to a drop of whatever adrenaline remained in our bodies, we would be asked to do it all again soon.

No matter how large an event loomed for us, it was only one among the multiple battalion-aid stations, field stations, field hospitals, surgical hospitals, and larger general hospitals in Qui Nhon, Saigon, and elsewhere. To think of it was overwhelming. To try to make sense of it was ludicrous. It all appeared to be part of a sick dream that would end only on the day we left that shithole. If only that were the case. The vision of the whole was surreal, and it made all the individual parts seem unreal as well. It only became totally real during the most basic part of it all—when we looked into the dying eyes of a young man who had traveled out of the safety of his mother's womb as few as eighteen short years earlier and had never experienced all of those wonderful and terrible things he's heard about, dreamed of, and dreaded.

If we look at only that primary, single, simple element, a soldier's life as reflected in his eyes, as the reason for everything we did, it made our jobs, our lives, and our sanity possible. It was never totally understandable but we could look at it reasonably enough to be able to eat and sleep and even love, at times, even though our minds were constantly fixed on the memory of those eyes. This seemed totally fucked up. The responsibility of each young GI's life remained ours until we were able to replace him with others who needed us more. The images were so numerous that it became impossible to associate a name, a face, an injury, or an outcome with it after the fact. But the eyes were always there, and they told enough.

Damage beyond Belief

—ɱ—

THE STEEL POT

As PRIVATE SIMMS WAS BROUGHT to a stretcher at the Seventeenth, he appeared to be in disbelief of the fact that he was telling me the story of his harrowing experience that had occurred just hours before "out in the bush." As memory permits, I share his story with you.

The birds and the tree frogs competed for first chair, and sunlight was nearly blotted to gray by the triple canopy of greens and yellows and the tropical sub growth of weeds and plants. The sphere of our existence was minimized to the unreal space of a fifteen-foot cube. Regardless of how fast we walked or how long we rested, it didn't change. Although it felt anything but right, we were too fearful to wish for it to change. It was safe so far.

The temperature was 102, and the humidity was so high that steamy clouds could be seen in the low pockets throughout that very green place. Humid smoke rose slowly from our backs and shoulders. Our fatigue jackets had been soaked for hours. We were accompanied by a swarm of mosquitoes that had already fed on us all at least three or four times, and each seemed to be replaced by twenty or thirty more as they drop off, so engorged with a banquet of blood that they couldn't fly. We were doused with DEET until we were certain that Charlie" could smell us a hundred yards before contact.

We were dripping in our own stew of sweat and small puddles of spilled blood that remained from the hundreds of leeches that sensed our presence and set up perfect ambushes yards ahead so that they could join the banquet. Our fatigue pant legs felt like concrete blocks from being soaked in the stinking green-and-brown algae from mud-bottomed bogs that appeared every couple of hundred yards, requiring us to expend what little remaining precious energy was left since our last rest. Our legs tugged each foot out of the knee-deep, quicksand-like muck and moved it forward just enough to gain twelve inches or so of progress. *God be with me if Charlie shows up while I'm in this shit*, I think.

It was beyond my recent memory of when I'd last had a shower or a bath. Recollection is vague, but it might have been at the Korean steam bath during our previous stand-down." For the equivalent of a mere two or three dollars, you could have a wonderful sponge bath, a massage, and a cold shower over and over until you were so weak you couldn't stand, and if you were so inclined to fork up another three to five bucks, a bonus boom-boom or a blow job. Maybe all of the misery of being a grunt was punishment for the terrible capitalism we had pushed onto this socialistic country. Or maybe God was pissed at all of us for the sins learned so soon by all of us eighteen-year-olds when, only weeks earlier, the most aggressive act of our lives was probably making a late hit on the quarterback at the Friday-night game or punching our younger brothers in the shoulder.

Because of the heat, the sweat, and the filth, the fungi and bacteria accumulating in the dark places that infrequently got the relief of fresh air performed a wild symphony of itching, burning, stinging symptoms that only seemed to creep further into our damp skin crevices, shrouded by the saturated clothing and armor we wore. The white, creamy, sweet-smelling exudate of the fungus of "crotch rot" and "foot rot" could put us out of operational order quickly. All of this, and Charlie" wanted to blow our fucking heads off to boot.

We wondered how many before us couldn't stand this shit. We thought about how close we were to that point ourselves. We cursed every little thing that went wrong, and they were many, on this imposed plight purposely laid out for us. Our lives were abso-fucking-lutely miserable.

Oh, and then there was the regulation shit that we had to carry so that we were prepared to meet any event we might encounter out there in the bush. All of it amounted to at least another seventy-five or eighty pounds, and sometimes more. It seemed unfathomable that anyone might expect a human being to carry all of this shit through that damp, dark, miserable, foreign hell.

The last and most ominous addition to these impossibilities had to be the steel pot—the regulation helmet and its liner—both drabbed off with the helmet cover in either OD green or jungle camo. At five pounds plus, it frequently became the straw that fucked up the grunt as well as the camel's back. It seemed to intentionally push us further into the earth and make our neck muscles ache and go into spasm. It pushed our boots further into the shit that tried to trap us there in the middle of this fucking, godforsaken place and at times would make us feel near panic if we didn't tear the fucking thing off our heads. The inner ridge of the helmet was a haven for mosquitoes, attracted by our exhaled CO_2 that concentrated in the space between the rim of the pot and our foreheads. The stinging and buzzing drove us nearly fucking crazy.

As the three FNGs in the platoon, we were granted no levity by either the sergeant or the lieutenant until we were able to prove that our liability to the platoon was less than our contribution and we were not apt to get everyone killed. The lieutenant had a pet reg that he constantly enforced through the sarge. Most all else was actually controlled by the sarge with the LT's blessing, as the LT had only been in country for less than a month while the sarge was on his second tour. The pinnacle of his authority was ensuring that we all wore our steel pots. Always!

We all tried to avoid his observation by falling back just a little or to move to the side a few trees distant, depending on our forward movement pattern. The bastard always seemed to catch us, and he would tell the sarge that if he didn't keep his men in order, he would have all of our asses on return to base camp. He seemed to garner great pleasure from this little bit of authority, and the sarge allowed him to keep it. This little quirk of the LT would result in an outcome for which I will thank him for forever.

My platoon had spent a miserable day in the bush, while without contact with the enemy, the contact with the elements seemed to triple as the day went on. There was a period of torrential downpour that raised the levels of the streamlets and deepened them, requiring extreme care in crossing. The muck was mid-calf below, and the water was to our armpits above. Two hours later, after climbing a two-hundred-yard, muddy embankment, clawing for every yard of elevation and often losing ground on every other attempt, so many obstacles had been encountered that the sarge suggested to the LT that we make camp on the high ground for the night.

All seemed well with the LT, so guard rotations were established and all of us settled down for a less stressful, if not more comfortable, night. We were now a stationary target for our nemesis, but after a short period of horizontally circulating blood and exposing my stinking, infected toes to fresher air, I just didn't give a shit about anything and fell asleep. My watch wasn't until near morning, and when I was awakened, I felt that I had been somewhere else and a great fear of not being alive swept over me.

Once I felt my own presence again and the reality of all that went with it—the mosquitoes, the heat, and the chorus of frogs that yet sang in the strange darkness just before daylight—I was almost disappointed that I was alive. Sleep was far better than the shit I had faced day after day in that stinking country. Now, I awoke just to continue with the same, almost unbearable miseries.

Finishing a round of rations, we assembled to make the last leg of our incursion before reaching our objective and then getting lifted out of this hellhole. We shortly came upon a well-used trail, and the sarge immediately took counsel with the LT. After a short discussion, we were ordered to advance in a V formation with the point man about twenty yards out front. I was third man back on the right side and already totally drenched in sweat and entertaining a host of parasites. I flipped my helmet from my head, as I felt I couldn't breathe with the weight of it along with the humid air pulling the oxygen from my lungs.

I made a few steps to make sure that the LT could not see me, when I felt a hard slap in the back of my head. I turned to see the sarge, silent but with pursed lips and a look of anger on his face. That immediately caused me to reach for my helmet and flop it back on my head. I suddenly felt a tremendous jolt that caused the light before my eyes to wane to pinholes and although it happened in a microsecond, everything seemed to be in slow motion. I imagined the sarge slapping me in the forehead and me wondering what the fuck was up with this guy hitting me again.

As I fell to the ground in slow motion, I seemed to rock backward and teeter on my heels. Sometime before hitting the ground, the light went out completely. My next memory was finding myself on the galvanized metal floor of a slick flying over the treetops at breakneck speed, my medic's face above me. I swear to hell that I really thought I had bought the farm and was on my way to a place I had never been before. The medic told me I was the luckiest motherfucker he had ever met and would bet his paycheck on my hand in a poker game anytime.

He explained about the sniper who must have been waiting for a clear shot at one of us as we filed through his shooting lane and how he had the scope of his rifle on my forehead as the sarge beat the back of my head. The sniper must have squeezed off just as my pot went back on my crown. The 7.65 mm bullet penetrated the steel outer layer and ran out of steam as it pushed against that sweaty piece of fiberglass that fit inside and held the liner straps that fit our stupid fucking heads so perfectly that it was even somewhat comfortable.

As the bullet had run out of forward momentum, it had spun around the liner inside the pot like a satellite orbiting the earth. It created mole-like, spiral indentations around the liner—twice. A ton of energy had been expended, but, phenomenally, not on my fucking head.

I felt like there was a garden hose in my mouth, filling my head to the bursting point, and my ears were ringing so loudly. My head was spinning wildly, and I felt like I might vomit.

—⋙—

He did vomit, several times, and with his moderate concussion, he bought a few days of observation and rest. After a week of stand-down and retelling his story to nearly every patient on the ward, he returned to his unit. I can still hear the story he told the FNGs about how he cheated death, and how if it weren't for his helmet, his Purple Heart (PH) would be on its way to his folks back in Ohio and he would have followed in horizontal position with the flag draped over him.

Struggling through the Brown Water and Quicksand[xiv]

THE PUNJI SPEAR

Late afternoon in the E.R. at the Seventeenth, and the triage area was cleared out as I stepped out to the back by the helipad for a smoke. I could hear the chopper coming from a long distance away and wondered how long it would take my mind and my body to forget that sound once I returned to "the world." As soon as the hint of the rotor came to my awareness, the endorphin high began. It stays with you for quite a long time, but after all is done, it makes you feel exhausted and wanting to hide from all of the shit.

Ironically, after being away from it for a while, you crave more. The difficulty of separating the tremendous horror from the tremendous high created by your body's own drug factory is contradictory, but it started on my first day of treating the wounded. It created confusion and self-investigation. What kind of person could get off on this shit that was so horrendous, so repulsive? It would later sit me upright in bed in the middle of a sound sleep. After all, how many times can a human physically tolerate watching, caring for and being responsible for another human in pain, in stress, in the act of dying or, worse yet, living?

Later, I understood how the brain drugs actually allowed us to function during those darkest times. Without them, failure was sure to follow. I no longer think of them as actual drugs; they were only the energetic feelings and confidence that replaced the depression and self-doubt that grew within us during the idle times.

I was joined by a SP-4 who had also heard the sound and couldn't stand to wait the long minutes before all of the details were related. We watched the chopper settle down like a bumblebee on the tip of a fragile flower, and two of our medics rushed out to off-load the patient. As they moved the stretcher out of the gaping hole of the open door of the chopper and toward triage, something appeared very strange as they got closer. I saw that the patient was actually on his stomach and a sheet was draped over his back, sticking up in the air over the middle of his body and making it appear that he was inside a white pup tent with his feet sticking out one end and his head out the other.

My medics moved the patient onto the ER stretcher very carefully and looked at me with raised eyebrows and anxious grimaces as they received a brief report from the field medic on the way to triage. They carefully removed the sheet, and I saw this huge length of bamboo sticking out of the patient's left chest, just below the lower edge of his shoulder blade and extending a good two feet above his body. He had met up with one of the most primitive of weapons used by the gooks: the punji spear.

Richard, an E-4, had been in country for about seven months. Other than a few bouts of jungle rot and a behemoth case of the clap, he, for all practical purposes, was still unscathed. He was a member of a small, five-man LRRP unit and was working just to the east of the Cambodian border—at least, that is where the slicks dropped him and his unit. His commander, while giving the coordinates for the mission, did so with a shit-eating, sheepish grin.

Days after, they were deep in the bush to the west and were most likely operating in another country. They were to travel for four days and attempt to intersect a large insurgent trail (Ho Chi Minh Trail) but not make contact. Rather, they were to observe and report on certain conditions that were given to them by the CO. All appeared to be going well through the third day, with the usual amounts of mosquitoes, leeches, spiders, and snakes. No contact had been made, and they were only about a half day out from their destination. Upon meeting their mission objectives, they would then hike out to an LZ pickup point well within South Vietnam.

To prepare for camp, Richard and a companion, Les, were assigned to go ahead and select the night defense positions (NDPs)—one for the forward location and then one for the rear. Richard was an excellent point man. He was revered and admired by the rest of the squad as one of the best. He most always was used to select the guard positions for camp. They proceeded up the trail to the west about twenty yards when Lester hand-signaled a halt.

After several seconds of freezing in place, Richard was motioned to come toward his friend. After a few steps, he could see what was causing the concern. They had found a punji pit, a fairly large hole dug about five or six feet deep. It was fitted with bamboo spikes that were driven into the ground with twelve to eighteen inches of pointed, sharp ends directed up toward whatever was to fall through the leafy, camouflaged cover placed over the hole. The pits were not necessarily intended to kill the victim but rather to cause horrid wounds that would require two or three comrades to attend him, thus disabling many instead of one.

The cover had been slightly dislodged by something, possibly an animal, and that is what had caught the eye of the soldier. Richard and Lester destroyed the camo leaf mat and blunted the sharpened stakes. They then filled the hole with debris and laid several bamboo poles over it. The freshly cut vegetation, along with the unnatural arrangement, would warn anyone who came close.

Thinking the job done, Richard walked around the opposite end of the now-destroyed punji pit and Lester, with his attention in the opposite direction, heard a sickening *thunk*. He turned to see Richard falling backward toward the hole with a spear sticking out of his back about two feet. Horrified, Lester braced Richard from falling full force and lay him down gently on his stomach. He then returned to the unit for the medic.

It turned out Richard had tripped a vine or string that was part of a carefully planned trap by the gooks. The camo cover had been more likely left somewhat askew to bring activity around the pit and distract from other, more dangerous traps that were discreetly hidden. The tripped vine had triggered a sprung tree or sapling that had been pulled back horizontally, nearly to the breaking point, to release at full force. Affixed to that sapling had been the nearly three-foot length of bamboo. It was about the girth of a fat stogie and honed to razor sharpness and had most likely been dipped in feces, urine, or some other nasty substance that would cause terrible infections in its recipient.

The spear had entered Richard's left lower chest region and went completely through him until only a nub of the rounded-off, unsharpened end could be seen nearly level with the surface of his chest. Not counting the ten inches of spear in Richard's body, another fifteen or so protruded from his back. The medic did exactly the right thing by stabilizing the protruding end so that it would not become dislodged or wiggle and cause more injury. Many people mistakenly remove such penetrating things (or try to), but that is highly ill advised. It's like playing Russian roulette.

Penetrating objects frequently pass through dangerously close to major vessels or organs and should be left alone until removed in a surgical setting. Richard was fairly stable, considering his injury. It was a good sign that the spear had not yet damaged major structures. The challenge now would be to move him to the predetermined LZ about four days away through Indian Territory, which was full of various traps and swarming with gooks. A lot of care and finesse would be needed to get Richard out alive.

The unit emerged at the edge of the LZ six days later. Due to the extreme caution and care taken by all, Richard remained stable throughout his care in the field. However, a chest through-and-through wound that is six days old is big trouble.

At the Seventeenth, Richard was given a head-to-toe examination, and his chest wound was the only one. Since the OR had been awaiting his arrival, we prepared him for surgery. After two large-bore IV sites were established, we gave him a liter of RL for hydration, started oxygen at four liters per minute by nasal cannula and administered several thousand units of penicillin IV. We boosted his tetanus immunization and wheeled him off to X-ray and then to OR. He was nearly crawling out of his skin after being on his stomach for six days, and we were very concerned about static pneumonia as well as a probable wound infection.

When Richard returned to the ward from OR, he had two tubes in the left chest, one for blood and fluid and one high for air. It turned out that the punji spear had missed his heart by about a half inch, and other than damage to lung tissue and some medium-size vessels, there was nothing else wrong. The surgeons were, however, very concerned about infection, and he was given high doses of penicillin as well as antibiotics for gram-negative organisms. A fairly significant lung tissue infection had already started, so a portion of the lung was excised and other tissue cleaned up.

Richard would have a rough road ahead and require much more support than a field hospital could give. He might well have needed a respirator and additional surgery to aid his left lung in staying inflated. He was sent to Saigon the next day. As usual, we never found out what became of Richard.

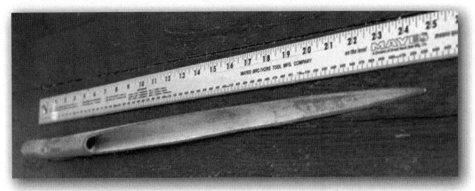

Actual Punji Spear Removed from Richard's Right Chest

ASCARIASIS

Vietnam held a host of entertaining and exotic viruses, bacteria, and para-sites. It was a haven for the microbiologist and the entomologist. There were at least two variations of malaria, dengue fever, and several other blood dis-eases carried by mosquitoes and other insects. God only knows what other pathogens constantly multiply in a pot of more than ninety-five-degree heat and humidity of 80 percent and above. Tetanus was still rampant in the country as well as rabies, leprosy, and several tick-borne diseases. Probably the most interesting, and the most disgusting in real life, was ascariasis.

To explain ascariasis, which afflicted as much as 25 percent of the indig-enous population, the life cycle of its nematode (worm) must be explained. First, its eggs are defecated by an already infected host. It then incubates in the soil and is inadvertently eaten by another person and soon-to-be host. Such a transfer was not too difficult in a country without sanitation. The eggs lie in the intestine for a bit until they hatch larvae. The larvae then get restless and bore out of the intestine and into the bloodstream until they reach the blood-rich tissue of the lung. There, they mature further, thrive, and then bore their way into the larger airways, up the bronchus, and into the mouth. They are then swallowed again to rest in the intestine, growing to six to twelve inches and the girth of a thumb. The adults lay more eggs, only to have them shit out once again, starting a whole new generation.[xv]

After laying their eggs, the mature worms eventually take one of two routes: if they like their host, they congregate in small, slimy, slithering balls in the intestines or the stomach, sometimes causing bowel obstruction. If they do not like the host, such as when he or she is poorly nourished or not permitted to eat while healing, they will crawl out of the stomach, up through the esophagus, and out the mouth (or nose, depending on which turn they take at the end).

My very first experience with ascariasis was while taking care of a Montagnard who had been shot in both lungs while fighting alongside the Vietcong. He had chest tubes in both cavities, a red Robinson nasal intubation for breathing, a stomach tube for feedings, and an abdominal wound open clear down to the viscera and held gaping open by five or six wire-retention sutures to watch for infection. He also had a Foley catheter.

It was about 2:00 a.m., and the coffee wasn't helping me at all. I had been in country for just over a month and at the 311th for just a couple of weeks, and my experiences with the indigenous common diseases and ailments of Vietnam were still at ground zero. I was working with an SP-4, an excellent corpsman but also fairly new to the country. As I glanced over at the patient from my chair at the desk, I thought saw a red tube on his chest. I thought for sure that he had pulled his endotracheal tube out or possibly even his chest tube.

I flew from the desk to his side, only to find a wiggling, fucking ugly worm about ten inches long on his chest. I had no damn idea where it had come from. As I looked at him and he stared at me, wide-eyed and horrified, emerging from his mouth was another critter heading out of Dodge. This one hesitated for a long time halfway out of his mouth, so I grabbed the fucker with a pair of hemostats and pulled him on out. The patient was horrified to see that these fucking worms had congregated in his body, and since he was Montagnard, he knew none of the crude GI phrases used by most of the native people.

He started shaking his head wildly from side to side as if trying to extricate all of the demons. Ultimately, he was so terrified, he flat passed out. I was fucking blown out of my head, and the corpsman didn't know what was happening either. I told him to go drag Capt. J., my boss at the 311th, the hell up there to tell me what the fuck was going on. Chuck showed up in his OD shorts, jungle boots, and helmet, and the sight of him alone calmed me down nearly enough to laugh.

Chuck was short and Buddha-like with chubby, little legs, and I can still picture him standing there in his boots with his belly roll nearly covering his boxer shorts and saying, "What the fuck is wrong with you? Haven't you ever seen a worm before?" He then busted out laughing, and we all laughed together—except for the Montagnard. The patient was boarded for an exploratory lap in the morning.

Upon talking with his surgeon before the procedure, he didn't feel he would heal well with all of his injuries plus the worms, and besides, they could cause real problems with his breathing. The operative report described a "ball of worms about the size of a softball" being removed from the patient. Our Montagnard patient continued on to a slow recovery lasting weeks.

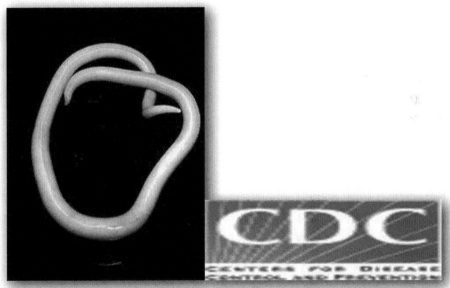

Ascariasis Worm. Photo from Centers for Disease Control, Atlanta, GA.[xvi]

FIRE IN THE HOLE

When you came near the end of your rotation in Vietnam, you took on an attitude that you'd seen everything and that you knew most everything related to your job and what was expected of you. Just as soon as that smug feeling set in, there was the major realization that you hadn't come close to seeing it all and you really didn't know shit compared to the big picture.

Don't get me wrong; most all of the comrades that I served with in the RVN were sterling at their jobs, and about 90 percent of them were wonderful people as well. The fact is, however, that in your most horrific nightmare or in your wildest of dreams, you could not begin to imagine the downright horrible things that can and do happen to the human body during wartime.

A short time after Christmas in 1969, we came back to earth with the sobering holiday vision that I am certain is still relived at least once a year by each of us who were party to the event. It's so vivid to me that I can hear the voice of Col. S. and the OR crew as they desperately worked to save this victim's life. I still smell the odors that permeated the OR suite and drifted through the meat-locker-like doors covering the OR entrance.

The mistake that had caused the injury seemed slight compared to its consequences. This was, however, frequently the case in a combat zone where some things are vital and need to be accomplished on schedule, or someone down the line would suffer and then someone further down the line even more, and so on, and so on. Here is the story about John and Larry.

Transport of everything, including food, water, and tons of munitions, was often delayed for up to weeks in the journey through the An Khe Pass into An Khe and beyond. If a major event happened in the pass, vehicular traffic would be backed up forever and be trapped there with no escape. To one side was the steep mountainside covered with former jungle coming back in various stages of growth, while the other side usually qualified as a scenic overlook, dropping several hundred feet to the same, snakelike road below—which would also be bumper-to-bumper with stalled, smoking, overheated, disabled vehicles.

The reason Charlie loved this scene so much is fairly obvious. Once you stop a large vehicle by disabling it and its crew, nothing can pass, sometimes for days. Once he gained this advantage, it was like shooting fish in a barrel, and Charlie would capitalize on this unavoidable event to the fullest measure. Everyone hated the pass except for Charlie.

It's not surprising that once supplies arrived to fill critical needs that had been delayed so long, getting them to the right unit by off-loading as quickly as possible was of the highest importance. The assignment of the day for PFC John and PFC Larry was to off-load six deuce-and-a-half trucks of long-overdue cargo for several of the Arty (artillery) units in the Central Highlands. John and Larry were in one of the Arty companies that for days had had to ration or deny requests for directed firepower in support of the grunt units that counted on them so much. Until the ordnance was unloaded and sent to the respective units, missions in the bush would continue to be greatly impeded.

Undoubtedly, critical need had great influence on how much care was taken in off-loading the dangerous ordnance. The testimony, after the fact, by John and Larry's few surviving coworkers, confirms that they felt that "major shit of a fucking horrendous nature" had been about to happen.

Artillery rounds were trucked and packed by standard procedure inside ammo boxes to protect them from contacting the hard edges of the container and each other, for obvious reasons. The packing material was frequently thick pieces of cardboard. It was a cheap, effective way to keep the rounds in place and separated. Unfortunately, given the rough roads, the twisting nature of the pass, the enemy contact that the trucks had endured along the way, and the weed that John and Larry were smoking all added up to a formula for disaster.

On top of that, many of the rounds were incendiary in nature, meaning that their prime component was Willie Peter (white phosphorus).

The stuff is extremely flammable, igniting at simple contact with the air. The cases were to be off-loaded onto pallets that were predesignated for to various artillery outposts, and once each pallet was loaded to capacity, a hi-lo would carry it to another vehicle to make the final delivery.

There was somewhat of a backlog, creating a wait for the hi-lo. After an extra-long break, John and Larry thought they might have fallen a bit behind. They began pulling the ammo boxes off the back of the truck with reckless abandon, some falling from their grip and onto the ground with solid thuds. They figured the contents had been well packed and shielded and there wasn't a big worry; nothing had ever happened up to that point—and that point was one of the cases fell to the ground end first, and all apocalyptic hell broke loose!

A sudden burst of glowing, white-and-yellow fire was followed by an explosion leading to a horrible, huge chain reaction that wiped out most of the trucks, John, and six other grunts. Many soldiers, up to fifty yards away, were wounded. Both of Larry's legs, one arm, and a small part of his right lateral chest wall was torn away in a millisecond while additional fragments and debris caused several penetrating wounds to his abdomen.

As the field medics arrived on scene, Larry was actually passed up for quite some time as being dead or mortally wounded while other GIs were attended to. When it was discovered that Larry was yet alive, his outcome seemed extremely dismal. When he arrived at the Seventeenth, a multitude of challenges presented themselves.

Larry was brought into the ER covered in a sheet that someone had found. I couldn't help but notice the already clotted blood hanging over the sides of the field stretcher, while there was no active bleeding through the sheet. Upon pulling the sheet back and observing Larry and his wounds, I was stunned by the horrific scene before me. Both legs were gone, the right one to the hip and the left one to mid-thigh. His right arm was gone at the shoulder, the wound extending into the axillary (armpit) chest wall with lung tissue easily visible. There were multiple penetrating entrance wounds into the abdomen, and through the dirt and the grime, it appeared that much of the remaining skin on his anterior body had been burned.

There were no IVs in place, and Larry had received one syrette of morphine in the field for pain. The field medic had been frantic that he could not find an IV site. This was no reflection on the medic, as there were several others who were in need of care, and Larry was triaged as "expectant" status. Since they had not been far from the Seventeenth, the medic hadn't attempted a lot of heroics in the back of their bouncing jeep. In all, only three others actually survived the accident; reports of the death toll continued to rise. Those three were transported by chopper to the Sixty-Seventh Evac Hospital in Qui Nhon.

Larry was immediately triaged with a total survey, and he was intubated by the anesthetist and given 100 percent O_2. The gore of the remaining wounds was beyond belief. Any semblance of normal anatomy had been blasted away. We searched through the dangling tissue of the right hip wound and found a couple of larger vessels that had been severed along with the leg. We strung number-sixteen intracaths into them and aspirated to see if we could coax some blood. Luckily, both produced enough to make us comfortable using them as IV sites.

We tied off the veins at the end surrounding the catheter, and they served just as well as cut-down IV sites. We immediately started NS in both to ensure the fluid didn't just run right out of Larry's existing holes. Once assured that it didn't, we started hanging up the blood. I really can't say if Larry was ever conscious from the point of his injury forward, as he had received the morphine, and that was enough, along with his decreased blood volume and his horrendously traumatic injury, to cause him to be nonresponsive. The only good sign thus far was a very faint pulse in his left carotid and the fact that a small amount of bleeding had started up in his arm wound after we ran a few units of blood. We placed a Foley catheter in Larry's bladder, and the return was bloody.

I couldn't help but notice a strange difference about Larry that I hadn't noticed in other severely wounded patients. Only later, after the fact, did I determine that his difference came from an odor I didn't recognize. Unfortunately, the OR crew would soon discover the source. Two surgeons and an OR staff three times larger than what we normally used to care for one patient worked on debriding and controlling bleeding on Larry's amputated extremities while a third surgeon worked on accessing Larry's chest and abdomen.

A tube was placed in the right chest wound and connected to suction until a more permanent one could be established when the wound was closed. There seemed to be fairly good aeration to the left lung; we had rise and fall of the chest wall with each squeeze of the Ambu bag. Much air was escaping into the right chest area, however. Bubbles emerged out of the chest wound synchronous with the bag squeezes. As long as we could keep him on enough air and fluid to the right places, we might have a remote chance in hell of getting Larry out of the OR. But then what?

We were expected each day not to ask that question. The answer might depend on where the victim came from, what he had been taught, what he believed in, who was in his life, and, most of all, the quality of life he might expect given the worst of circumstances. That is what we owed Larry: a choice, if we could give him one.

Just as the amputation wounds were coming along nicely, we were all jolted out of our already overly excited skins when Col. S., who was working on the abdomen, told us all to move away from the table immediately. None of us really knew what the fuck was up and thought he was crazy. Some did not move right away, and he repeated with clenched lips, "Get the fuck away from the table."

As soon as all were aside, the smell of burning blood, flesh, and bowel content seemed to hit us at the same time, and we heard a sound that resembled bacon sizzling in a hot fry pan. Several small pieces of Willie Peter had penetrated the abdomen, and once inside, they had been deprived of oxygen and lain dormant until uncovered by the surgeon. As each piece of WP was uncovered, it ignited and threatened whatever else was around it, including the explosive, gaseous environment of the OR.

The colonel asked for some of the medics to gather up all the metal, stainless, and kick buckets from the ER and something to cover each to keep out air. They broke scrub and left the OR, and it seemed forever before they returned with five buckets. The colonel stripped off his gloves, re-gloved, and approached the patient, calling in assistants as he needed them. He removed several pieces of the small WP from the wound, and they were still brightly white as he passed them into a bucket that was then immediately covered. The colonel decided to open the entire abdomen and to retain everything inside with only a few large retention sutures while he meticulously explored the intestines. This was necessary to control infection in the end anyway.

With two assistants with retractors, he opened the abdomen from the end of the breastbone to the pubic bone and explored the intestines from top to bottom by sliding the mesentery and bowel aside with long, blunt delivery forceps. This worked quite well for most areas, but deeper in the cavity required a careful examination for entry wounds. Each time a hunk of the WP was exposed, it burst into flame, of course. The internal tissue damage was significant. The staff worked as quickly as possible while several more units of blood were contributed to Larry's chance of living.

As the colonel finished with the abdominal wounds, we counted twenty-two pieces of WP removed from Larry's belly and left stump. They had done an overwhelming bit of additional damage, and even while we dumped blood into Larry's IV sites, his pressure continually dropped. After about one hour on the table, Larry decided it was time to go home. After several cycles of CPR had failed, the colonel asked for the rib spreaders, but before he made the huge, gaping chest incision, he looked down on Larry's body, shook his head in resignation, and said: "He wouldn't want this. Stop everything." We all felt empty but also greatly relieved, as the longer we carried on the horrendous misdeed on this poor soul, the more we realized that we were attempting to be something we were not.

Larry passed on, and the chaplain had his words with him. With the ER now empty, we washed up, walked across the street to our tin-roofed, plywood O club and drank until nothing much seemed to matter. Nothing more was mentioned of Larry. This had been his day.

Packing a White-Phosphorus Artillery Round[xvii]

Oh, That Tiger

—⚌—

A DAY OF NOTHING HAPPENING in triage was a day we deserved. The last four days had been a bit of hell on earth. We had cared for over a hundred GIs and forty Vietnamese civilians, and our entire unit was exhausted. The Fourth had tangled with a battalion-sized NVA force not far from Camp Radcliff, and it had been very close to a "supposed friendly" village. Unfortunately, the assault had involved one of the nastiest of the weapons of the war: napalm.

None of the grunts had suffered from the stuff this time, but unfortunately, the drops had been very close to the village, and civilians were caught by surprise while working in their fields by the rolling, orange, choking balls of fire. Upon touching you and clinging to your clothing and skin, it would spend itself by burning all of its fuel as well as all that could burn around it. The wounds of napalm are nothing like any other, except possibly those from white phosphorus found in artillery rounds and a few other inventive weapons.

As we have seen, white phosphorus is inert until it is exposed to air, while napalm burns only on detonation. Both are horrid and probably more sinful than war itself. Both create a horrid, evil stench upon burning the skin, the blood, the muscle, and the bone. They both burn deep, often to the bone and beyond to the other side. Remarkably, with third-degree, no pain is felt, but burn wounds never exist just as third degree. A goodly amount of skin around the wound is always second degree or first degree or both. The burn from napalm generally covers large percentages of the body, so it is excruciatingly painful with all three stages working on the poor soul at once.

Our most important goal in caring for these victims was to control the pain—attempt to get them through the first couple of hours without so much agony, at which point most of them would die. That day, that was exactly the way it happened. All twelve of the Vietnamese civilians with napalm burns died within a short time after the two-hour marker. It was a nightmare that was repeated several times throughout the remainder of my tour, but each time seemed like the first time and was just as horrid.

The outcome was nearly always the same. Fluids, beyond normal saline, were very valuable resources in the field, aid stations, and field hospitals, and for that reason, albumen, blood, and the rarest, plasma (blood without the red stuff—i.e., red blood cells), were rarely used on civilians. This policy seemed cruel, but I realized, soon after arriving in country, that the Viet civilians would suffer much worse deaths after surviving napalm if they were taken to civilian hospitals. They had nothing but custodial care—no medicine, few bandages, and no trained, full-time medical people.

Trained Vietnamese medical staff would go home at 1600, and family members were then responsible for the patient's care and feeding until about 0800 the next day. Most had no family, or the family had no idea where their loved ones were. Those who cared for the injured had the large task at 0800 to check every patient's vital signs and to remove the dead. I am certain that many families to this day do not know where—or even if—their loved ones or their remains are. My heart bleeds for them.

This and other anecdotes represent the horrid irony of life during wartime in Vietnam. Things were horrific beyond imagination. But somehow, the civilians' rationale on medical care seemed acceptable and tolerable solutions amid the circumstances that made Vietnam what it was. A few miles outside the major cities, there was nothing—no running water, no sewage management, no medical care, no hospitals—nothing. The people had lived generation upon generation under these circumstances and knew no better.

So, it seems that any medical care our military did, no matter how little or ineffective, was not only acceptable but much more than these people had ever expected. No reason for bad conscience here, right? My dad had had a favorite phrase for situations that turned out mostly bad even in the face of tremendous effort and attention: "You can't make chicken salad out of chicken shit!" How true, as cruel as that seemed.

There was the FNG lying in the jungle who "needed" morphine more than he needed oxygen in his lungs and the civilians burned terribly with skin hanging from their muscles, "needing" so much more but destined to die either now or later, because that's the way it was there. My mind remains confused. My conscience remains unsettled. I swore never to excuse myself for such things, and I have not.

But this day was a new day, a Sunday afternoon with barely a handful of grunts in the morning. A few infected scratches and scrapes, a relapse of malaria, and four with the clap (GC-STD). Some of them thought they would die, but after some reassurance and some penicillin, they were content to return to their units, promising to use the little foil packets that were available to them as readily as M&Ms most everywhere. Then the *wump, wump, wump* jolted us from our relaxed, sedentary state, and we awaited word from our com shack of what we might expect.

He was about twenty-one years old with dirty-blond hair and weary-looking eyes peering through the camouflage and orange dirt on his face. The whites of his eyes were blood red, apparently from sleep deprivation and pain. Although tense and exhausted, he appeared very much relieved to be here, under roof and under the care of army medics, nurses, and doctors.

Upon approaching him, I could see no obvious wounds above the waist from which there was any large blood loss. I proceeded with the usual triage inspection to rule out life-threatening wounds and/or injuries. A poncho liner covered him from the waist down. When I lowered it, I was stunned to see his right knee swollen to nearly the size of a soccer ball. It was flame red over a large area, and I noted three puncture wounds at various locations around the knee joint itself. Realizing the patient's obvious pain and the obviously infectious process taking place, we ordered an IV of NS at 200 cc per hour to help with dehydration and, more important, to deliver vital drugs such as penicillin and morphine.

As the IV was being started, I did a quick medical history to rule out allergies and, finally, determine what might have caused the injury to the patient's knee. What the young man told me was, at first, what I thought was his idea of a joke. But quickly, his account turned into a bone-chilling story of the most unusual of circumstances, nearly resulting in his death.

Mat, as we had come to know him, was a member of an LRRP team operating to the far west of An Khe, most likely in or near Cambodia. Their location was never confirmed, as they were not supposed be in Cambodia, but all the same, they were. An LRRP team is inserted, most times deeply, into an active enemy territory and is charged with collecting valuable intelligence on troop strength, type, and movement. Most often, they were not to make contact with the enemy but just to complete their objective, sneak back to a predetermined LZ, be extracted unnoticed, and report to their CO.

This team had been in the bush about fourteen days, and they were making their way back toward the LZ with just a short time left in their mission. They were bedded down in a circle in the jungle with no fire and covered with just their poncho liners to help with mosquitoes. Mat had rolled an extra pair of socks and balled them up in front of his steel pot. They sat just above his head, making a somewhat softer pillow than the ground.

This is what I remember of what Mat recounted:

—m—

I was dead tired from the day's hike, and we had been in some pretty close encounters that caused a lot of stress among us. We had several incidents of raw, angry nerves, but each of us maintained our cool, as we knew it was just a sign of being in this fucking place way too fucking long. I had last guard post, so I tried to drop off as fast as I could to get a good, long rest before my turn and then humping the whole next day and evening.

I fixed up my dry socks so they were bunched up against my pot and placed my M16 between my right arm and side. It was not long before I dropped off. I have no idea how long I was gone, but I was slightly awakened by an eerie, uneasy feeling that you sometimes get before an unexpected ambush or punji spear or some other fucking thing the gooks cooked up.

I had my eyes squinted halfway shut, and I looked to my left and right to see if anyone else was stirring. To my satisfaction, everyone seemed to be sleeping without concern. I closed my eyes once again, but the feeling just would not go away. I listened and strained my senses, trying to get a clue of what was going on, but just couldn't put my finger on the feeling or make proper sense of it. It seemed as though someone was breathing close by me—not normal breathing but long, deep breaths like I had never heard before. I could swear that I could hear rustling in the grass so soft that it was spooky, uncanny.

I moved my right arm to finger the trigger guard of the M16 and was assured it was at the ready as it always should be under these circumstances. I moved my hand away and, just as it came to rest on the ground, a fucking helluva commotion erupted with the grass swishing on the ground and a heavy vibration near my feet. I swear to God, an actual vibration on the ground and a *rumph-grumph* sound, and then a pressure in my right leg—not pain, just an ass-jarring jolt and pressure. My legs and hips were elevated, and my back was sliding along the ground toward the jungle edge. I felt helpless.

I let out a helluva scream, immediately thinking that it was a big fucking mistake, as I would most likely get shot by those gook fuckers or one of my own squad. At the same time, I smelled this horrid stench that was kind of like the garbage pit back at base camp—rotten, like when chicken has gone bad. As I became more aware, I realized I was moving out of the circle and toward the thick part of the tree line, skidding on my fucking ass while still holding my steel pot with both arms wrapped around it, thinking wildly that it would stop me.

I soon caught glimpses enough to see fur, orange fur, and I was totally fucking confused. The heavy breathing, kind of like grunting and huffing at the same time, seemed to get louder and louder as the edge of the bush came closer. I was abso-fucking-lutely terrified as things started to come together, and I realized that this was a fucking tiger that had me by the right knee, and he was about to eat me. *This can't be, can it? A fucking tiger?*

In desperation, I tightened both arms above my head around the steel pot so that as he pulled, the lip of the pot dug into the ground kind of like an anchor. The tiger gave several violent tugs like a dog pulling on a rope, and I felt as if my leg would be pulled off. It did slow him down a little. When he had had enough of that, he released my knee and came right over the top of me, head on. I was looking right up into the largest fucking drooling cat I could ever imagine. Strings of putrid, slobbered saliva hung from his mouth, some dropping into my eyes and ears and mouth.

Instinctively and full of adrenaline, I had the helmet sailing over me with both hands clenching it for dear life, and I fucking popped the cat right across the bridge of his nose. I swear, that fucking cat stopped dead in his tracks while straddling me and just glared into my terrified eyes. A long string of his drool spilled on my gut as he spun around so fast and so violently that he kicked a shithouse full of dirt and leaves into my eyes and mouth. I started spitting shit out and trying to rub my eyes clear so I could see if he was coming back.

What seemed like minutes but were only seconds from the beginning, the rest of the team was by my side, wondering what the fuck was going on with this writhing, piece-of-shit grunt spitting and sputtering on the ground, making all of this noise when on patrol. The only other person who had witnessed all of this was the guy on the far east side of our little slumber party, and by the time he grabbed his rifle and joined us, all he could mutter was, "Fuckin' tiger. Fuckin' tiger!"

Flashlights came on, enemy or no enemy, and our best-trained medical guy, Ron, cut my pant leg up the side where I told him it felt like I was oozing blood. It really didn't look so bad. There were two or three holes in my leg just above and on the knee. One hole was quite large and had the skin jagged and torn. The bleeding wasn't all that bad either, but my fucking nerves were about gone. Ron, the medic guy, was getting out a syrette of morphine when all of a sudden, two of our guys raised their M16s and opened up on full auto, scaring the living shit out of both of us. We crouched down so we wouldn't fucking die from whatever was now going on, and the rifle fire escalated into an all-out barrage!

Soon the whole clearing was filled with smoke and the smell of gunpowder, and three guys were standing upright with M16s pointed toward the opening in the bush about ten feet from me and Ron. I didn't know what the fuck was going on, but I watched them as they slowly moved toward the opening at different angles with one guy taking a stand off to the side with his rifle trained on something in that direction. The trail guard finally moved into the clearing from the other side and trained his rifle on the spot as well. It seemed to take forever for the two guys to reach the opening and when they did, I heard one of them say, "Holy fuck, it is huge!"

It was only then that I realized that while I was so intent on my injured leg and Ron likewise intent on caring for me, that fucking cat had come back to finish up the deal only to find four grunts at the ready. Even though they might have been as stunned and confused as I after the cat grabbed me, their quick response and judgment on all factors saved my sorry ass from being a cat toy, or even worse, a cat treat.

It's pretty shocking to be awakened from a dead sleep by someone screaming their fucking lungs out and to find someone rolling around on the ground like a fucking wild man—and then to be greeted moments later by nothing less than a fucking Cambodian gook fucking tiger running dead-on toward you in the middle of a jungle full of fucking

NVA gooks all wanting to kill you. It's amazing anyone still had the sense and orientation to shoot the fucking tiger dead, and I mean dead! That tiger had twenty-five or thirty holes in him, and thank God, 'cause that fucker wanted to eat me.

It was apparent to me and the rest of the squad that we had some work to do, and we had to do it fast. Our location was for sure being plotted as we spoke. We would be easy pickings for the NVA battalion that we had observed several times over the last few days. We sent out two LPs on trails leading to our camp and agreed to meet about two clicks to the east in about two hours. The plan was to have them out front, me on the litter that was now being fashioned out of bamboo and Para cord, carried by two and flanked by one about thirty or forty yards back. Our secondary LZ was about five clicks east of our location, so we figured we should make it there, given no trouble, in four or five hours. No trouble, right?

Initially, the bamboo poles broke. The guys had underestimated my weight by a least twenty kilos. The fucking broomstick-sized poles broke on the first lift. It had to be done over using thicker poles while we wasted a lot of our valuable travel time making our rendezvous. So now, much later than planned, we were just starting and well behind on getting to the LZ to meet up with the two lead guys.

Off they went with me while I cradled the heavy M60 lying on my back, facing forward, with two youngsters lugging my litter helter-skelter, weaving through elephant grass, bamboo stands, and God knows what else until we ran smack-dab into a whole shithouse of gooks. Fortunately, we three, plus our tail, thirty feet behind, were unseen. They literally tossed me into the fucking elephant grass, litter and all, with the M60 coming down heavy on my gut and balls. I had to clench my teeth to keep from moaning in pain. I couldn't see a fucking thing except my two guys taking up slightly rear positions to my right and left.

The tailer came to me, lay down, and rolled forward in the grass to knock down just enough so that I could see just the heads of the enemy about sixty yards ahead at the base of a slight rise. They appeared to be in a powwow of sorts. Based on our previous plans, two of our guys were out ahead, on the other side of the gooks to our east, and once we did not arrive at the first coordinates, they would come back toward us, not knowing about the gooks. A new plan was in order.

We decided to stay where we were positioned and to let the other two guys progress to a point of cover that looked most protected from our position. Upon their reaching that spot, we would open up on the gooks for just a short burst to alert our guys of the danger. At the same time, it would get the gooks moving. We estimated there to be maybe three or four squads—fifteen or twenty men—and we felt we should be able to handle that number.

Our estimate wasn't real good, and we soon realized we would be shooting pretty much inside a box with the good guys on most sides and bad guys in the middle. We weren't prepared to put our squad in that danger, and we decided it was lunacy under the present circumstances. Our squad leader gave the RTO some instructions that I couldn't hear. Within minutes, a Loach was in the area as well as an AH-1 Cobra gunship. A smoke canister was tossed out in front of us, and they zeroed in on the smoke well on the other side of us as the Cobra laid down several rockets and .60-cal. mini-gun fire to the right and left of the NVA. It seemed to us that it missed them, because from our vantage point, we had no idea we were dealing with an entire NVA battalion.

After about twenty minutes' work by the Cobra, he turned east and left with the LOH. We did not know that the bulk of the NVA battalion was now split to the right and left of the smaller group. Finally, upon realizing their numbers, we were very concerned about our six-man team surviving. If we decided to fight them the way we had originally planned, our mission would end much sooner than we had hoped and for all the wrong reasons.

While we pondered the shithole situation we were in, the screeching jet engines of a pair of F-4C Phantom jets at treetop level seemed to be coming directly toward us. We set out a canister of smoke to mark our positions and hoped that the fast-moving Phantoms would see it and avoid us. Several rockets rained down dead on the enemy to the north and the south, and the explosions, even from our more distant position, were deafening. On their second pass, they dropped their nasty death nail, and the ground lit up like a giant fucking firecracker, and a large, rolling ball of orange bounced like a beach ball at high speed among bathers.

The gooks were running everywhere, screaming and yelling and now ignoring our rifles as we all opened up on them. Surely, some who were victims of the napalm were wishing for a rifle shot to put them out of their misery. They were yelling, *"Chu hoi, chu hoi!"* (I give up, I give up) as they were greeted by another pass of the Phantoms. Whoosh, and another giant ball rolled down the alley, spreading certain death to those still alive.

The farthest-east team of two who, thank God, survived the aerial assault, was now firing on the running rabbits as they dipped in and out of the ever-thinning elephant grass. Some lay down on the burning ground and just remained there, lifeless even though not quite dead. We waited to see if there would be any immediate counter, but nothing happened. Once it was quiet, our RTO again contacted our commander regarding the large NVA force in the area, and we started out again with new coordinates.

We were more than content to have won that fight without a casualty. The remaining four hours were literally hell on earth because of very difficult terrain and no supplies. Most of our extra shit had just been left at the firefight, as we wanted to carry mostly ammo, what little we had left, and make up for lost time. Oh, yeah, and my leg was starting to ache like a motherfucker.

When we reached the LZ, an army dust-off chopper came immediately—the RTO had already called for it—and I was headed to some hospital in the Central Highlands.

And here I am at the Seventeenth Field Hospital with a tiger bite of the right knee that hurts like a motherfucker and is now swollen huge as shit. Hey, Doc, am I gonna lose this fucking leg?"

—w—

His brows were wrinkled and his face was contorted as he seemed to be holding back tears. Our surgeon, Captain G., came to him, put his hand on his shoulder, and promised he would do everything above and beyond what was necessary and would only take the leg if he felt it would take his life due to an infection. Mat nodded, and the morphine was on its way.

Just before he went to surgery, the surgeon numbed up the knee area and stuck a number-fifteen blade into the puffiest part, well away from the vital structures. We drained nearly a liter of yellow, brown, awful-smelling pus from the leg as the putrid, bloody stuff shot out of the wound under pressure. We caught most of it in a washbasin, minus about three ounces that hit the doc's lab coat dead-on. Mat said the pain was relieved a great deal almost immediately after the drainage, to the point that he was asking questions of some of his team members while waiting for surgery. Hopefully, we would see him in a few hours with two legs and one helluva tiger story to tell his ward mates.

Mat's fellow LRRPs had managed to get the cat back to Camp Radcliff. How they managed to return to the bush in the presence of huge enemy numbers, we'll never know, but I am certain there was involvement with a helicopter or two. They took tons of pictures for him to look at later and promised us some copies once they were developed.

When Mat was transferred to Saigon, a larger hospital, three days later and with two legs, they presented him with a Bronze Star, a Purple Heart medal, and the tiger hide, complete with its many, many holes. I do hope they let him take it back home to "the world."

The Orangutan Connection

—ෲ—

WHILE SERVING IN VIETNAM, SEVERAL things carried me and my memories back to safer, more enjoyable times in my youth, each deserving of its own story. This is one of them.

The air was thick with the smell of popcorn and cotton candy. All of my friends were here; this was one of the biggest happenings ever in my small town in western Pennsylvania. Aside from the Strawberry Festival and some other frivolous events self-created out of boredom with my cadre of friends, I looked forward to this day every year.

My friend Jack and I arrived at the carnival site early that morning just before all of the big tractor-trailer trucks with the fantastic graphics of lions and tigers and elephants and fat ladies and sword swallowers plastered all over the sides. We were overwhelmed with excitement. We anxiously moved from truck to truck, watching the sort of dirty and sometimes odd-looking men and women as they went about their work. We wondered how the scars and the crooked noses and odd-shaped legs and arms had all came about. Maybe they were soldiers and got injured in the war, or maybe just bums and beggars who lived life on the rough. We wondered if we might get one of those fabulous tattoos someday that covered their entire backs and went down each arm.

We watched as they unloaded the huge trucks of all kinds of equipment, including huge sections of canvas tied together with ropes and with neat colored pictures bigger than life. The canvases were stretched between and atop long poles, and before you knew it, you were looking at a tent complete with its own advertising. We watched intently as this new world was built in front of our eyes. I was truly excited, but Jack was even more so. He was nearly a full two years younger than I even though he was just one year behind me in school. I had been caught in the birth-day trap, and my parents chose to put up with me at home for another year instead of sending me off to school prematurely.

Jack and I were great friends even though his parents were a bit sus-picious of me. Whenever Jack got into trouble, it seemed that I was either involved or responsible. I recall one calamity when Jack and I went fish-ing in a little, narrow stream across town, just off a gravel road. It was pretty much at the limits of our distance away from home restriction, and we were nervous at the outset about doing something wrong.

We rode buddy style on my bike. Jack, who was a smallish boy for his age, sat on the handlebars of the twenty-four-inch Schwinn. We arrived at the bridge over the stream, hid our bike, rigged up our poles, and started downstream. We fished for a couple of hours and used up most of our bait of grasshoppers and red worms, so we decided to hang up the fishing and just take a walk further downstream to see what it was like, as we had never made it past the place where we'd quit.

We hadn't gone too far when I spotted a huge paper hornets' nest on a small, branched tree. I watched it for a while and didn't see any ac-tivity in or out. It was quite hot, and the afternoon sun was penetrating pretty strongly through the trees and onto the nest and area around it. I don't know what possessed me, but while holding the butt end of my rod, I grabbed the tip with the other hand, sprang it back, and let it whip against the nest in a huge snapping motion that cut the lower half of the nest clean off.

I immediately jumped back a couple of feet and stood motionless, but Jack took off running upstream toward the bike. Hornets poured out of the nest in a black mass and zeroed in on the moving target. I heard Jack yelp a few times and then nothing. I half sneaked upstream and found Jack sitting in the stream with just his mouth, nose, and small part of his forehead above the waterline. The hornets were still intently interested in Jack but were stinging him a little less frequently than before.

When it was over, Jack had been stung over ten times, and even though his face was swollen and very painful, he apparently was not allergic and had no horrid symptoms. I finally coaxed him out of the stream, led him back to the bridge, and got him onto the handlebars. He started to cry. I asked if the pain was really bad, and he said yes, but he was more concerned about his mom beating his ass for getting into yet another problem. Days later, my mom and dad sat me down and once again informed me that I was heading for reform school if I didn't shape up and that Jack's folks were really pissed and might not let us play together anymore.

Ironically, just about a month later, Jack, on the same handlebars of the same bike, on the same road with the same driver, was thrown violently into the air when we were coasting at breakneck speed down a hill. Jack had become nervous about the speed and squirmed around, causing me and the bike to go to the center of the road, where ashes and dirt were graded up into a ridge.

The front wheel wobbled out of control until it locked up sideways, sending Jack through the air and me off to the side. We were both wounded terribly, with blood oozing from several sites through the black dirt and disgusting ash ground into our bare legs and arms and faces. Jack had a terrible strawberry on his shoulder as well as many other wounds exposed through his destroyed white T-shirt. We truly looked like war refugees.

My Uncle Stew and Aunt May lived not far away, and we were both scared beyond reason to go home looking so wounded. We showed up at their house, literally scaring the hell out of my Aunt May. Now, let me tell you about Aunt May. She was young, with long, black hair and was extremely beautiful and sensual. All the men in my family would ogle her at all of the family functions, and I do believe Stew loved it, as it was a sort of sign of approval by the youngest and most insecure of the clan. He had picked a beauty for a wife. Stew fit easily into the slightly kinky category on certain things, especially the sexual ones, and he no doubt enjoyed the way other men looked at her.

Anyway, she was really a hot number, and I believe she loved to tease us older boys as well. She always left the bathroom door ajar a few inches, and my cousins and I would make several trips back and forth past the door, hoping to catch a glimpse of her naked. One time, she looked up just as we were glaring in, and she shook her head and did a *tch-tch-tch*. God, I thought I had gone to heaven. But this tragedy that Jack and I had just survived would turn out to be a day he would remember for a long, long time. Obviously, I still remember it also.

Once May recovered from the sight of us, she herded us into the bathroom as my uncle Stew was just heading out the door to work. He told May to make sure we got cleaned up and our wounds attended so we wouldn't get our asses beat at home. She made us both strip down to our undershorts and climb into a hot tub of water with Fels-Naptha soap. She leaned over the rim of the tub as she gently cleansed the multiple open areas on each of us with a washcloth loaded with Ivory soap. We couldn't help but notice one of her breasts exposed and the nipple on the other pushing out against her wet, cotton shirt.

Much of the ash was ground into our skin too far and would tattoo us for life, but she did get most of the grime from our bodies after about an hour of intent yet gentle scrubbing. Jack and I were numb struck with pain while still wishing our bath would go on forever. May gave us each a towel and instructed us to get out of the tub and dry off and to call her when we were done.

As we climbed out, we both had significant erections, even with all of the pain. I do believe it was one of Jack's first, as he was very embarrassed and suggested we put on our filthy shorts over our wet BVDs and leave when May left the room the next time. May reappeared, and she began to spread Neosporin ointment over our wounds. Once again, Jack, more than I, came to full attention as he went beet red and turned his face away from hers. She gave us each one of Stew's old, holey T-shirts and made us take off our wet undershorts before putting on our filthy outer shorts.

Jack's manhood was at full staff as we left the house, and he appeared mortified. On our way home, Jack couldn't stop talking about how kind my Aunt May was and how we should not tell about most of our adventure. We didn't, and it became our secret. And yes, after a few days when the pity phase died out, Jack did get his ass whipped.

We were mesmerized by all of the preparation at the carnival, and as we walked past one particular tent, an old man, supposedly a part owner of the carnival, asked if we would like to make some money and all the ride tickets we could ever use for the event's two nights. We asked what we had to do, and he swung his arm around, pointing to the marquee behind him. Part of it read, *Chico, the Bodiless Man from Mexico,* and another line there read, *The Wild Man from Borneo.* "Do you think you two could do that?" he asked.

We thought he meant we might have to feed or groom or do something with whatever lived in the cubicle he was now pointing out to us, but he said, "No, you will be those two freaks." Jack and I looked at each other in amazement. Our years of awesome belief in such unbelievable things as wild people, freaks, and half beasts seemed to evaporate with the circus owner's words.

But, though it sounded really weird to be freaks, we said, "Sure!" The old man told us to show up at the tent at 5:00 p.m. to get ready for the 6:00 p.m. show. We would have to work until ten and then again the next day for two shifts: 1:00 to 5:00 p.m. and 6:00 to 10:00 p.m.

He gave us a handful of tickets and said, "I am trusting you now. Show up here at five o'clock."

During our joy-filled ride fest that afternoon, Jack and I decided we didn't have to tell our parents about this. We wouldn't have to account for those periods, as we were pretty much somewhere else and away from home most every day anyway, and our parents knew we had been saving for the carnival for some time. We stuffed ourselves with cotton candy and hot dogs and soda and rode a bunch of rides until it was soon 5:00 p.m.

We showed up at the tent, and the old guy was elated to see us. He rushed us inside, and Jack was taken to his little cubicle just to the left of mine. I watched as they prepared him for his adventure. They dug a hole in the ground so Jack could scooch down inside so just his upper torso was visible above ground. It didn't look comfortable. They then placed a small, wooden end table with a round hole cut in the top to fit over his head. All four sides between the legs of the table were fitted with mirrors, so it appeared that one was actually looking through the legs as with a normal table. The carneys spread hay around all sides of the table so each mirror reflected the same view: hay. All that was left showing was Jack's head sitting atop the table. They wrapped a small, Mexican rug around his neck. His script was easy:

"Hi, I'm Chico. Chico, the Bodiless Man from Mexico." I would have to listen to that for four hours! I thought at first I would die laughing but soon felt sure I would instead go crazy listening to his chant.

I was soon to become the "Wild Man from Borneo," which did not involve a costume. I had fairly decent muscle mass on my upper torso from playing baseball and basketball, so the carney guy had me remove my shirt, shoes, and socks. He ruffled up my hair so that it stuck out in several directions and jammed some straw in it here and there. He sooted my chest and face and feet with some kind of theatrical paint, and last, placed a heavy, spiked dog collar around my neck. He attached one end of a rather large, heavy chain to a steel post driven in the ground and the other to the dog collar. He gave me some plastic teeth with long canines on them that slipped over my teeth. He then had me lie on my side in a pile of hay, and he covered my lower body with an old army blanket. My only instructions were to not expose my street pants and to growl ferociously from time to time. That was it.

All through our three-hour performance, I nearly cracked up several times listening to Jack's repetitive "Hi, I'm Chico. Chico, the Bodiless Man from Mexico." Yes, I did say three hours. It all came to a screeching halt after about that long. Jack had snitched to his younger brother, Rick, that this was going down, so Jack's parents, along with mine, had devised a plan to find us and get us the hell out, as the activity did not meet their approval.

They found the right tent with Chico and the Wild Man from Borneo. Rather than go inside, they paid the way for another of my best friends, Ron, my fishing buddy, to find us. I nearly died laughing inside when I spotted him coming. Maybe it was because of his very sheltered life and limited exposure, but he appeared not only fascinated and in awe but perplexed. After staring at both Jack and me for quite some time, he turned and left. Of course, we didn't know what was coming down but found out after the fact that he hadn't recognized us and suggested that they might have the wrong tent.

About a half hour passed, and things ended abruptly as my dad came through the tent opening and handed his ticket to the agent. He came directly to me, removed the dog collar, and asked me where my shirt was. I said I didn't know. By that time, the owner was all over us, yelling at my dad for ruining his show while Dad threatened to punch his lights out for taking advantage of two minors in a goddamned circus sideshow.

My dad, in a swoop, tipped Jack's table over and told him to get out of the hole and that we were *all* leaving. The owner gave Jack another fistful of tickets and disappeared. My dad would have knocked his block off had he stuck around much longer. We were led out of the tent to a cheering gang of friends, all except for Ron, who was sheepishly explaining, "I didn't recognize them in there."

After a few minutes of getting our asses chewed, Jack and I slipped away from the parents once they became distracted with each other, as they too were dear friends. Now, we could see how my uncle Dan was doing with the boast he had been bragging about all month.

The Orangutan Match was the highlight of the carnival for the older folks. They could actually bet fair sums of money, up to twenty bucks with odds, that a volunteer fighter from the crowd either could or could not stay in the ring for forty-five seconds with this fucking gangly, odd-looking monkey called an orangutan. It cost five bucks to challenge the ape, but you would get it back plus a share of the lost bets if you won. The bettors either won at the odds posted by the trainer or lost, depending on whom they bet on—the man or the monkey.

My uncle Dan was indeed a tough hombre. At eighteen, he had yet to lose a street fight that I knew of. Most guys on the streets in Oil City avoided him even though he was generally quite pleasant when sober—which was not often. His father, although small in stature, was solid as stone and in fact was a Golden Gloves champion for several years. He fought in the army as well and survived seven major battles as a member of the Bloody Bucket Brigade during WWI.

All winter, Dan saved his pennies, collected pop bottles, and did a few chores to save up his five dollars. He did push-ups and pull-ups and ran around the Tippery loop, a total of ten miles, nearly every day. Since no one knew of his plan but me, everyone thought he was fucking crazy, as no one did that shit back then. He had a tactic that he shared only with me: he would run around the ring and not let the monkey get his hands on him. He had noted, in years past, that as soon as the monkey got hold of the fighter, it was over in a matter of seconds. No fail! Sounded like a good plan, but in retrospect, he should have measured the size of the ring and the arm reach of that damned monkey.

Dan wore a pair of cutoff blue jeans and had covered his hands with adhesive tape. I don't know why. I guess he saw someone do that once. He climbed up into the ring, which was elevated over the crowd of about a hundred people. All were waving money and making bets with the ringmaster. A whole lot of money changed hands. I saw a local doctor bet a $100.00 bill—on whom, I do not know. It was supposed to be limited to $20.00, but doctors were highly respected back then and could pretty much have their way with everything.

When all was settled with the betting, the ringmaster and Dan whispered back and forth, and soon after, the ringmaster announced the fight over a megaphone. "And in the red corner, in the white T-shirt— Dan, a hundred and twenty pounds of solid muscle and a perfect record on the street. He is challenging Rufus, in the blue corner, a ninety-five-pound, dumb-ass monkey that is mostly hair and arms and would throw this fight for a banana. So, no bananas allowed."

The crowd was pumped up and cheering and drinking beer freely, as the ring had been wisely located adjacent to the beer tent. They handed Dan a bottle, and he sucked it down in no time, even though he was three years from legal age. They gave the ape one, and he shook it up and sprayed it all over Dan and the ring. The ringmaster stated a few rules, the most damaging being that Dan had to make contact with the ape at least once. I could see Dan's head spinning: what to do?

The bell rang, and the ape presented himself in the center of the ring with his arms down in an apparent vulnerable stance. My uncle Dan hauled back and smacked that monkey square in the mouth with one helluva punch. It sounded like a fist hitting the flesh of a watermelon. The ape was knocked back a bit, shook his head from side to side, and glared deeply at Dan. Dan, having made his contact, started around the outermost edge of the ring, dodging the ape's grasp a few times.

However, after Dan escaped the third corner, that ape reached out and grabbed a handful of his hair and literally pulled him into the center of the ring. He lifted Dan up like a baby, gave him a big sloppy, bloody kiss, and then hurled him down with brute force, flat on his face, onto the canvas. Dan did not move. The monkey nodded several times to the watchers and then proceeded to jump up and down on Dan's body with wicked force. Dan at one time tried to lift his head, but the monkey grabbed it on both sides and slammed his face onto the canvas. Red stuff began to ooze out from under Dan's head.

The monkey jumped on him a couple more times, and then the trainer took him to the blue corner while the helpers paid out the money to the winners. The ape drank a beer in record time and then went to Dan, picked him up, and gave him another huge, full-mouth kiss, even though Dan's face was a bloody mess. The orangutan's intentions for my uncle Dan were not really to cause him great harm but rather to win, doing what he was trained to do to get his beer and the love of his trainer.

Dan, however, had to be helped out of the ring, and he got nothing. He had a concussion with fairly serious symptoms for at least two weeks and didn't act right at all for some time. But at three weeks, he was devising a brand-new plan for whipping that fucking monkey the next year. His mom and dad never really got the details, only scattered remnants of a rumor. Whenever asked about it, Dan would just shrug in that "I don't know what you're talking about" manner that he used so many times and went on about his business.

—⟶ɷ⟵—

The Central Highlands of South Vietnam are among the most unusual places on earth. The jungle is lush and affords a wonderful place for birds, reptiles, and mammals to frolic about and possibly never be seen by the human eye. We certainly heard them singing, scuffling about, howling, grunting, and peeping, but we rarely saw them. I believe that was the plan for that particular ecosystem, intended to preserve its wild-life by separating it from humans.

As with all plans however, certain deviations occur that tend to spoil the purity. In this case, questions arose about whether certain elements even existed when sufficient physical evidence was not present. It would be one thing to see, interact, and even socialize with an alien creature, but it would be altogether different to see, attack, and kill it solely to prove it exists. So it was with the rock apes of South Vietnam. Although known to have existed by the thousands in Southeast Asia many, many years ago, they have become the mythical bigfoot of modern-day Vietnam.

At one time, the dense jungle afforded the luxury of a secretive existence, and many birds, reptiles, and mammals were hidden from human eyes. The war, however, caused intrusions into many such untouched places, creating significant change and conflict. The orangutan-like rock ape was nearly man sized and all too familiar to the natives throughout the Highlands as well as other locations where dense forests and rocky, rough terrain, and mountains hid their daily routines.

The night was humid and the moon showed full over the mountain as I, officer of the day, and Sgt. Handy, sergeant of the guard, started our night routine of walking the perimeter of the compound to assure all was kosher with the troops and our security. It was common at one time to man every other guard tower outside the first perimeter so that each tower would be covered every other night. We soon learned, after

suffering through red alerts and several actual infiltrations nearly nightly that Charlie had figured out our secret staffing plan.

In one infiltration, a Victor Charlie was killed, and one was captured. Turns out the woman who was killed was a mama-san for one of
the surgeons and the papa-san was a latrine worker (a.k.a. shit burner).
They had both worked inside our compound daily and were registered
with picture IDs giving them free access to the entire place during the
day. All Vietnamese were "shootable" after curfew if sighted inside the
compound, and that did happen on occasion. Once in a while, one
would be captured rather than dispatched and soon admitted that he or
she had accumulated information every day about our activities, personnel concentrations, mess times, and posting plans of the guard towers,
and so on. The info that they garnered while on the inside proved very
helpful to them on their secret visits after dark.

Because of the negative outcomes of the established routines for man-
ning the towers, security measures were changed nightly. Operations
were assigned at each evening's guard formation, and all the variables
were chosen at the last moment. If any special information was available
regarding enemy activity, it was shared as well. The walking rotations
were random and required only complete coverage of the perimeter several times a night.

So, after finishing our first round, the sergeant and I dropped into
the mess hall for a midnight brunch of that day's leftovers plus maybe
one new menu item. It was everybody's favorite meal outside of the club
feast, so the mess hall was quite busy around the witching hour. We had
just finished eating when we received word about some confrontation
going on in one of the enlisted barracks. We quickly headed out to the
building on foot.

The sergeant went in alone and after a short while came out stating
all was settled, no problem. This was frequently the case, as the sergeant
was influential with the enlisted men and could almost always settle conflicts without serious consequences for anyone. We decided to make a reverse round from that point and had walked about one-quarter around

the perimeter when we came to the darkest and most uninhabited part of the compound that abutted the sharp, stony-faced base of the adjacent mountain.

The mountain was a frequent source of problems. Its terrain consisted of dark stone boulders with vertical faces merging into pockets of thick, canopied bush. Agent Orange and burning was used to the maximum there, but the tree and grass growth was phenomenal due to the amount of moisture and heat that was present year round. Many areas could conceal a company of gooks for some time.

The sergeant and I were trying to see beyond the scattered perimeter floodlights when, all of a sudden, we were startled out of our wits by a heavy *clack, clack, clack* that seemed to start three-quarters of the way up the mountain and became louder and louder as it came closer. The sergeant carried his 16, and I had a M79 grenade launcher with grenade and white-phosphorus rounds. This combo on the "thumper" was common for harassment and incendiary (H and I) fire. The grenade rounds, of course, were just that, and the white phosphorus not only illuminated an area but also ignited anything flammable on contact. H and I activity at random night hours served not only to awaken and piss off our sleeping soldiers but tended to keep Charlie's misbehavior somewhat cautious, but, unfortunately, not always.

We watched for movement as the clacking came closer and soon discovered that it was being caused by rocks between fist and soccer-ball size. They carried along whatever loose debris of dirt, branches, grass, and smaller rocks with them, creating a small avalanche. A small, marble-sized rock actually bounced off my boot. The crescendo of rolling rocks picked up. They were coming down in quite a large number.

I truly believed that Charlie had taken to using rocks as primitive weapons instead of his usual arsenal of mortars, RPGs, and AKs. He was already ingenious in the use of punji pits, spears, and stakes, so rocks were not out of the question. The sarge and I separated from each other about twenty feet and peered up the mountain to attempt a visual on whatever was causing all of this commotion. On several, brief occasions, both of us were able to see with the naked eye figures moving among the rocks about three-quarters of the way up the mountainside. There was no sound and no other threat, just the rocks. We were convinced they were gooks, and they were up to no good.

Being younger and about half as heavy as the sarge, I elected to double-time it to the quartermaster shack to retrieve the starlight scope. It was a huge instrument, and we avoided using it except for situations such as this. As I finally made it back to our position, out of breath and with muscles aching, the sarge said he hadn't seen anything more since I'd left. He suggested we lay down some H and I fire to shake things up a bit so we might see what was actually up there. He emptied an entire clip on full auto, and I fired an illumination round up the hillside followed by a grenade round. Luckily, the first round was perfect in its arc, and the whole area lit up like a drive-in theater at intermission.

We were dumbfounded by what we saw. The hillside was sprinkled with fucking monkeys that looked about the size of small men. It was difficult to be sure, as they were a long way up. We judged them a little smaller than the usual gook and a great bit smaller than a GI. The grenade round had sent them helter-skelter, and the illumination round was about expended. We waited a moment, and I fired another phosphorus round, this time seeing fewer of the apes but getting a much better look at their profiles and hairy features.

They looked a lot like large orangutans. They had extremely long arms, shorter legs, and sometimes walked upright. They were extremely hairy and more toward brown than the usual orange-red tinge of the orangutan.[xviii]

We had heard stories from some of the guys from the Fourth Infantry and the K-Seventy-Fifth Rangers regarding rock apes but never paid too much attention. We heard many stories in the midst of the highs of alcohol and marijuana and the chatty lows of serious wounds masked by fear and unusual behavior. Neither the sarge nor I really had any interest in killing or injuring apes given their benign relationship to the camp, but we were soon to find that things would deteriorate.

It seems that at least once a year, the female apes come into estrus, and in the ensuing idiocy demonstrated by most mammalian males, the rock ape was not to be outdone. Their ritual was each male running back and forth across the flat tops of the mountain rocks as fast as he could go and then suddenly stopping and letting out a mating call that was not only shrill and loud but repeated for several minutes until he was out of breath. He would take a breather, and the whole process would be repeated over and over again for hours at a time. Many apes sitting above them on the rock ledges appeared to watch the goings-on just like the peanut gallery at the ball game on a Sunday afternoon. These were apparently the smaller, immature apes awaiting their turns in the hierarchy, taking in the scene below with great interest.

This routine would generally start around midnight and frequently went on until 0400 or 0500. It was somewhat novel in the beginning, and some GIs would actually go out and watch the monkeys howling and try to mimic them with their own version of the sex-crazed calls. However, after a short while, with the novelty of the situation gone and many hours of lost sleep, it soon became much more logical, right or wrong, to end the serenades early with a few rounds from the M79. I don't think any of us really tried to harm the apes, but I do know that on occasion, a game was played to see how close a round could be placed without hitting the animals. I'm sure, however, that the intention of "just fun" was not foolproof.

I hoped we would remain smarter than monkeys and keep making rational, adult, considerate decisions. But, hell, right then we were in a country thousands of miles from our interests and our homes, fighting a war that no one really wanted and where serious games of life and death were played out each day as we ruined the lives of those poor people for generations to come while our do-nothing, worthless Congress sat on its ass raking in the privileges of office. Obviously, we were not all that smart after all.

The Trail Guard

—◊◊◊—

THE NEXT PATIENT BROUGHT INTO the triage area was a young, Puerto Rican fellow from the LA area who was on his third tour in Vietnam. He was extremely anxious and was very difficult to manage in our small care area. He continuously climbed from the litter and disappeared into the remote areas of our compound where people normally didn't venture. He was found once in the munitions/weapons dump, a place where all soldiers' weapons and explosives were stashed when they were brought in for care. It was a bunker, well-fortified with sandbags and sand-filled fifty-five-gallon barrels intended to prevent injuries should accidental discharge of ordnance occur.

One of my medics found him at the end of the beam of his flash-light, lying on the rifles, machine guns, grenades, RPGs, and C4, most taken off wounded soldiers on both sides. John, we will call him, had two .45s tucked into his pants under his fatigue shirt, an M79 strung over his shoulder, a dozen or so grenades tucked into a medic's bag, and an M16 with ten clips jammed into a bandolier and his pockets.

Upon being disarmed, brought inside, and questioned on his plans for all of that armament, his story was eerie. Looking at his eyes, I could tell that mentally, he had been missing in action (MIA) for some time. They were wide, with pupils dilated to the max. He had a crazed, va-cant look like in old zombie flicks or horror movies where the beautiful blonde is impaled on a dagger while facing her killer. I couldn't help but remember a verse my grandmother quoted: "Our eyes are our windows to the world-They are a reflection to others of our soul". The soul I was seeing at the moment was very, very dark. His speech was extremely slow and deliberate and mostly made little sense except when he said he had to get out and go back out in the bush with his buddies, "'cause they needed [him] badly."

He asked us where his Browning shotgun was, and, of course, none of us knew what the hell he was talking about. Only after one of his unit buddies came in from the bush about an hour later did we learn that John was always one of the designated trail guards for his small LRRP team. He had sent for his Browning from back in "the world" on his first tour, and he used the twelve-gauge semiauto on his watch.

John had a much longer and in-depth story, however. By the time he reached us at the field-hospital level, his necklaces, dog tags, and anything else removable other than his jungle fatigues had been taken by the field medics. The shotgun he'd spoken of was determined to be with his best friend back in the bush, and that relieved him somewhat, but he was still very uneasy and wanted to leave. He felt he would die if he stayed.

His friend asked to speak with him alone, which we permitted. After a short while, John agreed to stay with us and have his leg debrided and treated for an AK-47 wound, through and through, of the inner part of his left upper thigh. Fortunately, nothing but muscle and fat were damaged, but it was a very ragged, dirty wound and needed timely care. We noted that John kept asking his friend where his necklace was. His friend seemed to avoid the question each time, scrunching his shoulders down and pulling his filthy fatigues over his open, upper chest area.

Later, we noted that the friend was also wearing a necklace, a very odd one. I moved closer to John's friend as if by accident, and my suspicions were verified. The necklace was made of dried ears strung on Para cord, one of the more macabre pieces of body wear popular with the grunts. The ears were in various stages of rot. Some were black and had a distinct odor of old, rotting flesh while others were dried and leather-like. Even though such war trophies were more than likely illegal, none of the commanders seemed to enforce it. After all, wasn't that what they were all about—killing gooks? The more ears, the more gooks. This wasn't any worse than the dangerous body counts they were forced to make after each fierce battle where the undead plugged you with a bullet or stabbed you in the thigh with a bayonet.

Over the next few days, John became more and more antsy, and we had to watch him closely. One of our doctors had a specialty in psychiatric medicine and definitely felt that something was very different with John. He was receiving a large amount of antianxiety medication and at times spoke through lips that barely moved while his eyes remained wide open.

One quiet afternoon, John and I sat down and had a smoke together and chatted about his beloved Browning twelve-gauge semi. I asked him why he found it so much better than his issued weapon, the M16, or an M79 with antipersonnel rounds. "I'm the trail guard for our squad, and no one has ever made it past my post." John took on a whole different personality when talking about his job. He said that he had killed twenty-three gooks while on trail guard alone. He qualified his tally by saying that some of them could not be verified to be NVA or Vietcong or Vietnamese civilians but had been in the wrong place for regular civilians and were probably involved with one of the other two anyway. More than likely, John was correct, but I'm sure it is a subject he shouldn't have discussed outside the theater of operations.

John then took on a very strange and somewhat scary demeanor and started talking about how much he liked what he was doing and how he was concerned that when the war ended, he would be lost without his role here and didn't know how he would deal with it. What he was actually saying was that he could not face a life of not killing humans. He validated this premise further when he told me about the challenges of the "surprise game" he played when he was doing trail guard. He and a couple of his friends, also owners of necklaces, developed and religiously practiced this very dangerous and very sick, dark game.

On the honor system, they competed to see how close they could let the trail traveler proceed before they stepped out and blew him away.

John told me that both he and his friend were the best, and both had touched the toes of their boots with the soon-to-be victim prior to shooting. John said, "I watch the fucking gook sneak up the trail without a clue that I am there. I'm in full camo and have used the trees and bushes and grass to the max so that animals don't even see me. I wait and wait, and for every fucking step he takes, I nearly come in my pants. It's so hard to wait, but when it happens, it is better than sex and better than anything I have ever done in my life. Man, the best one actually stepped on my boot when I finally blew the fucker's head clean off. I tried to wait just a little while to study the look on that poor fucker's face before he died, and then I touched off the Browning. Man, his fucking head exploded in all directions. A gob of his fucking brain hit me square on the forehead, and another piece hit me on the cheek. It felt warm, and it felt like I had his life in me."

John's eyes were glazed over, and I could tell that this boy was going somewhere other than back to duty. He went on, "I never got the little fucker's ears, and I don't know if they would've been any good for my necklace anyway. We sometimes use noses, or if it's really bad, the skin from their pecker. You know that ring of skin that sometimes guys' parents get whacked off when they are babies? These gooks don't do that, so that's always a last resort." John's eyes were filled with craziness, and I was almost fearful and somewhat sorry that my .45 was taken from me some time earlier, because I never cleaned it. This guy was a fucking loony tune and needed the best psychiatric care that could be found.

I excused myself from John and sought out our commander to ask him to expedite an evac for John to Saigon and then to Japan for some proper help. I was even fearful of his going back to the States and ending up living in my hometown near Pittsburgh, as he was going to be trouble even if interventions came soon. The commander said he would do what he could, and when I returned to my shift the next morning, John was gone. But not to Saigon, not to Japan, but out doing what he loved to do: killing "gooks," dirty leg wound and all. We never heard more of John. I truly hope he's dead, for everybody's sake back in the world.

Home. What Was It All About?

—⚬—

NO ONE LEAVES THE SAME. Although fear was expected to lessen each day there because of repetition and familiarity, it actually escalated until DEROS. It then ended in a blurry, surrealistic mindscape created by a cesspool of unbelievable events and the sick fucking emotions that surrounded each one of them. Self-hatred and lowered self-esteem seeped from our pores even while we assured ourselves that no human on earth could have done better in dealing with that horror.

Was that really so for me? No one would know unless they were there. Only my comrades could have answered that question, as they had the same cancer that ate at me. They didn't, though, because we were all separating to go to our individual, ignorant, and naïve places "back in the world." No one would want to know what it was like there, and no one could begin to understand anyway based only on my story. I couldn't tell it while in my safe, right mind without making it sound unreal, without the visual scenes, the sounds, the smells, and gripping your hand. It was far more horrid than even the worst hints fed to the public on sensationalized TV. Worse yet, my own program repeats itself over and over with just subtle changes, such as the shape of the face, the color of the hair, or the expression deep within the eyes. All this will be mine to possess and sequester, to handle on my own.

When I get back home to Pennsylvania, I'll show a few of my pictures, flash my Bronze Star, get a few kudos, and pack all of this baggage away for good. This was my great plan back then. But as I write, some forty-five years later, unless these visions somehow escape me, I will forever be a victim of the horrific chapters that lie deep in my brain. I may appear in my testimony to resent and regret my exposure to Southeast Asia, its people, and their private war, but that is not really the case. I am thankful that I could be there to contribute whatever small bit of hope and resolve that I could in an impossible situation.

It was what it was, an impossible engagement that was decreed by those who sat on their asses in Washington, sending me and 2.6 million troops into harm's way to save a corrupt and villainous regime under a totally flawed, politically managed plan of military engagement. In spite of all of this, we never truly lost a battle, and by some scorekeepers should have counted our work as success, spare the fatal intrusions of our politicians.

Above all, I mourn the 58,156 who did not return home. I still wait to this day for anyone, a stranger, a friend, or a relative, to ask anything about the year I spent away. Even as I consider that possibility, I am sure that I will weep as I try to remember the faces of each of them and hope-fully rid myself of at least a small amount of the toxin that has slowly taken me over.

Wars fought in years long past are frequently spoken of with wonder-ful warmth and admiration for those freedom fighters of the early and mid-1900s, as it should be. That is so much more healing than the pro-testing crowds that greeted me at 2:00 a.m. at Sea-Tac airport. Holding signs calling us murderers, baby killers, and crazed, drugged-up mon-sters who drank, smoked dope, and partied, killing innocent, harmless, defenseless families, they blocked our way into the terminal after our deplaning on the tarmac.

The rocks, the bottles, the soda cans full of urine that were meant to shame us for being alive were only precursors to our longer sentences of abandonment and punishment by our people and our government that were yet to come. No, we didn't have a parade or a salute or even a "Hi, how are you?" We had a fence protecting us, six feet high, and a private walkway that became public once we entered the terminal where two or three airport guards were posted. They ignored the protestors until bottles were thrown inside the actual terminal. The guards were even heard telling a couple of privates to hurry up and get the hell out of the main terminal after getting their flights arranged. They did not want a lot of GIs bunched up in one area attracting attention. Under their plan, they wouldn't have to manage a large crowd of people the whole night.

Finally, as I purchased my ticket to Pittsburgh, miserable upon being soaked with beer and feeling I had lost my right to even breathe here in my own country, a lovely, off-duty stewardess (as we called them then) from American Airlines directed me toward the professional lounge where the pilots and crews hung out. After a goodly amount of time in the washroom, I was pleasantly surprised to find her waiting in the small bar adjacent to the lounge. We drank JD Black on the rocks for a couple of hours and fell asleep in a booth until we were summoned by the bartender that our flight was leaving in thirty minutes and we might want to freshen up.

There were only six civilians on the flight plus two stewardesses, one being my new friend, and one soldier: me. When we boarded the plane, my friend disappeared for about ten minutes and returned with what I was sure was an illegal volume of whiskey, a carafe of water, two glasses, and some munchies. She set the stuff on the tray table before settling down in the center seat. I thought she was just going to set up the drinks and go about her job, but she had apparently spent some of those ten minutes arranging private time for herself for the two-hour-plus flight to San Antonio.

We had a couple more JD Blacks on the rocks. When the stewardess realized that I was not up for a normal social existence just yet, she suggested I lay over with her in San Antonio at her apartment for a day or so, as she would be off duty until Saturday. Oh my God, how I wished that I could accept her invitation, but I couldn't bring myself to cheat either her or my fiancée, Carole, who was still in Vietnam. We talked a bit more, and soon we were both cradled in our seats in a very innocent but hugely comfortable way. My God, how good it was to bump into this woman who sincerely gave her time and emotion to me, knowing I needed it so much. No sex, no loving or messing around, but rather, a warm, maternal association felt by a twenty-five-year-old man.

When the wheels touched down in San Antonio, I was still sleeping. When I awoke, my friend was gone, and no one was on the plane but the other stewardess and another passenger trying to get his bag out of the upper compartment. As I made my way past the cabin, the pilot handed me a piece of paper that read, "I really enjoyed our time together. If you change your mind, give me a call, home for two days. Thank you for what you do. Marci." I never saw her again, but hoped I would as I sat forever in the San Antonio airport, waiting for my connection to Pittsburgh.

So. I had been back in the world for nearly two weeks and other than a family get-together with the aunts, uncles, and cousins, not one single person asked me out for a beer or called me up on the telephone to ask how I was doing. Nothing. I realized that everyone had real jobs and school and tight schedules among time spent with family and girlfriends.

My mom became so upset with my boredom that she actually set me up on a date with a young girl that she worked with, just for dinner. I had taken care of a gentleman at Oil City Hospital, and his son insisted that I come back sometime to his restaurant for dinners and drinks for two. Well, I did take the young lady out to the restaurant, and I'm more than pleased that I did. She was the second person, other than my family, not to show disrespect for me since I had been home. We talked well into the evening over some JD on the rocks, and had I not already met and been mad about my fiancée, Carole, who had yet another six months to spend in Vietnam, maybe something would have developed.

During the period at home, I was idle most of the time. Issues plagued my mind, but I couldn't quite put a finger on their source. I had the ongoing, growing feeling that an energy within me was trapped and constantly making me restless, anxious, and irritable. Although my parents and relatives seemed attentive and watched my picture slide show with awe, especially the ones with the Filipino dancers with nearly no clothes, they couldn't begin to understand, let alone help me, with my conflicting feelings.

I had a very pessimistic attitude concerning Carole and me ever getting back together again, and I was not only depressed but fearful. The Central Highlands area was becoming a tinderbox full of activity as I saw from the secondhand reports on the nightly news. Then there were those handsome helicopter pilots constantly hitting on the female RNs. No, there wasn't a chance, but I wished I were there, even if it were to take her place for the rest of her tour. I had the same amount of fear for her as if I were there myself. At least I could help take care of her and she wouldn't have to deal with all of the danger on her own. She was terrified after the incident on November 15 and responded nervously to the slightest adverse event, although she tried to hide it from me.

My greeting at Sea-Tac had angered me nearly to the point of rage, and a good amount of animosity prevailed. Whenever I found myself in a crowd or group, the subject eventually always ended up at Vietnam. Somebody would bring up something from the news, and soon, everyone seemed to be trashing the soldiers with the familiar labels: murderers, child killers, and drug-driven psychopaths. Most times, company parted as emotions ran high on both sides and physical reactions seemed imminent.

In a nutshell, I found myself having to deal with all of the crazy, mixed-up emotions that I carried back to the States with me, and not a soul was there to help me sort them out. The army was ignorant of most things of this nature and knew nothing of PTSD. Those who acted out on these emotions to the max were treated by the SOP of whatever police department dealt with them, and that was it. The problems never got solved for most but rather, grew to monumental proportions.

I had a thirty-day leave and nearly became insane with the free time. If only the guilt and the fear, which were still my predominant emotions, would go away. I could deal with the pricks harassing me and attempting to deny me my liberties.

I contend that anyone who spent even a single week in Vietnam carried the fear of God in his or her gut, visible or invisible, admitted or denied. The basis of that fear for each of us was different but equally important. While everyone detested the thought of losing limbs, senses, or even life in that stinking, uncivilized, piece-of-shit country, the fear of not fulfilling one's responsibility and someone dying because of it was uppermost. It is fact that I and the majority of the nurses sent to Vietnam had minimal experience, especially in trauma. All of us carried the baggage of responsibility first for our fellow soldier, then the unit, then the commander, and ultimately, for the good ol' USA. If you made it through all of those responsibilities, all of the wonderful folks back home would greet you upon your return with parades, a pat on the back, a free drink at the local watering hole, and overall respect for just surviving the 'Nam. Just like after the "big war"!

For many nights, even after many years, I awakened in a sweat, hyperventilating and reliving some part of my year over there. The images and sensations were so vivid and real that I relived the horrid, terrible fucking stuff from the 365 days I spent in a rat hole where all the rats looked and acted just the same. So it was and is with a civil war.

The natives always had put-on, shit-eating, toothy grins showing destroyed, black teeth from chewing betel nuts, and they would bow and trot along at your side as you walked, selling or begging or secretly getting your rank for their reports on troop type and number in the area. Many held sincere hatred and determination to "do you in" along with as many of your friends as possible, and only then would you know the good from the bad.

Most of the bad ones were adults, but many were children as young as five through fifteen. This social terrorism was taught and planned and served the Vietcong and the NVA very well. You had no idea if you would survive a trip to the pisser or the shitter after dark, as there were no lights around the primitives. You had no idea if your mama-san, who washed your clothes daily and hung them on the barbed wire to dry, might help herself to your service .45 or your M16 while you were napping off and plug you in the chest. She hated you all that time while showing that black, toothy grin and having snapshots taken with her arm around your waist. She was always bowing to you whenever you returned to your hooch, and she even unlaced your jungle boots so you could quickly catch a few Zs before going back to duty.

Deep down, the Vietnamese had a love-hate relationship with American soldiers. They hated us for what we did to their country, their families, and their way of life while loving us if they were able to benefit from the higher standard of life made possible by working for the military, the black market, or as a whore. Only some realized this was a negative thing because inflation would eventually rip their "economy of little" to shreds.

All of these things perpetuated the terror mentality, ensuring that a soldier never spent a moment of rest in that fucking place where life seemed to be at such a low premium. All of this potential for hatred seemed to permeate the air like the fish-oil odor that hung in our nostrils. Add the nights that sleep was reduced to just a few hours after we decided that it might be OK to drop off when a young face popped to mind and we relived his end hundreds of times over until most of the sleeping hours were gone and the fatigue finally took us.

Or, even worse, the times that we didn't undress or shower because we crashed and burned from sheer exhaustion, only to awaken terrified that we had slept without taking all of the precautions: chair against the door, lights off, .45 under the pillow, M16 locked and loaded and leaning at the head of the bunk, boots spread open so Kevlar came between feet and the filthy fucking ground, flak jacket and helmet on the footlocker at the foot of the bunk—every night of the 365. Once reassured, you might give yourself permission to drop off at some point.

Then there were the frequent nights that we were threatened or visited by the rockets, the mortars, and at times the sappers that made all of the mental stuff more terrifying. The weight of all of this on top of our assigned duty of twelve hours plus per day, seven days per week, was the cross we needed to bear.

The constant, ever-increasing fatigue increased day by day, and I feared that eventually, the symptoms might well overtake me and make me lose contact with reality. I saw many of my comrades with that same affliction. You care little about yourself, your safety, and your purpose, finally reaching a point where you don't expect to make it back to the world. That was me, and I found myself volunteering for the most hazardous and dangerous duties just to break the perpetual pattern. So, what the fuck—survive the day, do what you might, but above all, don't fret and struggle over it. That was my plan.

Trouble is, that never worked. Our responsibility was for every minute of every hour of every day for 365 damn days. Even during the quiet times, you are strung as tight as an overwound watch in anticipation of what was coming next. Sometimes, nothing happened, but it felt like it did when you tried to sleep. Each night became shorter, each day became longer, and each poor grunt who came to you challenged your ability to do the right thing for him—or he often died, taking up more space in that dark, cold part of your mind. He was in your keeping, and he always seemed to have confidence in you and your comrades. He counted on you to pull him up out of that terrible goddamned hole where it was growing dark, where faces and objects were blurring and spinning around in a circle and making him so disoriented that he really didn't care which direction he ended up going, just so he got there. It was like being sick on the Tilt-A-Whirl. You didn't care if you fell off or got off normally, just so you were off. It was our responsibility to save him. It was our job to keep him from the darkness. I know these facts well; I did it all over again just last night. I am their keeper, their reluctant servant.

Carole and Me Shortly after Our Wedding in October, 1970

Back in the World, Some Things Don't Go as Planned

—⚶—

SNOWBOARDING IN NORTHERN MICHIGAN

IT WAS FEBRUARY, AND WE were receiving one of the record blizzards that we'd become so accustomed to in our Lake Michigan community. Nearly three feet of new snow on top of one and a half feet already on the ground put our county into that surrealistic, lazy, half-pace mode that takes hold because nothing will move any faster, period. The snow blanketed the trees, the roofs, and the telephone lines and interrupted or suspended electrical power to many areas of the county.

The hospital that I worked at the previous night was on emergency power most of the night off and on, and our workload had tripled because of all of the necessary extra procedural things that need to be done when you are not operating up to capacity. I arrived home late in the morning at about ten, but I couldn't get the car down my long drive through the cedar pines and the deep snow to my little chalet alongside the Platte River. At eleven, I was finally at my front door, cold and exhausted after struggling on foot a hundred yards through three feet of snow.

I made myself a cup of hot chocolate and tried to contact the fellow that plowed my drive, and after several attempts, I reached him. He laughed at me, saying, "I have a pickup truck, not a bulldozer." At that point, I was really concerned, as I not only worked 7:00 p.m. to 7:00 a.m. at the local hospital about ten miles away, but I was also a volunteer EMT who took calls during the day shift and on off-shift nights from the hospital.

The crew appreciated my presence as an RN since I was able to bring just a little extra to the service through the things I could do that were not permitted to an EMT. I really wasn't legally authorized to do those things, but the county endorsed me, and I was very careful with the way I used the skills—although, in retrospect, that might have been legally dangerous, legally. At any rate, I wouldn't be doing anything if I didn't get my driveway cleared.

My vehicle was nearly a half mile away at a turnaround point for the sand and salt trucks, and I would never be able to make it to the ambulance barn on time before the unit left. As I started my second cup of hot chocolate and watched the branches of the huge bush in front of my house bend closer and closer to the ground, I recognized the scraping and grating of the county snowplows, huge V plows with concrete or steel ballast that were capable of moving near-mountain-size piles of snow. One sounded like it was in my drive!

I put on my soggy boots and my down vest and plodded out into the cold once again just in time to see Rich, one of the other volunteer EMTs, who also worked for the road commission, making a beeline for the bank of the river, pushing a huge pile of snow. After raising the depth of the river by an inch or so (just kidding), he made one more pass back toward the road, finishing a beautifully cleared runway for my Toyota four-by-four. Rich gave me a Santa-like wave as he turned the corner and drove out of sight. I knew we would see each other several times over the next few days.

I took a quick shower after retrieving my truck, put on flannels, and stretched out on the couch with my golden retriever, Chelsea, and told her all about my night. She was only about one and a half years old and couldn't get enough of the hospital stories that I shared with her each morning. I had slept merely minutes, it seemed, even though it was two hours, when my wife awakened me with the news that my ambulance radio was going off.

I listened. It turned out to be about the first of several car accidents and other "chest pains" of the day, none of which resulted in death or serious consequences. It snowed nearly all day, making conditions even worse for travel, and I was pleased that no more ambulance runs occurred after 4:00 p.m. I had the night off at the hospital, so I had my mind set on a relaxing dinner with the family, some TV, and an early night to bed.

At 2:00 a.m., the ambulance radio screeched again, and I knew my night was about to turn from comfort and warmth to misery and ball-chilling cold. I put on my hunting compression underwear and another thermal layer and finally my goose-down parka and my Rockies and headed down the stairs, boot laces hitting the paneling on the way. I heard my wife complaining angrily that we would never have a normal life with me chasing four jobs at once.

In addition to the three I've already mentioned, I was also a certified EMT instructor and taught a full basic course as well as refresher courses. At one time, I had five jobs at once, as there were few instructors in our rural area and ongoing refresher sessions were required to keep licenses current. It was a pace that I did not intend on keeping for very long, but the money was excellent, and I felt that I was fulfilling a needed service. My friend Terry was the director of our county ambulance service, and he was very well connected with most of the elected and appointed officials, so our service never suffered from needed equipment or fair pay.

When I arrived at the ambulance barn, the bus was already outside, spewing foggy, hot exhaust into the cold, bone-chilling air. The snow had stopped, but a cold wind was blowing in from the west, moving snow clouds over us that appeared extra black against the full moon. It was an eerie sight typical of a Poe setting. The crew was still scant, with Terry driving and Dick and me as the "back caregivers." We always preferred a fourth for extreme weather or conditions out of the ordinary. Keith showed up in his pickup, sliding sideways into the parking lot. He hurriedly piled in, and we were off.

Terry shook his head and grimaced when he said, "You're not going to like this one." It so happened that the run was to an elderly gentleman's home on the hill overlooking Crystal Lake. Most of the residents on the lake were senior-citizen snowbirds who rarely stayed in the area during the winter. On occasion, out of just being too old to care or for other important reasons, some stayed and tried to tough it out in the harsh, northern Michigan winter. This could be a very difficult situation because the roads to most of these homes were rarely kept open during the winter, and it was very difficult to gain access with the big rigs we used for EMS.

We were told to wait for the county plow to go ahead of us in hopes of accessing the home normally from the road at the top of the large hill. The very first attempt at the huge snow load found the county truck hopelessly stuck and calling for another larger unit to pull it out so that he might pound his way in, in tandem with the rescue truck. We quickly decided from our post position after listening to the radio traffic between the snowplow and the county dispatch that we could not wait. Dispatch was now telling us that the call had turned from a "chest pain" to a "man down." Never a good sign.

We raced toward the bottom of the hill on the hard road and slid completely through the stop at the bottom, through a small, unwooded area, and nearly into Crystal Lake. We bailed out of the ambulance, breathless with the anxiety of the near mishap, and proceeded to load a backboard stretcher with gear that we would need for a resuscitation. The air was so bitterly cold that it burned the inside of our chests even with the shallowest breath. In the meantime, Terry called dispatch and told them to call out a truck to the bottom of the hill to pull the ambulance back onto the roadway.

With the bobsled backboard loaded with our supplies, we looked up the hill. It was dispiriting to watch the tiny headlights of the two tow trucks and the single home light through blowing snow. We lunged on each and every step, making progress but very, very slowly. Terry was a pretty big guy and was monumental in making a three-man path. I must say, he had a helluva constitution considering his size. It took more than an hour to make the hill, and when we were nearly to the top, dispatch called and said there was no problem in recovering the ambulance but that we should not plan on the roadway being cleared at the top.

They had also received another call from the wife saying that the man was still on the floor and could not get up. They said the lady was unusually calm and didn't sound like she was appropriately alarmed about her husband's condition. This gave us a brief feeling of relief, thinking his condition was not that grave, but that comfort would soon vanish. When we got to the base of the home, we encountered a long, twenty-foot set of stairs that ended on a platform just past the corner of the house that then took a ninety-degree angle to the left and another twenty feet to the usable door in the back. The steps were, of course, piled high with snow nearly to the handrail, and it was just a guess as to where the steps actually were underneath.

We slogged through in single file, pulling the backboard sled behind until we finally reached the top. We encountered the wife upon entering, and she very calmly and politely led us to the back bathroom where we found her husband lying on the floor with his drawers down and in a pool of urine and blood at the other end. She told us that she had last seen him just after the news at 11:00 p.m. She had gone to bed, but he went to follow his usual routine in the bathroom before retiring.

It was obvious that the man had had a catastrophic event when he was on the commode and had fallen forward into the plumbing of the sink, making a considerable gash on his bald head before falling to the floor. It was also obvious that the poor soul was quite dead and probably had been since shortly after the nightly news. It was now nearly 4:00 a.m.

Terry immediately took the wife aside to the living room and tried to explain that he felt that her hubby was gone, but it just didn't seem to register with her. He explained this several times, but she insisted that we do everything to save him because she "needed him badly and didn't know how she could live without him." Terry asked me to give it a try. I found myself speaking to the little, pathetic, vulnerable woman, who was clearly very senile and needed a much better setting in which to deal with the loss of her spouse.

I suggested that we proceed with the patient as if he were still viable and remove him while the wife was relatively calm. All of us thought this an excellent plan, so we loaded the poor man onto the backboard and put a couple of blankets on him and strapped him securely to the board, which seemed to please the wife.

We started out into the night onto the first set of twenty stairs with Dick straddling the patient to fake CPR. The patient was eased down the first few feet with Terry anchoring the whole operation with a rope tied to the backboard and the other end wrapped around his waist. As he slowly moved down the steps with the patient and Dick ahead of him, all hell broke loose.

Terry's foot went through the space between two steps, and he lurched forward and lost control of the rope, letting the bobsled with Dick and the patient free slide for the fifteen or so feet down the steps. They hit the landing, and the wooden railing at the end exploded as they crashed through and plummeted out into the night, much like a ski jumper might take flight. We looked at each other aghast and dumbstruck as they disappeared into the darkness.

Fortunately, the wife was still indoors, unknowing of the disaster going on outside. According to Dick, he and the patient careened down the hill at breakneck speed until they finally piled up against a tree trunk about three-quarters of the way down. Dick would tell us that it was like an explosion as the backboard shattered. The man was thrown to the side, still strapped to part of the board, and he and the equipment flew in all directions.

By the time we all made it down the hill to the site of the carnage, Dick was sitting in the snow, laughing his ass off. He had sustained a nasty arm bruise and a scrape on his cheek. The patient was pretty much the same as before: quite dead. Terry said, "No one would ever believe this story in a million years." We all decided that it should remain a secret among the four of us until it no longer mattered. And so, more than thirty years later, we are all old enough not to care.

DETROIT IS NOT ALL THAT BURNS ON HALLOWEEN

October was my favorite month in Northwest Michigan on the Platte. The weather was most often pleasant and warm—what we called our Indian Summer. The salmon had nearly finished running upstream by this time, and the beautiful steelhead were generally heavy in the stream, gorging on the thousands of eggs laid by the spawning salmon. There was always the occasional brown trout taking advantage of the feast, and usually, they were pigs (quite fat and not proportionate in length or weight). Also, bow-hunting season opened on the first of October and continued until the first day of firearm deer season on November 15.

This country was truly heaven, and throughout my ten years of living in this outdoorsman's paradise, I pondered how lucky I was to have a great job, a wonderful chalet on the river, a wonderful wife, and a young, beautiful daughter who was and remains—excuse the expression—the light of my life. I loved the outdoors and spent a lot of my spare time enjoying all that my little slice of heaven offered. I fished literally off my back porch, hunted in my backyard, and never felt cheated of options for entertainment.

I worked as a night nursing supervisor until my promotion to director of nursing and assistant administrator at the local hospital about ten or twelve miles away. It was a big part of my wonderful, made-in-heaven situation until the corporate-takeover bullshit became the way of the land. We had two major hospital systems within sixty miles of our facility, and the competition for the occasional specialty patient that we transferred was intense. It became so intense that after a few years of bribing our old-guard board of directors and kissing ass with the physicians, one of the hospitals offered to take over the small facility. It led us into a huge expansion project full of debt and then insisted on managing the hospital in a somewhat peaceful takeover. Of course, all of the administrative staff, of which I was now part of after my promotion, was replaced by the larger hospital's corporate clones.

I was offered a job several levels down in the pay scale. Ironically, it included the same responsibilities that I had before, only with a different title and a lower salary. I accepted it bitterly, but only while I secretly scouted out new ground in the state of Florida.

It was during this period that folks who had poured their hearts and souls into our facility, even though still doing a fantastic job for the patient, really didn't give a flying fuck about the ownership and management bunch. Most said that if the takeover had been more above the table, they would not have felt so cheated and thus would be more inclined to work for the new "suits." I don't know. I don't believe that would ever have happened, as our old management was a group of good ol' boys, and while our work was very difficult, we had a whopping, super time as employees.

We had accomplished a bunch for the hospital by planning and building on a new ICU and ER. We had applied for and received, after months of work by yours truly, sole community provider status, which increased our Medicare reimbursement by nearly one million dollars a year. We held many functions, including fund raisers for the hospital and for disadvantaged groups. We had employee poker nights that cost $10.00 to play and drink all night where half of the up-front money went to a nonprofit and half was up for grabs to whomever of the twenty to twenty-five guests did best at several poker, roulette, craps, or bingo games. It was always a great time when we were all together.

One October, I worked the night before Halloween and had the actual holiday off. The night I worked was hellish, and I was late getting home, only to have to make an ambulance run almost immediately after changing clothes. After the run, I collapsed onto my bed in the upstairs room and slept until late afternoon. When I awakened, I looked out into the drive to find my Chevy Blazer completely covered with several layers of toilet paper. All the trees around the house had streamers of white, green, and yellow toilet tissue. My house windows were soaped and had "Hello, how are ya" messages written everywhere along with "Happy Halloween." I suspected it was the doing of my work mates, as we frequently traded treacheries. I believe I was up on them by a couple until that afternoon.

I knew there was a lingering danger that holiday, as I was on ambulance call, and the Blazer was the only vehicle I had to my avail. I figured the quickest way to get rid of the paper and clean the soapy windows was to use the garden hose to soak it down. That removed half the streamers, but it stuck the other half to the surface of my vehicle.

I removed a large amount of the soaked, sticky toilet paper and was in the process of trying to scrub the soap off with a plastic putty knife when the ambulance radio went off. I was paralyzed momentarily just at the thought. I jumped into the Blazer and answered the call. I learned that just three roads down from me, a man was acting strangely, staggering and passing out. His grown daughter was very concerned, as he had never behaved this way before.

His house was beside the river on a sandy, unimproved, narrow, two-track road. There were several little turnoffs on the road leading to small clusters of trailers, which were on cul-de-sacs. The daughter was going to meet the first responder at the end of the road where it met the blacktop and lead them through the maze to her father's house.

I made it there in little time, just as the daughter was approaching the hard road. She was visiting her dad from downstate and really didn't know how volunteer ambulance services did business. She was very reluctant to believe that I was a first responder with the service. My Blazer still held many obvious traces of dried toilet paper clinging to the black paint, and I could tell that she had very serious concerns about getting into the vehicle. Ultimately, though, she agreed to lead me back to her father's place.

We bounced along the sandy, tree-rooted road, and she was quiet other than telling me where to turn. She was not at all convinced this was legit, and I saw her looking at the door handle several times as though assuring herself of an exit strategy.

I had just made a turn as directed, and we hit a humongous root. We both bounced a bit on the old Blazer's well-worn suspension. When the body of the old thing bottomed out with a thump, the dash-box door flew open, and another of the Halloween pranks from the group at work reared its ugly head. A tampon flavored with ketchup popped out right onto this lady's lap. She let out a scream and proceeded to tell me what kind of a lame, goddamned outfit this was and that she really didn't expect much good to come of this day. She cried while screaming out an indictment of me, my truck, the ambulance service, this hick country, and all else that went with it.

I tried to console her, but it was hopeless. So I just went for the home run and told her, "Just get me to your father, and I will make sure he makes it to the hospital."

When we reached the house, the little, old man, who would weigh all of seventy-five-pounds soaking wet and with a belly full of Bud, was sitting in his easy chair. He was a nice, old guy and introduced me to his daughter, who was standing in front of him, still dumbstruck. I, of course, was already checking out his systems, and the big clue came almost immediately upon checking his pulse. His heart rate was very slow, and the beat was very heavy. He stated he was very weak and felt short of breath. I immediately felt that he was in complete heart block.

When he and I, and, yes, his daughter and my Blazer met with the ambulance at the hard road, the monitor immediately confirmed third-degree heart block at about 38 per minute. We started oxygen right away, and I put in an IV line. I did not have access to a pacemaker at this level of care, but I did have some emergency drugs. After I contacted the hospital ER, they gave me permission to use Atropine as the condition warranted. His BP was stable but low at 100/50, and with the oxygen, his nail beds seemed passably pink. I learned long ago, if it ain't broke, don't fix it, so I held back on the Atropine for then. His daughter was directed to go ahead to the hospital and start giving helpful history to the Emergency Department staff while we finished up the prelims and came behind.

We secured the old man onto our comfortable stretcher, but I placed an arrest board under him so that it would be ready to go if needed. The gentleman was very nice and more concerned about me not having a comfortable place to sit alongside him rather than about his condition. The monitor continued to show a heart rate with a junctional pacemaker at 36 to 38 per minute, and I put the heart alarm on 34. It seemed when he was talking, his rate stayed up a bit, but I think that was just a coincidence. We started out with Terry once again driving and Dick in the passenger seat up front. There was little that more than one attendant could do in the back.

We traveled only a mile or so, and I began getting faint whiffs of what smelled like plastic. It would come and go, at times stronger than before. I leaned through the pass-through to see if the guys were doing anything that would cause the smell. I asked Dick, "You aren't sneaking a cigarette, are you?" He looked at me weirdly and blew it off.

I monitored the patient, and his heart rate was just bumping on 34 at times, and his BP was now 90/48. His color was still OK, but he complained of a little chest tightness. I got on the radio and asked the hospital ER for permission once again, based on the new vital-sign numbers, to give the Atropine. They advised me to give 0.5 mg Atropine IV if we were still a good distance out. I opened my discreet drug box and was rooting through my syringes and needles when I got a big whiff of something burning. I yelled at Terry and told him that I smelled smoke for sure and we needed to check it out.

Terry and Dick were not real keen on making the run to the hospital any more drawn out than necessary. Neither of them really had any experience with the more intense levels of care involving the use of drugs on cardiac patients, and both were understandably worried. Terry nonetheless pulled the big rig over and got out to inspect the unit. He walked around it several times and then looked under the hood. He peeked into the care compartment and told me he could find nothing.

Just as he was to get back into the rig, a passerby stopped and asked if there was anything wrong and could he help. Before Terry could answer, the guy said that he could smell a fire somewhere. Was that what we were going to? Terry was perplexed. After the passerby left, we continued the drive to the hospital. My patient's heart rate, in the meantime, had gone back up to thirty-eight to forty, so I decided to use verbal stimulation instead of the drug unless he absolutely bottomed out.

We had traveled about a mile or two when the stench of burning plastic became so strong that my patient said that it was making it harder for him to breathe. I replaced his regular O_2 face mask with a rebreather mask, turning up the O_2 flow to twelve liters a minute. Just as I was about to take his BP and after turning the soft interior light on, I looked up to see this brown spot on the white vinyl headliner gradually get larger and larger. I told Terry to pull over immediately, as we were definitely dealing with a fire.

He asked if we shouldn't just go like hell for the remaining four miles instead of stopping as I recommended. While he was speaking, I noticed that we were going faster and faster, while the brown spot was growing larger and larger. I told him to pull over. "*Stop now!*" By the time the ambulance came to a complete stop, the brown spot had gone from about four inches across to a hole the size of a watermelon. We could see flames sparking between the hard metal roof and the headliner, and soon, just as we cleared the old man from the unit, the roof burst into flames.

Terry called for the FD and backup ambulance while Dick worked on the fire with the portable extinguisher. There was smoke everywhere, and we had to keep moving the poor little man further and further from the unit, down the asphalt pavement of M-22. They set up emergency lights all around the unit, and I continued checking the patient. It appeared the excitement was doing him good, as he maintained a decent BP at a heart rate of 38.

Three or four vehicles came by while the ambulance was in flames. Terry, Dick, and I were lined up on the hard road with the patient on the wheeled stretcher. Each of them slowed down for a better look and asked whether anyone was injured or if we were the only vehicle involved, assuming that it was an accident. No one questioned that a man was covered with blankets, lying on a stretcher sitting at the side of a rural road with an ambulance ablaze thirty feet away.

Terry, Dick, and I chatted with the old man while waiting for what seemed hours. In reality, it was less than twenty minutes before the fire truck arrived. A sheriff's deputy was right behind, and within a few more minutes, the backup ambulance arrived. The old man's heart rate was now well above 40, and his pressure was holding at 100 and above systolic. We had a grand time chatting with him and continued our conversation about the largest brown trout ever taken out of the Platte River, the wonderful gift of nature that we both were lucky enough to live alongside.

Upon loading the patient and our gear into the new ambulance with Terry and Dick squeezed in as the extra fourth and fifth passengers, we slowly headed toward the hospital about four miles away. As we pulled in, the man's daughter was waiting at the ambulance entrance door with her hands on her hips, and she was a wreck. Terry managed to lure her away for a moment while we whisked the old guy into the ER, closer to all of the lifesaving equipment he might need.

It so happened that the old guy spent the night in the hospital and never had any further difficulty. He was transferred the next morning by ambulance to our referral hospital for a permanent pacemaker insertion. Upon a visit by Terry the next day, according to the old guy, his daughter was ready to lay us out and give it to us royally, but he insisted she not go there. He felt he had had excellent care, and none of the circumstances could have been prevented. He, of course, did not know of the tampon and the glitch that his daughter and I had first started out with.

Ironically, his daughter sent us a donation in his honor and remembrance a few years later, earmarked for the ambulance service. The note said, "Thank you for giving my dad the greatest of memories during his last years here on earth. He told me that he, for once, felt like a person, not a patient, while he was in your keeping. He never felt like he was in danger at all. Knowing all of the circumstances and details of that night, you guys and your service must be a bunch of fine people who do what you love, taking care of folks in need. Thank you. Pauline, in memory of George, my father."

Almost as Good as New

I always hated it when the ambulance radio blared out, "Injuries from domestic dispute." The components of these calls were challenging. There were obvious medical issues to deal with, but there were also the hidden psychological issues without clear-cut solutions at our level of care. Additionally, there were frequently children and bystanders that needed attention, if not care. This run had all of the elements and all of the bone-chilling variables to handle, leaving one scratching his head afterward and saying, "What the fuck am I doing in this type of work?"

We were directed to a mobile-home community alongside the main road outside of Honor. We had been there many times before. It is home to many families struggling to enter the middle class through difficult labor, lower-paying jobs, and, most important, burgeoning debt. Most of the folks there were making it, but just barely. The sheriff was called there frequently on "domestics," and on some of those occasions, we were called as well to attend injuries.

On June 4, 1991, we arrived at the scene. It was like a circus. Police tape encircled the forty-foot-long mobile home, and a perimeter had been created another three hundred feet out around it, putting many people, including children, out onto an adjacent street. Some were lucky enough to have a relative in another part of the park where they could go, but I believe most stayed behind the crime-scene tape just to see the damage that might have taken place. They would wait for some time.

The emergency-rescue unit was not permitted past the final perimeter until the state police could ensure that all threats had been removed. According to our report, the wife and two young girls of about three and six remained in the home with the father, who was the suspect for domestic assault. We talked with the lieutenant for an up-to-date report and were told to turn off our flashing lights, sit back, and relax until we were given the OK to move in with our equipment.

After chatting among ourselves for a bit, the three of us found comfortable spots in the ambulance and fell asleep. After what seemed like only seconds and an eternity at the same time, the lieutenant tapped on our window, telling us it was OK to enter the building and that the mother and two girls had been removed safely.

We entered the open front door, and as I got to the bedroom at the end of a long, narrow hallway, a large state-police officer was gathering some evidence. He looked at me, pale and shaking his head. Without speaking, other than with his eyes, he suggested that this guy had bought the farm; he was gone.

My mind quickly tried to adjust from two hours of waiting, wondering, and being asleep to a white room with a yellow, bare bulb in the dresser lamp casting eerie shadows on the walls and ceiling, capped off by a worn, dirty, white carpet. Mixed in with the yellow-tinted-white everything, on the other side of the room, were very detailed marks in blood in a pattern that appeared to have been painted there. The splatter was everywhere on the bed and the ceiling. The bedroom was extremely small.

Apparently, the entire family had been held hostage there, sitting on the bed while the father had rambled on in a thoughtless rage about not being fit to raise such a wonderful family and that they would be far better off without him. According to the testimony his wife had given the officer in charge, he had lost two jobs in the last three months due to drinking problems, and they weren't even making lot rental with the wages he made. His mother had purchased him a $500,000 life-insurance policy in his youth, and he had made the decision to make at least 75 percent of his family happy.

He apparently had threatened this act several times in the past, but tonight, with his family sitting on the bed, he had placed the butt of the twelve-gauge, double-barreled Winchester on the floor, leaned his chin out over the barrels, and in spite of his wife pleading and his children crying, "Please, Daddy, don't do it, we'll be good, we promise!"—*Kabooom*!

This all had taken place just after the police arrived in response to a domestic involving a firearm. When they came storming into the trailer, they were appalled at the horrific scene that awaited them. Assuming the victim to be dead, they moved the family to the other end of the trailer to the kitchen and would not permit the family to change clothes or to wash up until all evidence was collected and photographs taken. They were transferred to a local hospital by the police for medical examination and psychological support.

As I moved around the bottom of the bed, a large glob of bloody brain tissue fell from the ceiling, landing on my shoulder. The policeman said, "Don't touch. I'll take that for evidence." I first saw the man's two feet as he lay face down at the bottom of the far side of the bed. As I walked alongside his body toward his head, my heavy-soled shoes crunched small pieces of bone from his face and skull into the cushion of the carpet. The sensation and the thoughts that went with it nearly made me vomit.

One side of the man's jawbone was nearly intact and lying on the blood-splattered dresser. As I stood watching him, I thought that I saw his shoulder blades rise ever so slightly. The cop saw me watching and assured me that he was one dead man, as he had been here for nearly a half hour, and he hadn't moved.

I gently turned him over on his back, and the man immediately began coughing and choking. His massive head wound was causing his own blood to pour down the small hole deep in the crater of flesh that was the opening to his airway. I was both surprised and completely overwhelmed with a sense of duty to save a life versus dealing with a horrendously disfiguring, self-inflicted shotgun wound of the head. I turned the patient onto his side so his airway would remain partially open and leaned over to speak to him. "Do you want to live now?" Surprisingly, he heard me, and he nodded yes.

His lower jaw was completely gone, as was the majority of his upper maxilla, leaving a cavern of injured, destroyed, bleeding tissue. His nose, left ear, and a part of the frontal portion of his forehead were gone. Gray matter mixed with the oozing blood from the gaping hole in his skull pooled into the cavities of his face wound. The bleeding was massive, with small arterioles pumping out his lifeblood, which had formed a huge clot on the floor and most probably had saved him up to this point by forming some type of channel allowing air to be taken in through the small, nickel-sized hole deep in the bloody, red tissue. Large air bubbles of blood were expelled on each expiration, and I surmised that the volume of air he was getting into his lungs had been at least temporarily adequate, though barely. He was able to move all of his extremities slightly when asked to do so.

My immediate challenge was to establish and secure a good airway and to prevent the patient from aspirating and choking to death on his own blood. I radioed the other EMTs on scene to bring all of my airway equipment and the oxygen delivery-on-demand device into the room. Before I finished my list of needs, most of it was lying on the bed in front of me, opened and ready to go. Our unit was phenomenal at working together and anticipating each other's needs.

I grabbed a soft, red Robinson cuffed nasal-tracheal tube about the circumference of my index finger and gently fished the tip through hamburger-like tissue until I was able to see the opening of the airway, which was, in this case, a small ring of trachea one band above his larynx. I slid the tube down another two inches, causing the patient to heave his body, retch, and cough violently, sending blood spatter all about the room, into my face, and my EMT partner's face. Even though we were well aware of the possibility of blood-borne pathogens, especially HIV and hepatitis, we continued working feverishly to establish the airway before attending the mess.

I gently inflated the cuff on the tube, and more coughing evolved for just a short period. I listened at the end of the tube, and a good flow of air was moving in and out on each breath. He had good breath sounds on both sides, so I had one of my helpers hold O_2 tubing near the opening with liter flow at eight per minute while I tied umbilical tape around the tube, preparing to secure it in place. The bleeding continued quite profusely, and I packed the cavity snugly full of gauze fluffs.

Once I had a mountain of gauze over the entire face and skull wounds and around the endotracheal tube, I gently but snugly wrapped Kerlix around the entire head to secure the dressing in place. I then tied the endotape together near the back of the head to keep the tube from moving or becoming dislodged. We all shared doing the remainder of the patient survey so we could safely transport the patient. We were soon loaded, and with a three-police-car escort with lights and sirens, we raced to a Traverse City hospital about twenty miles away.

When we arrived in the ER, the doctor and the nurse attending were surprised that we had a patient still living. His vital signs were stable, although reflective of blood loss and excitement, at BP 100/60 and pulse 110. When the ER doctor started to remove dressings from the face, I suggested that they have a bunch of new ones on hand that could be used quickly. The doctor looked up at me and said, "We'll be taking care of this patient now, if you don't mind!"

I said "No, I don't mind, as long as you do it well. If you need any more information, we will be out on the bus." After about an hour, Terry went back into the ER and was gone for some time. As we later learned, once the patient had left the ER for surgery, Terry and the doctor had a face-to-face confrontation. The doctor conceded that he was wrong and had been rude because he was nervous and upset over the injury. He said we did a fantastic job and most certainly saved the man's life. He offered apologies to all of our crew.

Months later, our crew was attending our monthly emergency service meeting, and Terry reported that the man had had a complete turnaround psychologically. He was in rehab and learning skills using his hands. He was blind and mute and had to feed through a tube and breathe through a tracheotomy. He said the man had found God, and with the support of most of his family, he was in a much better place than before and wanted to move on with his life. Amazing how much one must sometimes sacrifice before realizing how valuable what's left over adds up to, especially when it's a matter of life.

CHRISTMAS IN FLORIDA

It was a beautiful evening in mid-central Florida. There was a soft, warm breeze on the starlit night as I drove to my job in Tarpon Springs. It was my turn to work Christmas Eve and the holiday, and I was somewhat disappointed that I would be spending them away from my family. Christmas has always meant a great deal to me and my family as a time for reaffirming our love and trust in those who ultimately stay standing beside us as we face our most difficult times.

My childhood memories of that day of the year are the greatest. I still recall the sounds, the smells, and certainly the vision of our huge family get-together at my Grandma Slater's house. But most of all, I remember the feelings, a peace not felt on the other 364 days of the year. Only on this day did all of my very stubborn, pig-headed uncles struggle to keep opinions to themselves that so frequently in the past had shattered relationships for months at a time. Christmas was a time for laughter, fun, devotion, good eating, and sharing, not for bad things like arguing and bickering and complaining. It was a time to live, not die.

For the first time since I'd worked at this particular hospital, our night-shift crew had decided that along with the usual bring-a-dish routine, we would dress in holiday attire. The other two nurses dressed as Mr. and Mrs. Santa, and I dressed as an elf complete with green leotards, green shorts, a white shirt, and green vest, all topped off with elf ears and the standard elf hat. My daughter and my spouse had spent a lot of time finding all of the components that might come close to fitting a forty-year-old jolly elf, and they were quite proud of the finished product. It added a little blush to my cheeks.

The shift was going along quite nicely, with the usual stuff. There were a couple of drunks, a chest pain or two, a few with abdominal pain, and the usual drug seekers. The west coast of Central Florida was huge in the illegal-drug-traffic trade, and we got our share of all the things that went wrong as a result—everything from gunshot wounds to near drowning to overdoses and any one of a hundred other complaints.

One drug dealer of fair significance to law enforcement had inadvertently left his address book at the bedside of his girlfriend, whom we treated for an illness. When she was discharged, we looked inside for a telephone number to call and let the boyfriend know he had forgotten the book. We discovered hundreds of first names and incomplete addresses of scheduled hookups for what we figured were drug sales.

We photocopied the entire book, called our good friend Brad from the local police department, and he was there in a flash. He asked that we keep the address book, as the guy would most likely be back and we were to give it to him as though nothing happened. Sure enough, within the hour, the girlfriend called, asking about "her" address book, and we said, yes, we had it. They picked up the book, and all went well, with no apparent suspicions from her or her boyfriend, the dealer.

At that point, the evening went to hell in a hand basket. With me in my elf suit, we received back-to-back ambulance calls. One forty-five-year-old patient had chest pain, and another patient had walked through a sliding-glass window at one of the famous fast-food places. Of course, both units arrived at the ER at the same time, and concurrent to their arrival, we were summoned to the reception area for a guy who had been dropped off outside our entrance covered with blood. He said someone had stabbed him at the local bar during a robbery attempt.

The two Santas and I put our present patients at rest with a brief explanation that if we didn't show for a bit, we hadn't left but would be with others and assured them they would be cared for properly. They smiled. After all, they were dealing with Santa, his wife, and his elf.

The Santa family took on the ambulance patients while I attended the stab wound in the reception area who was quickly growing weak. I took a wheeled stretcher there and helped him lie down. He smelled heavily of alcohol and urine. While I assisted him, his blood-soaked shirt smeared all over the front of my elf outfit, and I was leaving bloody handprints all over him and myself while struggling to get him on the stretcher. It was truly a mess.

The guy was becoming frightened by the amount of red stuff he was spilling on the floor, but I assured him we would take care of him. I wheeled him into one of the care bays and immediately started a large-bore IV with normal saline running at a good clip. Before starting the fluid, I relieved him of several tubes of blood that would help us later with the status of his blood volume and his alcohol level.

I examined the wound a bit closer upon removing his shirt and found that he had a puncture wound in the right upper quadrant of his abdomen. He complained of no pain but repeatedly swore about the motherfucker that had done this to him. He denied other injuries, but I completed a patient survey to ensure that was the case. The more he chattered, the more obvious it became that he knew his assailant, and it probably hadn't been a robbery at all but rather an argument gone long and wrong.

The ER doctor took a look at him, checked his charted vital signs, and ordered a CT scan to attempt to determine the amount of intra-abdominal bleeding and its source. I took him to X-ray, and had just gotten him on the table when the phone rang. The folks in the ER needed me stat, meaning five minutes before the phone call. I informed the CT tech to call me immediately if anything went wrong, as I knew he was experienced and trustworthy. I tore over to the care area to find chaos had broken loose.

The chest-pain patient, whom Santa had thought to be settling down and probably would turn out to be indigestion, was in and out of ventricular tachycardia. Santa had already bolused him twice with lidocaine. I nodded to her to prepare the paddles, as the man was now unconscious and needed a more advanced step in our protocol. We shocked him three times. He was now in ventricular fibrillation, and a full cardiac code was called.

As soon as the code team arrived and Santa felt comfortable with her patient, I proceeded to the man who had fought the plate-glass window.

He was a black man, and the skin color around his mouth and eyes were gray. His speech was slurred. A large piece of glass had broken off and hit the underside of his upstretched arm, more than likely in a natural defensive posture, and it had cut a deep swath to include veins, tendons, and arteries all the way up his forearm until burying itself in his right axilla (armpit).

The piece of plate glass had shaved a large piece of his forearm, about the size of the tongue of a work boot. A second shard of glass had found its mark dead-on in the poor man's axilla. A small piece was protruding and it bounced at the pace of his heart as it sat on or in the gentleman's brachial artery. Ends of arteries were sticking out from the flesh, pumping precious stuff onto the stretcher but very weakly and very slowly. The character of the blood loss was not a good sign at all, since the injury was horrendous and blood was barely dripping now.

I instructed Mrs. Santa not to remove the glass shard but to start a second IV, get a hemoglobin and hematocrit (H and H), type, and cross-match for four units of blood and four units of fresh-frozen plasma. She was to elevate the arm and apply pressure on active bleeders while avoiding the shard of glass, start oxygen at ten liters per minute by mask and run in a liter of NS at wide-open rate and a second to follow at 150 cc until BP stabilized at 100 systolic. Such was the beginning of our Christmas fiasco.

I retrieved our man from CT, and he was looking a little more comfortable with oxygen and some replacement fluid on board. The bleeding had not soaked through the dressing I had applied. This did not mean he wasn't bleeding, as he had a gut to fill internally, and that kind of bleeding wouldn't be nearly so obvious. By the time I got him settled in his spot back in the ER, the surgeon on call had arrived and was looking over his chart. The CT tech brought the films to him in the ER, and he immediately called in the OR crew for an emergency exploratory laparoscopy with probable liver repair.

I explained that he might want to consider our second patient as well, and upon seeing the man and the arm injury, he summoned the backup surgeon on call and a second OR crew, as these operations would have to be done simultaneously and would take a goodly amount of time. While the nursing supervisor watched over the two surgical patients, who were a little more stable, I returned to the code just as they were calling it unsuccessful. He was pronounced dead at 10:40 p.m. This would not be a good Christmas for his wife and loved ones who sat waiting in the quiet room.

As I stood among the family of six in the visitors' quiet room, which was used by the families of patients who awaited extremely long procedures and family members whose loved ones had serious events requiring intensive care in the ER, I wondered what a nurse in an elf suit might say to a family that had just lost a loved one. I trembled at the thought. I had gone through this terrible task hundreds of times, but never in an elf suit.

I twisted my mouth into the most serious grimace I could imagine and looked the wife dead in the eye. I told her that I was extremely sorry to inform her that her husband had not survived the heart attack. She and her daughters broke into mournful wails, and I stood silently to give them a period to grieve. Allowing undisturbed time to the family after announcing the death, I had learned, was golden, for their sake.

The wife eventually asked if he had experienced a lot of pain, and I said that I didn't feel it had been the case. I assured her that we had tried every possible procedure, that her husband had been a real fighter, and that we had felt that we might have a chance to bring him back, but it was not to be. I finished my sad task with them by saying, "Again, I am extremely sorry to have to give you this very sad news while dressed in this ridiculous suit. It really bothers me, and I apologize for that." After a short cry by the relatives, they thanked me, and the wife said that she really didn't mind seeing the efforts of the elf and Santa doing all they could for those in need.

Several days later, she informed the administrator of our wonderful work, even while in our holiday dress. Although she had been more than pleased with her husband's care, the administrator wanted to discuss our choice of work clothes later.

The ER was empty at the moment, and I stepped outdoors into the warm, breezy night. Looking up at the magnificently starlit sky, I recognized our significance, and the level at which we shared ourselves with our loved ones and friends became thought provoking in the scheme of all things. I smoked a Winston and returned to the mess inside that would take hours to put back in order. The night was yet young.

The man with the liver wound recovered, but slowly, because of his alcohol abuse.

The man injured by the glass window received many vein and artery repairs but survived to order many more burgers.

The drug dealer was arrested for felonies three months later. The police had documented several of his sales with photo evidence and cut deals with the buyers to testify against him in court. The book scheme had worked out well. The police reminded us to keep our eyes open for any others that might turn up.

Afterthoughts

—⚡—

UPON REFLECTION, I REALIZE THAT I was cast in a mold influenced by many people at various stages in my life. Discounting the DNA that I was born with, the first influences were the will of my parents and the era in which I spent my childhood. The frivolity of youth competed with my parents' expectations of me becoming an adult while they tried to survive in very difficult times. Given a little more time, we might have come to agree on those expectations. The rate at which they expected real contributions from me created conflict. It pushed me toward adulthood much sooner than I wanted. I did, however, gain a remarkable confidence in myself that remains with me to this day.

My college days provided the second of my life lessons—the enlightenment that all people are not entirely good or fair and that not everybody has your best interest in mind. This was a particularly difficult one for me to comprehend and accept. Even though I had some very difficult times in my youth with my parents' frustration in trying to provide me with as much as possible with very limited resources versus my stubbornness in wanting to remain a kid, I totally trusted them. Given the underhanded, secretive tactics of my clinical instructors, I learned about distrust and the uncertainty and danger of counting on others.

My third stage of maturation was molded through life in the military and the realities that went with it. Though I had succeeded at very difficult tasks against very tough odds in college and felt extremely confident once I had earned my degree, the much larger arena of life after school held even more unknowns and tests of my confidence.

My military career went quite well, in spite of the army screw-ups with my pay and my assignment orders, until the horror of war suddenly confronted my innocence in April of 1969. After a very long, peaceful airplane flight, I was thrown into a situation in which my life could end at any moment, and there was nothing I could do to prevent it. This fact suddenly became clear, and it was devastating. Stark reality was even more challenging in the hostile environment of heat, humidity, insects, stench, filth, a foreign language, and finally, the constant attempts to end my time here on earth by an enemy I had not even seen. I felt I had reached the very bottom that night in the bunker at Bien Hoa Air Base in April,1969, but, once again, I was wrong.

Possibly the most dramatic stage of my life, which still affects my beliefs and tenets on major life issues, began on the first day that I treated a wounded combatant. That day was reinforced by repetition, day after day, week after week, until the lessons were impregnated deep within my heart and mind. The intense facts of what war really meant at the critical, bloody, human level, far away from the politics and the hype and the protests, came into clear focus. I wondered at the onset what could really be worth putting these young, innocent humans into the horrendous risks of battle. The same question was appropriate for those we battled. It meant the same to all of us, only under a different flag and a different ideology.

One might ask the same question as we speak: what the hell was it for? What the hell *is* it for, even today? In spite of my disillusionment, I hung on to my trust in the army and the supposedly sage decisions by which we were led. I maintained a blind justification for all the horror happening throughout the country and concentrated on my ability to function at least enough to ease some of my patients' pain.

However, buried in all of my rationalization and not permitted to come out until after years of recurrent dreams when I was taken back to those dark times, I lived with a psychological flaw that I don't imagine that I alone carried. Until my hands actually touched those who needed me, I was terrified of not coming up to the standard needed to take away the pain, give back the breath, and replace and pump the lifeblood. I labored under this anxiety so intensely that, at times, I attempted to compensate by spending endless hours at work, suffering the entire next day from exhaustion. The problem was that once the ball started rolling, the pace became faster and faster, and the numbers who needed you escalated higher and higher until it seemed that failure was probable. The most amazing part was, however, that I did not fail. But I became more and more addicted to the seemingly endless flow of adrenaline that came along with holding the lives of others in my hands.

Upon returning home after my tour in Vietnam, I poured the lust for this strange energy into learning as much as I could in the medical field by saturating my resume with critical-care courses, certifications, and licenses. I soon realized that it was not nearly enough, and my life, even with a wonderful wife and daughter, had a huge, vacant hole in it, making me feel useless, unfulfilled, and still guilty. Only after I joined the crew of a small-town ambulance group in northern Michigan did that old feeling of partial redemption again return.

In an attempt to fill my emotional vacancy, I juggled and managed several critical care and E.M.T. jobs at once for nearly four years and after spending another three years as the Director of Nursing Services at the local hospital, my family and I moved to Florida.

I reestablished my clinical presence in a couple of high-volume emergency departments. It reminded me once again that I was indeed deeply and terribly addicted to the adrenaline that came with the intense times, but never would I have access to as much "dope" as I had been supplied through the horrors I experienced in Vietnam. My forced rehabilitation from the chemical was even more evident when Carole and I left Florida to rejoin remaining family members in Michigan.

In preparation for retirement, I elected to work in a small, low-volume ER. After only weeks, I was horribly injured by a patient, causing me to retire prematurely at age fifty-seven. My life plan changed dramatically in a domino effect: I was diagnosed with a litany of medical problems involving heart, lungs, and, ultimately, cancer of the prostate. Most importantly, my source of the wonder drug was gone.

In conclusion, a very significant portion of pain and guilt remained part of me for the remainder of my professional life. However, after my imposed retirement and the difficult, cold-turkey withdrawal from my brain drug, my mind was finally at peace, and I directed my purpose more healthily. Only a small, nagging requirement remained: to declare, thankfully and humbly, that I am no longer a "reluctant servant."

The Author, Dennis V. Neely, Seventieth Birthday (February 10, 2015)

The End

FOOTNOTES

i National Vietnam Veterans Foundation.org/statistics

ii National Vietnam Veterans Foundation.org/statistics

iii FDR Inaugural Address, March 4, 1933.

iv Public domain, US Army.

v US Army Corps of Engineers Map Service, Printed by the National Geographic Directorate, Vietnam.

vi US Army Corps of Engineers Map Service, Printed by the National Geographic Directorate, Vietnam.

vii Wikipedia.org/wiki/hearts and_ minds_(Vietnam)

viii http://amvif.com/government/Veterans/Dapsone/Dapsone.htm

ix https://www.google.com/search?q=free+pictures+of+ac+130+spectre+gunship

x http://www.dc3history.org/puffthemagicdragon.html

xi Report, US Military Whole Blood Program in support of Combat Operations South Vietnam, 1965-1970, prepared for the Deputy Surgeon General, February 1971.

xii Report, Administrative Division, 406th Medical Laboratory, USAMC, Japan,1970.

[xiii] http://www.history.army.mil/books/Vietnam/MedSpt/chpt9.htm

[xiv] Public Domain, US Army

[xv] http://en.wikipedia.org/wiki/Ascaris

[xvi] http://en.wikipedia.org/wiki/Ascaris/CDC

[xvii] Public Domain, US Army

[xviii] The rock apes, orangutans, apes, monkeys, or whatever one cares to remember these wonderful creatures as, are actually not acknowledged to have existed during the Vietnam War or for thousands of years before that, according to the book-taught folks who know everything about this and most other subjects. In fact, even though hundreds of accounts of these apes were shared by many GIs and Vietnamese alike, the rock ape is considered to be in the category of cryptids—the same category as the yeti, abominable snowman, chupacabra, and the like. Explanations of the nonexistence of the rock ape state that it is all a matter of available habitat that is not bothered by the silliness of man. All of these creatures are very secretive and expose themselves only in moments of their audiences' drunkenness or desperate plights. In fact, I believe that the rock apes, with the invasion of thousands of people into their mountainous jungle, were displaying a type of modified behavior. Acquiring necessary but diminished resources necessitated unwanted associations with humans, resulting in aggressive, protective behavior. At any rate, I and hundreds of grunts, "gooks," and civilians saw what they saw: the rock ape of the Central Highlands. See also http://en.wikipedia.org/wiki/Batutut#Sightings_during_the_Vietnam_War.

UNCLASSIFIED
AD NUMBER
AD509537
CLASSIFICATION CHANGES
TO: unclassified
FROM: confidential
LIMITATION CHANGES TO:
Approved for public release, distribution unlimited
FROM:
Controlling DoD Organization. Assistant
Chief of Staff for Force Development[Army], Washington, DC 20310.
AUTHORITY AGO D/A ltr, 29 Apr 1980; AGO D/A ltr, 29Apr 1980
THIS PAGE IS UNCLASSIFIED SUBJECT:
Operational Report -Lessons Learned, Headquarters, 4th
Infantry Div~.uion Artillery, Period Ending 31 January 1970 (U)
BY ORDER OF THE SECRETARY OF THE ARMY:

AVFDD-AC 31 January 1970
Subject: Operation Report-Lessons Learned, 4th Infantry Division
1 Enemy Action Binh Dinh in the area of Ankhe, enemy activity was
limited to harassment and interdiction of supply routes and occasional
attacks with mortar and B-40 fire. Few significant contacts were made
with the enemy. A sapper attack on Camp Radcliff on 15 November
resulted in the destruction of 19 helicopters. Additionally 129 mm
rockets were employed by the enemy, in the area for the first time.
Numerous contacts to the northeast of AnKhe beginning the 3rd of
January indicated a large force of enemy in that vacinity, tentatively
identified as elements of the 18th, NVA Regiment.
The most significant activity during the period was a ground attack on
the outermost part of Binh Dinh, FSB Hardtime. Other enemy units
identified were part fo the 2nd VC Regiment and the 407th Sapper

Battalion. Terrain in the area and and the hiding of the enemy in Dense vegetation of the jungle canopy and the rough terrain provided concealment from observation and provided areas in which the enemy couod hide from unfriendly elements. The rugged terrain and canopy also limited movement of friendly elements and hampered both ground movement and aerial assault.

The operation terminated on 29 December and the 6/29 Artillery Tac CP returned to Camp Radcliff. Operations in the vicinity of Camp Radcliff during the Tac CP's absence consisted of search and destroy ambushes, and LRP's in the immediate proximity of An Khe. the Battalion Rear CP, under the command of the Battalion Executive Officer, provided command and control for the batteries support of Task Force Bravo. Two significant incidents occurred during November and December. Camp Radcliff was attacked by sappers, losses resulting in 1 US KIA (AVN) and 3 US WIA. Equipment losses included 15 helicopters totally destroyed and 2 damaged. On 12 December Camp Radcliff received 6 82mm mortar rounds. All rounds landed in the 6/29 Artillery area. Damage was 1 US WIA and an RTT destroyed

N/A OACSFOR, DA, Washington, D.C. 20310
UNICLASSIFI ED

A P P E N D I X   B

PROPOSED CITATION

PRESIDENTIAL UNIT CITATION

AWARD OF THE PRESIDENTIAL UNIT CITATION BY THE PRESIDENT OF THE UNITED STATES OF AMERICA TO THE FOLLOWING UNIT OF THE ARMED FORCES OF THE UNITED STATES IS CONFIRMED IN ACCORDANCE WITH PARAGRAPH 194, AR 672-5-1.

THE 17TH FIELD HOSPITAL, 67TH MEDICAL GROUP, USAMEDCOMV(P).

THE CITATION READS AS FOLLOWS:

THE 17TH FIELD HOSPITAL DISTINGUISHED ITSELF BY EXTRAORDINARY HEROISM IN ACTION AGAINST A HOSTILE FORCE AT CAMP RADCLIFF, REPUBLIC OF VIETNAM, ON 15 NOVEMBER 1969. ENEMY MORTAR AND ROCKET ROUNDS WERE DIRECTED AT THE 17TH FIELD HOSPITAL AS A COVER FOR A SAPPER ATTACK AGAINST THE HOSPITAL BILLETS AND THE AIRFIELD AT CAMP RADCLIFF. THE PERSONNEL OF THE 17TH FIELD HOSPITAL DEMONSTRATED EXTRAORDIANARY HEROISM IN REPULSING THE ENEMY FROM THE HOSPITAL COMPOUND WITH SMALL ARMS FIRE. EXTRAORDINARY VALOR AND DETERMINATION WERE ALSO DISPLAYED IN THE MANNER IN WHICH ALL ABLE HOSPITAL PERSONNEL EVACUATED THEIR COMRADES FROM THE BURNING AND EXPLODING BILLETS WITH A DISREGARD FOR THEIR OWN SAFETY AND WELL BEING. ALTHOUGH STUNNED BY THE ATTACK, ALL ABLE HOSPITAL PERSONNEL CONTINUED TO FUNCTION AT

MAXIMUM EFFICIENCY AND EFFECTIVENESS TO CARE FOR AND TREAT THE MASS CASUALTY SITUATION THAT DEVELOPED FROM THE ATTACK ON CAMP RADCLIFF. NONETHELESS, THE ADMINISTRATIVE, ANCILLARY AND PROFESSIONAL FUNCTIONS OF THIS RUSTIC, 125-BED HOSPITAL LOCATED IN THE CENTRAL HIGHLANDS WERE DEVELOPED TO A LEVEL OF EXCELLENCE ENJOYED BY FEW HOSPITALS IN THE REPUBLIC OF VIETNAM. THE FACT THAT THE 17TH FIELD HOSPITAL'S ANNUAL GENERAL INSPECTION WAS COMPLETED SO SUCCESSFULLY ONLY THREE MONTHS AFTER THE UNIT BEGAN OPERATION AND SUFFERED A SEVERE ENEMY ATTACK REFLECTS GREAT CREDIT UPON THE DEDICATION, LEADERSHIP, AND DETERMINATION OF THE 17TH FIELD HOSPITAL. THROUGH THIS UNIT, THE AMERICAN IDEAL AND DREAM HAS BEEN PRESENTED TO THE PEOPLE OF VIETNAM, THROUGH ITS MERITORIOUS DEVOTION TO DUTY AND GENUINE CONCERN FOR THE CARE AND TREATMENT OF THE PEOPLE OF VIETNAM AND ITS ALLIES. THE DETERMINATION, DEVOTION TO DUTY, INDOMITABLE COURAGE, AND EXTRAORDINARY HEROISM DEMONSTRATED BY THE MEMBERS OF THE 17TH FIELD HOSPITAL ARE IN KEEPING WITH THE HIGHEST TRADITIONS OF THE MILITARY SERVICE AND REFLECT GREAT CREDIT UPON THEMSELVES AND THE ARMED FORCES OF THE UNITED STATES.

RALPH R. CHAPMAN

COL

MC

Incl 3

Commanding

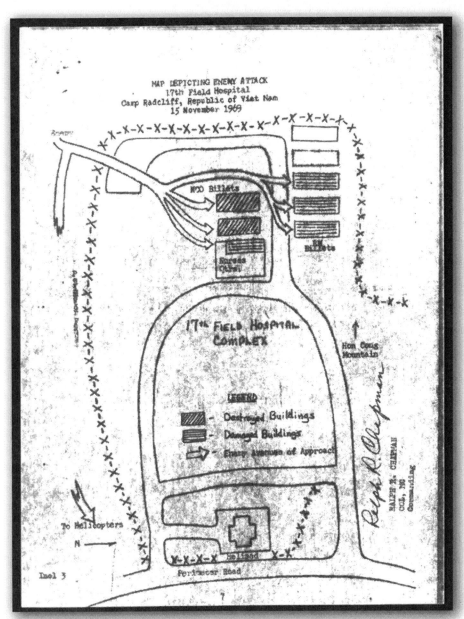

Map Depicting Sapper Attack on Seventeenth Field Hospital

42676600R00151

Made in the USA
Middletown, DE
19 April 2017